A POSTILLION STRUCK
BY LIGHTNING

Self taken by my father one morning at *The Times* for the
audition at the Old Vic, August 1939.

A
POSTILLION STRUCK
BY LIGHTNING

DIRK BOGARDE

BOOK CLUB ASSOCIATES
LONDON

This edition published 1977 by
Book Club Associates
by arrangement with Chatto & Windus Ltd.

Printed in Great Britain by
Butler & Tanner Ltd,
Frome and London

This book is for
My Father and Mother, Elizabeth,
Gareth, Tony and Lally.
With my love.

D. v.d.B.

CONTENTS

ILLUSTRATIONS

Endpapers

A View of the Cottage, Great Meadow, the Church, 1931

The 17 pen and ink drawings that appear throughout
the text are by the author

PREFACE

IN 1968 when I left England to live abroad, I suggested to my father that I might perhaps start to write a book about my early childhood. The severance had not been very easy, and I felt that by recalling some of the intense pleasures of the early days the break might be somewhat soothed. He agreed, but reminded me that as far as I was concerned my early family background was very hazy. He felt that I would receive little help from the Scottish side, apart from my mother, and that there was no one left on his side save for himself. Consequently, if I liked, he would start to collect as much information as he could to assist me in what, he said, would be a very lengthy task. I accepted with pleasure. It was only after his death, in 1972, that clearing up private papers in his studio I came across a packet and a cigar box labelled simply "For Dirk". He had been as good as his word and had assembled a wide collection of diaries, letters, school reports, photographs, glass negatives, cuttings and written notes in his own hand on dates and times. It is from this carefully amassed selection from a life that this book has, in the main, been written. For the rest I have had to depend on my own memories and those of my English family and my friends.

Where it was impossible to remember a real name, I have substituted another: and also where I have felt that this might save embarrassment. Street names and some identifiable town names have likewise been altered. Otherwise the events, as I remember them, all took place as written. Although, clearly, many of the conversations have been re-constructed, these are the words we used, the phrases we used and the way we were then. Part One is a condensation of at least two summers, but Part Two is "as it was" to the best of my recollection.

I am indebted very much to the following people for assistance with "remembering", and for the use of their own letters and diaries: Mrs G. Goodings; Mrs A. Holt; E. L. L. Forwood; W. A. Wightman; and G. van den Bogaerde. And to Mrs Glur Dyson Taylor who was "godmother" to the book.

To Mrs Sally Betts, who typed it, and corrected my appalling spelling, punctuation and almost indecipherable typescript, my warmest thanks and gratitude.

DIRK BOGARDE
CHATEAUNEUF DE GRASSE

PART I

SUMMER

Summer 1930

I

WE were almost halfway down the gully when my sister screamed and called out, "I've found him!"

But she hadn't: it was just an old rusty can gleaming wet in the dew among the leaves. It wasn't George by any stretch of the imagination: I'd know George anywhere and he wouldn't be down the gully, of that I was pretty sure. He'd be up top, in the Great Meadow where the grass was fresh and tender, and there were hosts of dandelions which he liked.

Not in the gully, which was deep, and dry, usually, and lined with great ash and oak, and chalky along the edges full of warrens and, down at the bottom by the road, old cans and bedsteads and stoves which people dumped among the nettles. George was the kind of tortoise who thought for himself, and he would never have thought to wander so far from the house when the Great Meadow was bung full of food and surrounded the place in which he usually lived. He wasn't a complete fool.

I struggled up the side of the gully and broke through the nettles and elder bushes into the field. I was soaking with dew. Down below in the valley the first chimneys were smoking and the meadow lay still in silver light, a good hundred acres of it. It was going to be a bit of a job to find George among all that grass.

My sister was behind me, having scrambled painfully through the elder branches, whimpering from time to time. I didn't take any notice. If you said anything the least bit kind, or helpful, or sympathetic, they started to snivel, and after that cry. And you might as well have said nothing, because then they only did a whimper or two and, seeing you didn't care much, stopped. So I didn't say a thing to her. She rubbed her stung knees with a dock leaf and pushed her hair from her eyes.

"Why did we have to get up at dawn to look for him?"

"Because."

"But because why?"

"Because it's the best time to find them. That's why."

"To find tortoises!" she scoffed, rubbing away at her wretched knees. "You'd think you'd been hunting them all your life."

I started to hum and sing a bit.

"And you haven't," she continued, "because they come from Africa and you've never been there."

I left her and started walking down the long slope to the valley, peering at molehills and under tussocks of ragwort, and generally trying to seem as if I had a pattern. Pretty soon she'd get windy left up there by the dark old gully and she'd come trolling and skittering down to join me.

I found a large rabbit hole, and stooped to search it. Once, a month ago, he'd got out and stuck himself in a rabbit hole in the orchard.

She wasn't far behind me now, singing a bit, and brushing the long wet grasses with her skinny brown hands. She grabbed some sorrel leaves and chewed them.

"If he gets stuck in a hole again, we'll never find him, there must be five hundred million in this field. There must be."

I got up and dusted my hands and walked on singing my bit of humming-song. She was right, but I wasn't going to let her know that.

"We'll just have to search every single one."

"Well I won't!" She stopped some paces behind me, waving her arms like a windmill. I walked on, looking and kicking about the big grass clumps.

"It's not my tortoise. And I'm soaking wet. My sandals are all slimy. You'll be sorry!" she screeched.

Patiently I turned and looked up at her against the morning.

"It's half yours," I said politely, but coldly. "Uncle Salmon gave it to us *both*. So it stands to reason that it's *ours*. Not just mine."

She shrugged, but was silent. I stared at her. She suddenly bent and started to unbuckle her sandal. "Well, I don't want my half of it. You've got the part with the head. That's the best part." She sat down in the wet shaking her old brown sandal. I could see her knickers, but I didn't bother to tell her. She was so rotten.

"Well, go on home and I'll look for him alone. And when I find him I'll have both halves and you'll have to lump it." I turned and ran away down the hill . . . in case she tried to follow. She didn't, but she screeched again.

"The head part is the most interesting part. You said so. I don't like the tail part. And if I go home alone Aleford's stallion could get me."

I reached the edge of the meadow and threw myself on to the grass under the ash tree and lay there looking at the sky and puffing a bit. It was quite a long run down from the top.

It was only yesterday evening that I had carefully washed his shell, and then put a little olive oil on it so that it shone and gleamed like a great golden brown pebble on the beach at Birling Gap. Only yesterday that he'd had the very innermost heart of a lettuce. The pale, yellowish-whitish bit. And only yesterday that Reg Fluke told me to put a little hole in her end of the shell and fix a bit of string to it. "Then he won't wander," he said.

But I didn't, and here we were in the dawn, searching for him, in vain it seemed.

There was a thumping in the earth under my back, and I could hear her running. Her feet thumping along in the grass. She slithered down beside me clutching her soaking sandals and peered at me. Her long hair hung over her face, and brushed my cheek. She looked like a hideous witch-thing: she crossed her eyes at me.

"Don't!" I said in alarm. "You'll stay like it."

"Not that you'd care. You left me up there and the stallion might be anywhere. You just don't mind about me. I won't help you look." She leapt to her feet and ran barefoot through the field, jumping over molehills, waving her skirts about, and singing very loudly indeed. This was not to impress me, but to frighten away Aleford's stallion, which we had never actually seen, but which we'd been told about in great detail by Reg Fluke and a boy from Woods, the butchers in the village.

And the telling was bad enough. I wasn't exactly anxious to see it myself. But I lay on, listening to her singing away in puffs and gasps as she ran furiously uphill.

The sun had been up only a little while and beside me, close to my face, so that it was actually all blurry and looked like an eagle, was a burnet-moth on a bit of grass, feeling the sun, and waiting for the dusk to come. I rolled over on my stomach and looked up the hill. She looked quite small now, leaping over the grasses, and jumping about with her long legs and the sandals held high, as if a great dog was running beside her trying to grab them.

A blackbird was singing in the ash tree and I was just wondering if there was a nest nearby when I heard her: it was rather frightening actually. She let out a terrible shriek, and then another and another as if someone was stabbing her.

5

I jumped up and stared. She was standing quite still, staring at the ground and holding her sandals close to her heart. Shrieking.

It must be George, and of course, he must be dead. Horribly, by the way she was yelling . . . I started to walk up the hill towards her.

"What is it? What's happened?" I called.

"Come quickly . . . come quickly . . . it's ghastly! Hurry! God's honour, it's the biggest one . . . it's the biggest! Quick."

I ran. The wet grasses stinging my legs, and the tussocks and molehills tripping me. The yelling stopped but she was staring at me with great beseeching eyes.

"Come quickly!"

"This is as quick as I can. Is it a snake?" That was it, of course. An adder. And we'd both be bitten. "If it's a snake," I said, stopping immediately, "come away. Don't stand there gawping, come away. It'll kill us. Just run."

"It isn't a snake . . . it isn't a snake . . . it's terrible!" She hadn't moved, so I went on, rather reluctantly, but cheered that it was nothing too beastly . . . obviously not George mangled by a fox or something, otherwise she'd be snivelling. But now she was crouching in the grasses, staring at it like a mad rabbit.

Then I was beside her, my shirt had come out of the top of my shorts, and my shoes were soaking too.

"What is it? What is it then?"

When she spoke her voice was sort of roughish and very low with wonder. "Look," she said, and very gently parted the grasses before her. "Look, it's the biggest mushroom in the world. Look!"

And it was. It must have been about as round as a dinner plate, quite. And it sat in a little hollow with some others around it; but they were smaller, this was a giant.

"Gosh!"

"Isn't it *huge*? It's the biggest in the world."

"It might be a toadstool, or something."

"Well, let's pick it and take it home and they'll tell us."

Very gingerly I reached out and pulled the great shiny brown top . . . it smelt like a million mushrooms. It was golden brown in the sun and underneath it was pink and white, and damp. We smelt it carefully and she opened her skirt like an apron for it, and we walked breathlessly up to the house.

"It's like a beautiful parasol," she said.

In the kitchen there was a breakfast smell. The kettle was steaming away on the Primus stove and Lally, plump in a print dress and tennis shoes, was sitting at the table buttering toast.

We stood on the brick floor looking at her, willing her to look up at us, but she went on scraping off the burnt bits and singing a song to herself. My sister deliberately dropped one sandal and then the other. Lally stopped singing and said: "Go-and-wash-your-hands-why-haven't-you-got-your-shoes-on?" all in one breath, but still not looking up, although she must have seen us.

My sister said in her Old Maid's voice: "We have something rather strange to show you."

Lally looked briefly at her bulging skirt and said: "If it's living throw it out and if it's dead likewise. Kettle's boiling."

"It's alive and dead at the same time, sort of," I said.

"Well, we don't want it in here, do we?" said Lally, stacking up some toast and cutting off the crusts all round. "And I'd be pleased if you hurry up before the Prince of Wales is here."

"It's a mushroom," said my sister, moving across the floor with the bundle and laying it on the table among the crusts and the butter crock. "And it's possibly the biggest in the world . . . or anyway in Sussex." And she carefully opened her skirt and showed it.

Lally took a look and then was interested. "Jerusalem!" she said. She always did when she couldn't think of anything else, or if you had surprised her, or if she was quite pleased but-not-going-to-show-it, or if she didn't understand clearly. And she didn't

7

understand this. For a moment we all looked at it in dead silence.

"Well, it's big I grant you, probably wormy too. What do you want me to do with it?"

My sister removed it very gently from the cloth of her skirt and, wiping her hands together, she said: "We could all have it for breakfast, couldn't we?"

"Fried," I said.

"With bacon sort of," said my sister.

"Be tough, I shouldn't doubt, you'd better ask your mother: it might be poisonous and then where should I be? Never get another job, not having poisoned a whole family. It's very large," she said. "Give it a good wash and we'll see."

Well, you could tell she was impressed because she forgot to remind us to wash ourselves, and taking down the big iron frying-pan she started singing her song again.

Carefully we washed it at the big sink and smelled the fresh damp smell of it and admired the pink underneath part, and there were no worms.

It was about the best thing I've ever eaten. Cut in strips, like bacon, and fried in butter with tomatoes and a bit of ham and soft toast.

"Where did you find it then?" Lally asked.

"We were looking for George in Great Meadow and she found it." I indicated my sister with a flick of jealousy.

"It was sort of in a little hollow place, right in the middle," she said.

"It's a wonder Aleford's stallion wasn't about," said Lally, wiping round her plate with a bit of bread: she said this was all right to do ever since she came to France the first time with us. Anything the French did was all right by her, which shows just how ignorant she was. "That stallion could kick you to death with a look: there was a boy lived up at Teddington when I was your age, got kicked in the head by one. He was loopy all his life." She cleaned the edge of her knife against the plate and stuck it in the butter. "Any cows in the meadow?"

"Some," I said. "Right down at the bottom."

"Well, you need cows and horses in the same field for mushrooms," said Lally. "If you don't have it that way you can't get mushrooms."

"Why?" asked my sister.

8

Lally was spreading damson jam all over her toast. "Because when you get cow dung and horse dung in the same field you get mushrooms, that's why," she said and bit into the jam.

My sister looked white but a little scornful. "Dung," she said.

"DUNG, dung," said Lally. "You ask anyone, anyone you like. Ask Aleford or Beattie Fluke down the bottom, or the Prince of Wales. They'll all say the same thing. Dung."

For a little time we were silent, except for the clink and scrape of knives and forks and the kettle lid plopping up and down. Sunlight streamed through the windows, across the table and the bumpy whitewashed walls.

"Do the French eat them?" I asked.

"Wee," said Lally, nodding her head.

"Well, it must be all right for us to, I mean if they do it must be," I said.

"They're the best cooks in the world, aren't they?" said my sister. "So they'd be bound to know if it was all right or not."

Lally eased up from the table and started stacking the plates. "Can't all be right at the same time," she said, going across to the sink and dumping them into some water. "Can't be right all the time. Even the French. Remember one thing," she said, taking the soap up from the shelf. "The French eat snails too."

We helped with the drying-up in a thoughtful silence.

* * *

We lay on our backs under the ash tree by the top of the gully and watched the crows wheeling and gliding in the wind. All around my head sorrel, buttercup and long bendy plantains shimmered and nodded. I crumbled a little empty snail shell, transparent and silvery. My sister had her eyes closed, her hands folded on her chest like a dead Plantagenet. She had the same kind of nose, poky and long; her hair was scattered with pollen.

I leant up on one elbow and sprinkled the snail shell all over her face.

She screamed and hit me with her fist.

I fell back into the grass and lay still, staring at the crows. She was mumbling and brushing her chin.

"Stupid fool," she said.

"I merely wondered if you were feeling sick yet. That's all."

"Well I'm not." She lay back. "Are you?"

"No. Not sick. Full."

"I think Lally is a liar anyway."

"I know she is," I said. "Look at the Prince of Wales."

"What about him?"

"Well, you know: she's always saying he's coming, or she met him at the pictures, or Victoria Station. And she's always talking to him on the telephone. She says."

"Well, that doesn't say she's a liar," said my sister, rolling on to her stomach and squinting at the sun. "Not like Betty Engels. She's a liar properly."

"Why . . . I mean how do you know she is properly?"

"Because," said my sister patiently, "because she said her father was a millionaire and I know it's a lie." She knelt up and picked some grass.

"How?"

"Because I saw him actually riding a bicycle."

"Well I should think Lally is just as much of a liar as Betty Engels . . . I bet she's never even seen the Prince of Wales. And not at Victoria Station."

"Why not Victoria Station?"

"Because to go to Sunningdale you have to leave from Waterloo."

We lay still for a while, comforted by our proof and by the fact that we did not feel sick. After a little while I sat up and tucked my shirt into my shorts. Away across the meadow the Downs were smudged with the morning sun and a little red Post Office van went bundling along the lower road and got lost in the trees. You could just see it shining red here and there in the gaps and then it turned right up to Peachy Corner and disappeared. I got up. "I'm going to have another look for George. Coming?"

She groaned. "All right, coming," she said. "And then we'll go down to Bakers and get a bottle of Tizer, I've got threepence." I pulled her up and we ran howling and laughing down the meadow: a linnet shot up at our feet, spiralling into the sky like a singing leaf, and as we whooped and leapt over the tussocks I could see the river sequinned with sunlight. I gave a great big shout of happiness . . . we weren't going to be sick and it was going to be a beautiful morning.

2

HERBERT FLUKE said that they weren't really canaries at all. They were ordinary sparrows dyed yellow, sometimes pink, and stuck in their cages. He said he knew because his brother Reg had a friend who used to catch them with bird-lime on twigs every year when the fair came to the village.

But I wanted one very badly. Basically because they were birds, and I worshipped birds, and also because the cages were so terribly small. They hung all round the stall in clusters . . . little square wood and wire boxes about eight by eight with chippering, tweeting little yellow, and sometimes pink, birds flittering and fluttering against the bars while you rolled pennies down a slotted thing on to numbers, or lobbed bouncy ping-pong balls into glass jars for twopence a throw. If you scored thirty or over you got a bird . . . the most you ever seemed able to score was a five or a three which together made eight, and for that, the lowest amount, you sometimes got a matchbox with a fishing set in it or a black and a pink celluloid baby with a little bath, with "Japan" printed on their bottoms.

But sometimes people did win a bird, because I saw them. Farm boys, with tightly belted trousers and shiny hair and fat maid-girls giggling on their arms, swung a little wooden cage in their free hand as they loped and lumbered across the shadowy, trodden grass to the swings. So people did win them sometimes; and I had two and sixpence which I had pleaded, hinted, saved, and on one occasion, which I remembered with a scarlet face, thieved, from around the household. Once, when my sister and I were changing the water in the flower jar on the altar in the church by the cottage, I pinched fourpence left by a hiker in the box: and spent four days of agony before I threw the scorching and almost molten coppers wide into the barley field on the way to Berwick. A fat lot of good thieving did you.

But tonight I had two shillings and sixpence intact . . . and in coppers: we'd gone into Bakers in the village on the way and changed it all, to make it easier at the stalls. Lally's mother, Mrs Jane, was with us: tall and respectable in black with a high black hat bound round with a shiny ribbon and a big coral pin her father had brought from Naples. Lally had on her tennis shoes and socks, and a nasty blue speckly frock which she wore always when we went shopping or out on any sort of social trip, and carried the black and red shopping bag with the candles, the rice and the pound of Cheddar for old Mr Jane's supper.

My sister was wearing her shorts, and whistling like a boy, which she hoped everyone would think she was, and jingling her one and fourpence in the pockets.

"What are you going to try for?" she called above the jingle-jongle of the roundabout. "Bet it's a canary-bird. Well, I'm going to try for one of those camels . . . a blue or a red, I don't care which, so long as it's a camel." She hadn't bothered to wait for my answer. Naturally.

The camels, which she had envied ever since she saw them here last year, were ghastly things, covered in spangly silver paint, and with baskets on their backs to put flowers in. You had to roll pennies for them too, only the top number was eighteen.

Lally was sucking a Snofruit and in between licks singing to the music on the roundabout . . . "I'm Happy When I'm Hiking." And Mrs Jane was picking her way carefully through the tumbling, rushing, laughing people, very tall and black, and holding her umbrella like a diviner's rod before her. I think she was enjoying herself, but you couldn't really tell with her; she seldom smiled unless it was over some rather old and boring story of when Lally and Brother Harold were children.

The canary stall was some way off from the roundabout, and quite near the lych gate of the church. People were sitting about on the gravestones in the flickering light from the fair petting and giggling, and putting paper flowers in their hair. Mrs Jane was a bit put off by all this.

"Fancy!" she said. "No respect for the dead at all. I'm very glad it's not me or your father as is under there on an evening like this."

"You wouldn't know, Mother," said Lally. She enjoyed a fair. "And what you don't know you wouldn't care about."

"I'd know. And your father would know for all he's deaf," said Mrs Jane.

"Would you be a ghost by then?" my sister asked in a soppy way.

"I'm not saying what I'd be," said Mrs Jane, pushing a large collie dog out of her way. "But sure as there's going to be thunder tonight, I'd *know*."

12

We had got to the stall, the lights and the little cages all bobbing and jingling about, and people all round the barrier shoving and counting change, and rolling pennies down the little slotted bits of wood. In the middle was a large woman with a black and white apron with a big satchel bag round her neck, and every time a coin landed on an unnumbered square she shovelled it into the bag without looking and went on calling out, "Eight to score Thirty for a Dicky." And all the while her eyes were scanning about the fairground as if she was looking for somewhere to go.

I rolled my first three pennies, my arms rigid with fright, my eyes concentrating on the square with "C" marked on it. But the pennies rolled down the slotted thing and just wobbled like old bicycle wheels on to the black or white squares and the woman in the middle shovelled them up without a look. The fourth penny tumbled on to number three and my sister smirked and said, "Ten times that and you'd have won." And I pushed her so that she fell over a lady with a pushcart and started to whine.

"Behave yourself!" said Mrs Jane.

"You'll get a thick ear if you don't," said Lally and gave Mrs Jane her Snofruit to hold while she helped my sister to her feet.

The fifth and sixth pennies rolled down on to a black and a white and now I only had two shillings left.

Why don't you have a go on something else, then?" said Lally. "You won't have anything left for the roundabouts."

"I'll just have a few more tries," I said, and moved round the stall to another place to bring me luck. Just in front of me my sister stood, hair across her eyes, tongue sticking out, stiff with concentration trying for her camel. Mrs Jane stood behind her like a black witch, her glasses glittering in the electric lights, and the pink pin in her hat winking and bobbing as she craned to watch.

I got a five, a three, a black, and a six. Fourteen, another black, and then my last penny wobbled across the board, teetered about for a second that seemed an hour, and finally settled just into the magic square C. But it lay cruelly exposed to all and sundry with its edge just over the line. "Doesn't count," cried the lady in the middle, her fat greasy hand poised over the offending coin. "Got to be right in the centre. Jam bang in the centre!" she cried triumphantly, scooping up my coin and hurling it into her bag. "But you got a fishing set," she said and slung the rotten little matchbox across the squares towards me. Glumly I shoved it into my pocket and pushed my way through the people. Lally called after me, something about don't get lost and they'd be coming, but I was heavy hearted, and didn't really listen. Above the glaring lights of the fairground the swifts swung and screamed, swooping in and out of the flags and banners. The Downs were hard and blue against a copper sky, big clouds crept up, like smoke from a great fire miles away, and a little cool breeze came whiffling along, making all the lights swing and dangle, and sending paper bags and chocolate wrappings scampering and eddying about the trodden grass. People ran past laughing, with red happy faces; girls with bows in their hair and braying boys wearing paper hats. The roundabout clonked up and down and round and round, the brass angels in the middle banging their cymbals together every few moments and turning their heads slowly from left to right with wide brass eyes gleaming at no-one, while the white and yellow horses, the pink pigs, and the racing, startled ostriches swung round and round petrified in enamel. Around the canopy went the words "BROWNRIGGS PLEASURE RIDE FOR FAMILIES" blurring into a ribbon of red and gold and yellow, and I went over to the stall where you threw balls into glass jars, had three go's and won a stick of rock with Ilfracombe written through it.

Down by the dodgem cars there was a rather nasty girl with red hair and glasses. Her name was Alice McWhirter and she was new to the village. Her father was some sort of artist, and they had taken old Mrs Maiden's house up at Elder Lane, and, as far as we were concerned, they were foreigners. She had come and talked to my sister and me when we were fishing once, and, although we were as rude as possible, she wouldn't go, so we'd brought her home for tea, given her a jam sandwich, made her walk along the top of a wall by the pigsty, pushed her in the nettles and sent her home alone. But she still came back for more. Lally said she was lonely and "an only child" and that her father was an artist and what could you expect with no mother, and we were to be better behaved to her because we had each other, our father was a journalist and we had a mother. She was awfully soft at times. And so we sort of got to know her a bit, and once she asked us to her house which was very small and untidy, and smelled of linseed oil and cooking. Her father was very tall, had a red beard and bare feet and swore at us, which was the only time he ever spoke while we were there. After we'd looked at their privy, her collection of moths, all lumped up together, dead in a jam jar, and a photograph of her mother, fat and laughing with glasses, and a pom-pom hat, who was also dead, she asked us if we'd like some orangeade. We said "yes" and followed her up a rather rickety stairway to the bedrooms. Although it was about tea-time the beds were still unmade, and there were clothes and old shoes all over the place. One room was very small, where she slept, and the other quite large and full of paintings and leather suitcases and a dreadful old camp bed in a corner covered in dirty sheets where her father slept. On a marble-topped table there was a big white china mug which she brought over to us very carefully. "Here you are," she said, "Kia Ora." And handed me the mug. It was full and heavy. And orange. I was just about to take a sip when she suddenly threw her skirts over her head and screamed, "Don't! It's not Kia Ora at all, it's pee!" and fell on the camp bed laughing and laughing, with her legs going all sorts of ways.

I put down the heavy white mug, and we just stood there staring at her for a bit. Suddenly my sister said, "I'm going home" and started off down the rickety stairs with me behind her and the awful girl still laughing on her father's bed.

After that we kept out of her way and never spoke to her again, but she made friends with Reg Fluke and we sometimes met them birdnesting or down in the meadow looking for slowworms.

I stood looking at the dodgem cars clonking and bumping into each other, and the people screaming and laughing and I felt Alice McWhirter moving along towards me. She was wearing a sort of velvet dress, and her legs were bare and scratched, and her glasses shone in the lights and all the dodgem cars were reflected in them as she peered up at me. She really was frightfully ugly.

"Hello," she said, and smiled.

"Hello," I said politely, but coldly to show her I had not forgotten the orangeade part.

"Reg is on number four," she said, indicating the car with a nod of her head. "I wouldn't go on, I'm too scared."

I didn't say anything.

"I've got sevenpence and I'm saving it for one go on the swings and one go on the horses, only I want a cockerel," she said, edging closer.

"I've got two shillings," I said in a pompous voice, "and I'm going to spend it all on rolling pennies."

She looked amazed. "TWO shillings! What do you want to win?" she asked, her nasty little claw-like hand clutching the dodgem rail.

"That's my affair, I wouldn't tell you," I said, and I was just moving away when she grabbed my arm with her horrible little hand and cried: "Look what Reg won at the rolling." And there, in her right hand, which had been hidden behind her velvet skirt, hanging in the air between us, was a little wooden cage with a canary fluttering and beating against the wires. "Isn't he beautiful!" she cried. "Reg got it for four rolls!"

My heart was thudding, my mouth dry, the little cage bobbed and wobbled in her outstretched hand between us. The thing I had most longed for was in the grasp of ghastly Alice McWhirter, and Reg Fluke had got it in four rolls.

"It's very pretty," I said. "But the cage is too small."

Alice McWhirter laughed a scornful laugh. "We're going to make it a bigger one, in our garden, out of an old orange box. I know where the wire is, and we'll put in twigs and grass and things. This," she laughed, swinging it disdainfully above her head and frightening the bird out of its wits, "is only for fairs and travelling and that. You couldn't put them all in orange boxes!"

And then Reg Fluke was clambering over the rail, his face smiling and country-looking, and red and shiny.

"Showing you my sparrer, is she?" he asked, pulling out a dirty handkerchief and wiping his forehead. "Cost me four rolls, that did . . . and this," he indicated the dodgems with a jab of his head backward, "cost me sixpence and that's me skint."

Alice McWhirter wagged the cage about in front of my stiff face. "I've got sevenpence you can share," she said.

"Coconuts is sixpence for four balls," said Reg. "What'll you do with a penny? Save it for a pee?" He roared with laughter, and Alice McWhirter smirked away. Funny how pee kept coming up with her.

"I'll give you one shilling in coppers for it," I said, blurting it all out. The music was very loud, the cars banging and crashing into each other. Reg's jaw was stuck open with surprise. "How much?"

"One shilling," I said very loudly indeed, "in coppers."

"For a sparrer?"

Reg took the cage from the clutching hand of Alice McWhirter

16

and peered into it. The canary skittered about again, and a feather fell out.

He handed it solemnly over to me. "Where's the bob, then?" He crammed the pennies into both his pockets, and with a wink to Alice McWhirter he pulled her off into the crowds.

My heart bursting, my face red, the cage pressed close to my chest, I shoved and pushed through the people until I caught sight, over the heads in front of me, of Mrs Jane's black hat.

"Great Heavens!" she cried, seeing me. "You got one! Well I declare. Lally . . ." she turned and cried above the music . . . "the boy's got his canary!"

They stood round me in a circle, the three of them, staring at my prize. My sister clasped her hands with joy, and a glimmer of liking flickered in me for her, until she said: "It'll just wash off in the rain, all that yellow, and be an ordinary sparrow you could have got for nothing." And hate glowed deep in the coals of my heart. Lally cuffed her head lightly and said, "Well I daresay you've spent all your money, and Miss Know All here's got her camel, so we'd better hop, skip and jump it home." We turned and threaded our way through the thronging fairground. The roundabout was playing "The More We Are Together" and the little wind flapped at the legs of my shorts, and jiggled the black ribbon on Mrs Jane's hat. My heart was full, thumping with happiness. My brain reeled with all the plans for my canary—a cage next, a large cage with perches, and a jam jar full of seeding grasses; a tin tray for sand and a bowl for bathing in; and maybe, later, a mate; and nests, and babies. Oh! Lord! What joy.

Lally looked up into the dark blue of the night, and sniffed. "Mother?" she said. "You said there'd be thunder, and I reckon you're about right. Shouldn't wonder if we have a storm before we reached home. Good job you got your brolly."

"Always bring my brolly everywhere," said Mrs Jane. "Ever since I got wetted at your Aunt Gert's Silver up at Shepperton that year. Blue crêpe it was, and I got so wet you could see my stays right through. I thought your father would do himself a hurt he laughed so much."

We had got to the path which led to the white wood bridge across the river. Behind us the glare of the fair was like a big bonfire, the twinkling lights like embers, and the smoke from the roundabout drifting up into the night. Ahead all was dark and still, and the trees and hedge blurry shapes. The white planks of the bridge were like whales bones. It was very still again: the little wind had stopped.

My sister said: "How much did it cost, your bird? All your two and six?"

"All," I said flatly.

"Throwing balls or rolling?"

"I got a stick of rock throwing the balls . . . it's in my pocket. You can have it if you like."

"I would like. Don't you then?"

"I don't mind it. It's got Ilfracombe all through it."

"Wherever's that?"

"I don't know. Cornwall, I think."

We were crossing the bridge now, in single file, Lally ahead, swinging the shopping bag; Mrs Jane and her umbrella; my sister holding her camel and myself. The river was low, the lights of the fair rippling faintly on the surface. No sound save our feet clonk clonking over the hollow-sounding boards, and now and then a gurgle gurgle of water round the struts.

"Struth!" said Lally suddenly. "It's close though. Ilfracombe's in Wales by the by. And what that's got to do with Sussex rock I don't know. But those Gippos are all cheats."

Far away, over Wilmington, was a low grumbling rumble of thunder. We had got to the path now, and our feet crunched over the gravel.

"Good job you brought that brolly," Lally's voice came back from the dark.

"Always carry a brolly," said Mrs Jane.

My sister was scuffing her sandalled feet, swinging her blue camel by its legs.

"I gave Reg Fluke a shilling for it," I said in a lowish voice.

"What?" She spun round and I tripped over her.

"Get a move on you two," called Lally, "there's going to be a storm along any moment."

We walked along for a bit in silence. Suddenly there was a flash of white light in the sky, and the great hump of our hill was suddenly pale green in the night. Mrs Jane gave a little cry and hurried on.

My sister did a sort of jog trot behind her, and I kept up.

"It's cheating not to have won it. I rolled for mine, and it cost ten tries," she said.

"Buying's not cheating, and anyway I've got it, so there."

18

There was another rumble of thunder over Wilmington and another and another, and we hurried in a zig-zag way along the path, across the main road and through the little iron gate into our field.

"Don't touch the gate, children!" cried Mrs Jane. "It's iron and you might be struck. Lally! Mark what I said to the children here, you'll be struck if you touch the gate." We slid through the opening and up into the field: another blinding flash burst down out of the sky, lit up the whole field, grass, nettles, molehills, all suddenly reared into violent light and colour against the sky, and as suddenly faded away into utter darkness, leaving us blinded and staggering, stumbling over tussocks, and blundering into each other. My sister started to whimper and Lally was just about to shout something at her, because I heard her say "Don't be . . . ," when a great roaring crash from the heavens descended upon us, bursting over our heads and splitting the world into a great hurling roaring blast of sound. And with it came the wind whipping through the grass and tearing through the trees in the gully. Staggering and clutching together, the four of us struggled in the dark up the hill, holding each other for some kind of protection and comfort from a world of which we seemed to be no part.

My sister was crying noisily by now, snivelling along, her beastly china camel banging my knees, while I struggled on, holding the cage tight to my chest, and wondering desperately if the canary would be dead before we reached the shelter of the house. Just as the first great plops of rain started to thud down on us we saw the lamp-lit windows ahead, and bending our heads to the wind and the now pelting rain, we pushed through the wooden gate into the orchard, along the slippery brick path and round to the kitchen door. Another great roaring raging crash tumbled about our ears and made the earth shake, as Lally fumbled with the latch and burst us all into the mellow golden light of the white-washed flint-walled kitchen. She slammed the door hard behind us, her face wet, and her hair straggling down over her eyes . . . "Father? We're home safe and sound and the boy got his canary!"

3

THE float suddenly started to bobble about, red and white with a bit of feather stuck through it, and then it swirled and whirled away under the surface with a grey waggling shape before it. My sister turned a somersault and landed, knees wide apart, in a clump of water mint.

"A bite! A bite! You've got a bite."

I was swiftly, nervously, reeling it in . . . playing it gently, carefully among the weeds and trying to bring it close to the bank. It seemed to be quite a big fish . . . it was lovely and heavy at the end of my line.

"Throw it back if it's too little," said my sister, peering down into the water, cupping her hands round her eyes in order to see to the bed of the Cuckmere; squinting, and puffing. Her hair fell over her face like an old skirt.

Gently I began to wind him up to the bank; a little breeze riffled the water and the rushes rasped and clattered like paper swords and in a second I had him flopping and wriggling on the grass. Instantly my sister was upon him, her hand round his fat white belly and the other hand wrestling with the hook—something I never very much liked doing. Taking out the hooks. She never seemed to mind at all.

"It's only gristle. That's all. It's not like lips or anything. They don't *feel* it." Expertly she yanked the hook away and, grabbing the empty lemonade bottle, she hit him smartly and swiftly on the head. He lay glistening in the sunlight. Cool grey-green, creamy white belly. Red fins, wide glazing yellow eyes. A roach. About seven inches.

We knelt there in the grass and counted the catch of five of varied sizes. They smelt muddy and cool—and sweet. Like cucumber sandwiches.

"Will that be enough?" I asked.

"Well Jesus fed millions with five, didn't he?"

"He had bread, too. Anyway it wasn't Jesus, it was a miracle."

"Well, whoever it was." She got up, and started to button up the flies of her shorts. They used to be mine and were too big for her, but she was having her "being a boy" day. "I think it'll be

The Cottage

enough. We'll have to FHB if it isn't, that's all." We were collecting our bits and pieces. The fish I wrapped in grasses and reeds and
put into my old school satchel, and she picked up our bottle, the
bait tin, and a Woodbine packet full of spare hooks, and we walked
through the trees to the road.

"I think we're jolly nice going fishing specially for her," said
my sister, clambering over the rickety iron fence and opening her
flies again. I laughed and hit her with the satchel, and she screamed
and wobbled and fell into a bit of a ditch.

"You silly fool! I've lost the hooks now. Serves you jolly well
right." We scrabbled about in the grass and leaves in the ditch
and found the Woodbine packet which I shoved into my shirt
pocket.

"It's silly to push people off fences when they're climbing them,"
she grumbled. "That's how people get their legs and things
broken." She pushed through the gate and up into our field and
we started to climb the hill to the cottage. The sky was high and
blue and clear, with little lumpy clouds trailing about and making
round black shadows on the grass. Everywhere the grasshoppers

were scissoring away, and at the top of the field you could just see our highest chimney shimmering in the sun.

"But I mean," said my sister, a bit puffed with the clamber, and holding her shorts round her waist with one hand, "I do think it's jolly nice of us to go fishing for her just because it's Friday and she's Catholic."

"Well I like fishing anyway."

"I know. But it is *nice*. Why does she have to have fish because it's Friday?" She always wanted to know difficult things at difficult times.

"It's a rule," I said shortly.

"A Bible Sort of Rule?"

"Yes."

"I know."

But she didn't really. We walked along in silence for a bit; well, not really silence because she was doing one of her songs and I was whistling little bits here and there, in case she thought I was puffed. Which I was. At the top of the field the cottage roof stuck up with its chimney, and then the flint walls and the two rather surprised windows in the gable looking down to the farm. Round the cottage was a rickety wooden fence with bits of wire and an old bedstead stuck in it, and some apple trees and the privy with its roof of ivy and honeysuckle and a big elderberry. The privy had no door, so you just sat there and looked into the ivy; no one could see you through it, but *you* could see them coming along the little path and so you were able to shout out and tell them not to in time. It was really quite useful. And better than a door really, because that made it rather dark and a bit nasty inside. And once a bat got in there after Lally had closed it and she screamed and screamed and had a "turn". So we left off the door for summer and just sort of propped it up in the winter, to stop the snow drifting and making the seats wet.

There were three seats, like the Bears'. A little low one, a medium one, and the grown-up one. The wood was white and shining where we used to scrub it, and the knots were all hard and sticking up. No one ever used the smallest one, we had the paper and old comics and catalogues for reading in that; and the medium one just had a new tin bucket in it with matches and candles for the candlestick which stood on a bracket by the paper roll, and a cardboard tin of pink carbolic.

There were lids to all the seats, with wooden handles, and they had to be scrubbed too—but not as often as the seats; which was every day and a bit boring. Sometimes at night it was rather nice to go there down the path in the dark, with the candle guttering in the candlestick, and shadows leaping and fluttering all around and the ivy glossy where the golden light caught it. Sometimes

little beady eyes gleamed in at you and vanished; and you could hear scurrying sounds and the tiny squeaks of voles and mice; and once a hare hopped straight into the doorway and sat up and looked at me for quite a long time, which was fearfully embarrassing, until I threw the carbolic tin at him and he hopped off again.

We squeezed under the wire and into the garden and down the

brick path to the kitchen. My sister was singing very loudly and happily because it felt like tea-time and we'd caught so many fish, and I joined her, because I was looking forward to seeing Angelica Chesterfield eating the fish I'd caught her and thanking me for being so polite and remembering she was a Catholic and that this was Friday.

We were making a marvellous noise when Lally appeared at the kitchen door wiping her hands in her apron. "For the love of dear knows who shut up!" she said, her elbows covered in bubbles. "You'll have us all arrested with that noise, anyone would think you owned the whole hill the way you carry on and your tea's on the table." She said this all in one breath and then turned and marched back into the kitchen. "It's rhubarb and ginger today."

The kitchen was low and cool; white walls, pink brick floor. There was a smell of paraffin and butter and scrubbed wood and washing in the copper. Tea was scattered about the table, a plate of bread, the jam in a jar with a little white label saying Summer 1929, a big brown teapot with a blue band, cups and saucers and Minnehaha, our cat, quietly washing his face.

"What," said Lally, after we had washed and were all seated, and she was holding her cup in two hands, her elbows on the table, blowing gently at the steam, "what have you been up to? Nothing good I'll be bound. I said to your mother and father in my letter today, they'll be up to no good I'll be bound." And she sucked her tea pleasantly down.

"We caught five roach for Angelica's supper this evening," I said, spreading big lumps of ginger and rhubarb over my bread.

"Because she's Catholic and today is Friday," said my sister.

"Fancy," said Lally, blowing at her tea and not looking at us at all. "Fancy it being Friday," and settled the cup into its saucer. "And who is going to have to take out their innards and cut off their heads and that, I'd like to know? Who has to wash them and take off the scales with a sharp knife and do all the cooking of them? Answer me that or tell the Prince of Wales if you won't tell me." She buttered herself a piece of bread. "And," she said, putting on her posh voice, "supposin' 'er 'ighness Angelica Chesterfield doesn't like muddy tasting little roach which should have been left alone in the river: supposing *that*! *Then* what do we do about 'er Catholic meal?" She took a big bite out of her bread and butter. We watched her chew away for a while. I put some sugar in my tea and said as politely as possible, "Well, she could always have tinned salmon, couldn't she?" Lally shook her head slowly, "No," she said, "no tinned salmon in this house, your father says it all comes from Japan and they put ptomaine poison in the odd tin. We don't want that do we?" She wiped her lips with the back of her hand, hit my sister a blow for swinging her feet at table and started to clatter about with the tea things.

Munchoka in the Kitchen

We washed up in silence, Lally washing up, we drying and putting away. She wiped her hands and lifted my satchel off the dresser and started to take out the roach. "Well, we'll have to make haste," she said, breaking a longish silence and handling the fish with a practised hand, "because Miss Angelica Whassername will be here directly. She'll be on the six o'clock, and I've no doubt she'll want her supper sharpish after that long journey."

The five roach didn't look much after she'd done all the innard thing and cut the heads off. She smelt them deeply, mentioned that they must be fresh, it was just the mud, and washed them under the tap and flipped them on to an old blue plate. The innards and bits we gave to Minnehaha. Lally told us to get out from under her feet.

We went out and lay on the grass. If you looked straight up you saw the blue sky and one cloud: if you looked a bit to your left you could see the grass stalks as big as bamboos and a nodding scarlet poppy as big as a duster, and if you turned your head to the right you would see my sister wrinkling her eyes and picking her nose. I hit her.

"My finger was up my nose! I could have poked my eye out." She lashed a fist at me and I rolled over and we fell into a struggling heap, laughing and howling and trying to sit on each other. In a little while we lay spent, breathless, giggling: our faces pressed into the grass, sniffing its greenness, and feeling the sun on the backs of our legs.

* * *

The Seaford bus was just rumbling into the village as we got to the Market Cross and stood waiting under the chestnut tree. It used to stop for a second outside Bakers to deliver odd packages or papers, and then it would trundle up and start reversing round the Cross so that it was pointing towards Seaford and the way it had just come. It used to arrive every evening at about six and leave again at six-thirty, and in the morning it arrived at nine-thirty and would leave again at ten and that's all it ever did. As far as we knew anyhow. Sometimes you could change buses at Polegate crossroads and go in a quite different direction, to East-bourne, which was a very exciting thing to do. But usually we met it . . . and occasionally caught it in the morning, washed and combed with sixpence in our pockets from our father for shop-ping in Seaford. Which wasn't so exciting but was quite decent really because there were one or two good junk shops, and some-times you could buy bound copies of "Chatterbox 1884" for 2d. We used to take a picnic lunch and eat that on the beach after we had done our shopping and a bit of swimming, and then we'd have tea at the Martello Tower, which was a very curious and dampish place but where we got lovely raspberry jam tarts and sometimes lemon curd ones. Lally used to have bloater paste and toast. But my sister and I just had an American Ice Cream Soda and our tarts. Two each. And a smell of tea from the silver urns hissing on the counter, and hot butter and varnished wood. After tea we'd walk along the front a bit, have a look at the shops in Sea Street, and then back on to the bus for home.

The first person off the bus was Miss Maude Bentley in a grey wool frock and a black hat with a ribbon, and behind her, clambering down slowly as if she was being lowered on a rope, came Miss Ethel. And baskets and walking sticks which were handed down to her when she was safely on the ground by Fred Brooks the conductor. "There you are, my darlings," he'd call out. "Off you go and don't get into trouble." They were the rector's sisters and they had a little gift shop in the front room of their house. They sold writing pads and pencils and postcard views of the church and painted ones of Jesus and Mary and Mabel Lucie Attwell little girls. In the front hall, in a big china umbrella stand painted with bulrushes and yellow flags they had Lucky Dips for tuppence. You gave Miss Ethel or Miss Maude your money and then, while they watched to see you weren't cheating by squeezing the packets to tell what was inside, you could bury your two hands in the bran and fumble about for a little paper-wrapped parcel. Blue for a boy and pink for a girl. It was really a bit soppy and the prizes were rotten for tuppence. All I ever got was the three monkeys not seeing, speaking or hearing evil. That's all that boys *ever* got—except once I did see a boy get a very small penknife with a picture of "R.M.S. Majestic" on it—but usually it was the monkeys. They must have bought millions and millions of them. We said "Good evening", and then some more people came off and there was Angelica Chesterfield. Angelica had very, very long black hair, and long legs and long arms and a long nose. She was altogether long, and a year older than us. She wore a black knitted cap with a red pom-pom and a long blue coat and shiny London shoes with ankle straps and white socks and we all smiled stupidly at each other and then I took her suitcase and we started to walk.

"Was it a boring journey?" I asked. She smoothed her hair, moved it over her shoulders, adjusted her pom-pom and said: "Not fearfully. Mummy put me on the train at Victoria and I had some books to look at and when we got to Seaford a lady said, 'O! This is Seaford!' And I got off and said to a very nice man with a dog 'Where does the bus go from,' and he said 'Here,' and I got on and now I've got off." She tripped over a stone in her shiny black shoes and smiled. We turned down the lane towards the river and my sister said: "We've thought of some lovely things to do while you are here. We've found a very creepy caravan where a witch lives, and we'll take you to a sort of cave up by Wilmington we found and we know where there's a punt and we could go along the river and pick some waterlilies." Angelica smiled again at us, pushed her hair over her shoulder again and said: "I like to read quite a lot."

"Not all the time?" I said.

"Not *all* the time," she agreed quietly, "but I do like it."

"But it's summer. It's holidaytime!" said my sister. "You don't *read* on holidays."

But Angelica smiled away and didn't say anything. We clattered across the bridge, her brown suitcase banging my legs and my heart sinking with every footfall. It was going to be a hateful week.

Lally was at the gate looking red and singing, a handful of wooden clothes pegs, and a big basket of washing in her arms. "Well! Here's Her Highness!" she called. "Have a good trip did you? I expect you're quite tired out and with that walk too. There's ginger beer in the kitchen and supper's at eight."

The room where Angelica was going to sleep was through our room, through Lally's, and then through a little cupboard place. It was very small, with a bed, a chair and a table with a drawer. The window looked right down the meadow to High and Over; and on a clear day you could sometimes see the sea like a piece of silver paper. I put her suitcase on the table and said: "We have to tell you something. If you have to go to the lav in the night it's under the bed." Angelica went white. "You've got the prettiest one," said my sister reasonably. "It's got a pheasant on the bottom." Angelica looked nervously round the room as if she expected it to rush out from under the bed or somewhere and peck her.

My sister humped the chamber pot on to the bed and looked at it with pleasure. Angelica did a wrinkling thing with her mouth and gently pulled off her pom-pom hat. "It's very nice," she said flatly and smoothed her hat with her long thin fingers. I thought that she was going to cry. She often did. Usually did, in fact. Once when we were all on holiday together in Wimereux she cried and moaned all day because our father and her father were going out fishing in a little boat together, and she wanted to go too. And

28

they had to take her, and she was most dreadfully sick all day and we were jolly pleased. Because none of the rest of us were allowed to go, and she was the eldest and rotten. And here she was wrinkling up her mouth and smoothing her hat and blinking away, and I knew the tears were coming and just because of an old chamber pot.

"We caught you some fish today."

She went on blinking. And smoothing.

"Because you're a Catholic," said my sister.

"They aren't very big, but big enough, and Lally has cleaned them and everything."

She stopped the blinking thing and sat on the edge of the bed.

"Thank you," she said in a sort of twisty voice.

"Perhaps," said my sister, "if you go to the lav just before we go to bed you won't need to use it. And then," she said happily, "I can have it back." She was holding the chamber up in the air like a tea-cup and looking at the marks on the bottom. "Or else I'll have to use my camel I won at the fair, and it's small."

Angelica snuffled and buried her face in her pom-pom hat.

★ ★ ★

Sitting under the apple tree was rather pleasant after that. It was a lovely tree, old and sort of leaning away from the sea winds. The bark was all rumply and covered with moss and lichens, and on one branch there was a bunch of yellowy-green mistletoe growing. And that's why it was our most favourite tree. My sister was squashing the scarlet berries from some cuckoo-spit in a tin. She squelched them round and round with an old wooden spoon. We were making Hikers' Wine. When we had squashed them into a pulp we poured them into an orangeade bottle, with the label still on, and then filled it with water. Then we used to go and leave it in the gully at a good place, and hoped that a hiker, feeling thirsty, would spot it and think how lucky he was. And of course it was deadly poison and if he drank it he'd probably die, which was fearfully funny. We had done this with about five bottles and they had all gone when we went to look the next day. The gully was full of the beastly people all clambering up in khaki shorts and green or yellow shirts, to see the smallest church in England. And we thought that Hikers' Wine might put them off. Or kill them off. And it looked exactly like orangeade . . .

had the same colour, and little bits of skin and orange-sort-of-stuff swirling about in it. It was better than setting rabbit traps for them, which we did . . . but they always seemed to avoid them. Feet too big, I think.

"The trouble with her is," said my sister, squashing away, "that she's potty."

"I think it's because she's a Town person . . . and because she's going to be a Nun."

My sister stopped squashing and looked at me with a mouth like an "O".

"In Czechoslovakia," I said.

"You're a fibber!"

"God's honour."

"Who said?"

"I heard Aunt Freda tell our Mother."

"Why is she going to be one in Czechoslovakia? Why not in Hampstead or somewhere?"

I took the tin away from her and did a bit of squashing, because they weren't quite mixed up and some of them looked like cuckoo-spit berries still.

"I don't know," I said. "Probably that's where you have to go to be one. Probably it's a sort of factory place where they specially make Nuns." We cried out with laughter. The sun was getting pale and a wind came shuddering up among the grasses making the lupins bend and nod like people agreeing. From the house was a good smell of frying. We squashed the berries into a paste and started to pour them into the bottle.

"I've seen Nuns in England. In Hampstead, in the Finchley Road and on a bus," said my sister. "They can't all come from the same place. Anyway," she added, pouring very carefully so that the "muck" didn't slide down the outside of the bottle and spoil the label, "anyway . . . they're jolly well welcome to her."

I lay on my stomach and ate a bit of grass which tasted like liquorice. Right down at the bottom of the meadow stood a clump of cows, brown and white, all standing looking at nothing. Sometimes they stamped a foot to move the flies, or tossed their heads and mooed; their tails swung and flicked; and there they stood chewing and blinking and looking at nothing, round the little iron gate. If Lally or our mother saw them round the gate like that they turned right in the road and walked a mile and a half up the chalk road to the house. They were so frightened.

My knees were cold; I rolled over and saw that my sister had got most of the stuff into the bottle, poured some water in, and was swirling it round and round, with her tongue sticking out like an adder's.

"That's it!" she said happily and shoved the cork in with a thump of her fist.

We took it and hid it in the scullery so that it could stand all night and settle. Otherwise it just looked like a sort of soup.

But in the morning, about midday when it was hottest and the hikers were scrambling up the gully, it would look like a lovely cool bottle of orangeade left behind after a picnic. To make it look a bit like that, we used to scatter a few bits of paper about, and screw up some cake boxes and things; sometimes an eggshell or two, so that it looked more real.

And the bottles always disappeared.

★   ★   ★

We all sat round the kitchen table in the soft glow of the evening light. It was too early to light the lamps, and the pink sun outside the windows just glanced on the knives and forks and the amber handle of the brass kettle on the range.

Angelica was pale but a bit more cheerful at the sight of food. She had changed her travelling clothes and combed her hair and washed her face, because she smelled of soap, and we wondered if she'd done any more than that, caught each other's eyes and squirmed with giggles.

Lally banged the fish server against the side of the pan.

"That's enough!" she said. "You two mind your P's and Q's or I'll take the back of my hand to you." She knew something was up, she always did.

The roach had sort of shrivelled up a bit; not enough for us all as it happened. But *we* had pilchards on toast while Angelica picked her way through the bones of her fish. But it didn't worry us because it made us look a bit more polite, and anyway we'd eaten hundreds of roach and liked pilchards best.

"They went specially out to catch these for you, these two," said Lally, waving her fork at us. "So you know they must be fresh; can't abide them myself, too muddy," she went on, "but I must say I like a nice pilchard, for all they repeat till Thursday forenoon." Angelica fiddled away at another bone.

31

"We're not actually supposed to have pilchards," I explained, thinking she might be interested, but all she said was "Oh."

"Because," I went on, cutting through a crust, "because our father won't have anything in the house in tins."

"He says everything in tins is Japanese and they kill people," said my sister.

"And if you so much as open your mouth and say anything about this," said Lally with a glinting look at us both, "I'll fetch you a wallop on the side of your heads as'll give you both a mastoid."

4

EGGSHELL had a humpity back, long white hair and a black coat down to her ankles. She never spoke to us, just hurried past with her head wagging and a funny black hat like half an egg pulled down to her eyes. So we called her Eggshell.

She lived up at the top of Red Barn Hill in a wooden caravan with big wheels and a little door at one end which opened in two pieces like a stable door. The caravan was just outside a little elderberry wood right on the edge of the hill; it was painted red and the wheels were blue, but that was a long time ago, and now they were faded down to almost pale pink and grey. There was a pointy little chimney sticking out of the roof, and sometimes you could see the smoke coming out with a smell of cooking, which made her seem a bit more real and not frightening. To get to the caravan you had to go up a little path, high up the hill from the gully, and then into the elder wood, and along another little twisty path all among the rabbit burrows, and then you'd see an old rusty milk churn, a little bit of garden, about as big as a box, and then the steps and door of the caravan. And that's as near as we ever got; it's as near as anyone ever got ever. Even Reg Fluke, and he's braver than I am, only got as far as that—so you can see that she *was* a *bit* frightening and of course she would be, because she was a witch.

We knew that because of the long hair and the funny hat and coat and all the cats. She must have had a hundred cats at least. Well, perhaps not a hundred exactly but really millions of them. You could see them sitting round the caravan: playing, sleeping or just sitting. And they were all colours; not only black like a witch's cat.

Once when my sister and I were up there hiding in the elders watching her, we saw her feeding them and heard, actually heard, her talking to them! That was a bit amazing really because we never heard her talk to anyone in all our lives. Just the cats. But we couldn't hear what she said; it was just a mumbling sort of sound, and she bent her way among them giving them bits of something to eat from a bag. We were a bit disappointed because, clear as clear, you could see the words "Home and Colonial" written on the bag and that didn't seem to fit in. But my sister said it had probably been left behind by some Londoners on a picnic and she'd stolen it. I said that I didn't think it could be stolen if she had found it and they had left it behind not wanting it, and my sister said: "Well, how do you know they didn't want it? She most likely stole it. Witches do. Remember about children. They give them to the Gipsies." And I fell silent, remembering what I had heard. But wanting to like her anyway, witch or not, because she liked the cats.

Reg Fluke, who lived at Farm Cottages in the valley, said that his mother, Beattie Fluke, used to go and see the witch, when she was a girl, because of her chilblains. Reg Fluke was a Village Boy, and we weren't, strictly speaking, allowed to play with him because of that. "They'll spoil your speaking ways," said Lally, and "They'll get you into mischief and do things you wouldn't like to tell your mother about," which made Reg Pretty Exciting. But actually he was a bit soft in the head and we didn't want to play with him anyway.

His mother was a bit different. And she was grown up. We sometimes used to meet her outside the Magpie in the afternoon, walking a bit funnily and with a bit of a red face as if she had been running. But she was always very friendly and used to carry a big white jug full of beer home for her husband's tea. She had a squashed face like a red orange, full of little holes, and a huge fat nose and no teeth, and she laughed so much you couldn't see her eyes, which got all squeezed up and ran with tears, so that she was forever wiping them, and her nose, with the back of the hand which was not carrying the jug.

"She's a witch all right," she roared with laughter when we asked her. "Been a witch all her life for all she's called Nellie Wardle and had a son as went to the war. Seen her about on her broomstick many a winter's night." We were sitting with Beattie Fluke on the river-bank, just beside the bridge. It was very hot, and she was having little sips of her husband's tea and fanning herself with her green tam o'shanter. "When I was a girl my mother used to take me along to her for my chilblains. I can't tell you what I had to *do*, that wouldn't be very nice, now would it, but it worked a treat. Oh! she had spells for everything . . . toothache, and harvest bugs and nettle-rash and never-you-mind-what-else. There's many a lady in this village as has got a lot to be thankful for to Nellie Wardle—and they don't go round the graveyard laying no wreaths, I can tell you that!" She roared with laughter and had some more of Mr Fluke's tea.

"But she doesn't really fly, honestly Mrs Fluke?" said my sister.

Mrs Fluke lay back in the grass and started laughing so much she spilled her jug. "Sometimes I actually seen 'er loop the loop!" she said, shaking with laughter and the tears pouring our of her screwed up eyes. "Loop the bloody loop, right over the church with streams of fire coming out of her behind." And she laughed until she choked and sat up slowly. For a moment the three of us looked at each other in silence, and then Mrs Fluke made a rather rude noise and said: "I can almost see her this minute . . . with all the flames . . . twirling and twirling and twirling." And she stopped, put her hand to her mouth with no teeth and said: "Now you run away and play, I'm going to have forty winks." And laying back in the grass, she put her tam o'shanter over her face and started to snore.

We walked along the path to the bridge in silence, pulling at the tall summer grasses and scuffing the stones along in front of us. Presently my sister said:

"I think she was lying. You couldn't possibly have flames coming from there, you'd get burnt."

"And anyhow they don't fly on brooms . . . that's old fairy tale stuff. They just live in dark places with cats and do spells."

"They *do* have cats," agreed my sister, "and she's got hundreds."

"And I bet she does spells. I think Mrs Fluke was right about that because Reg said she'd told him. About the chilblain part."

"Oh! I'm sure she's a witch, she *looks* like a witch to start with. Anyway let's make her a witch, it's more creepy like that."

So Eggshell was a witch from them on. We leant over the bridge making spit gobs and watching them float under our feet, rather like Pooh-Sticks, only we couldn't be bothered to run to the other side to see which of us had won.

"I think she's quite *vulgar*, don't you?" my sister asked.

"Mrs Fluke? Awfully. Saying 'Bloody' and making that noise. Awfully."

A moorhen went dibble-dabbling along the sedge and, seeing us, scurried into the willows.

"Behind seems quite a rude word," my sister said.

"I bet the Prince of Wales never says it."

35

"Do you think he's got one though?" my sister asked thoughtfully. "I don't think Kings and Queens have them."

"How do they 'go' then?" I said. "They must have."

"I suppose so. It's too difficult. But I do think 'behind' is quite a rude word," she said.

I made a very big gob, sucking in my cheeks to do it, and watched it swirl slowly down until it went splot in the water. "Bum is much ruder," I said.

My sister gave a shriek of delight and spun round on one foot. "Oh! yes!" she cried. "Bum's much ruder," and ran away laughing up to the road.

★ ★ ★

So we decided to take Angelica to see the witch. The week was pretty dull so far. When I showed her how to blow an egg she'd had a coughing fit and we had to hit her on the back quite hard; she had been quite polite and nice, and interested in, the slow-worm, but not anxious to touch it, and enjoyed a picnic in the big haystack in the yard, but hadn't liked the prickles, and come for a walk down the gully but found it damp, and generally was a Londoner. Lally said one evening that she was homesick, and that people who lived in towns usually were in the country because the quiet got them down. But my sister and I thought that she was (a) stuck up, (b) a cissy, and (c) soft in the head. Whoever went for walks, and quite long ones, in shiny London shoes—or read in her room on hot days when the larks were up in the sky wheeling and swooping and making it all loveliness? And Holy books at that. One we saw in her room was the Life of St Theresa. And there was a picture of a droopy sort of lady in brown, holding a bunch of roses and looking up to see if it was raining.

However, we decided on the witch. And it was a wet day. Pouring wet.

★ ★ ★

Lally was folding the tablecloth and my sister was clattering the forks back into their drawer when I said,

"Let's take Angelica up to Red Barn Hill."

"Oh! Let's!" said my sister and went to find her wellingtons in the shed. Angelica was up in her room writing her diary. That's another thing I didn't like about her, she always got out of washing up.

"She's a year older and the guest," said Lally, taking sides.

My sister came clumping back in her wellingtons, pulling on her old mac.

"Whatever do you want to go up there for, on a dreadful afternoon like this?" said Lally, blowing hard on a spoon and polishing it on her apron.

"We want to show Angelica where the witch lives," I said.

"Stuff and nonsense!" said Lally, huffing at another spoon. "There's no such thing. And don't you go putting the fear of God into Angelica or you'll catch it."

"She's got that already," I said, pulling on my boots.

Lally shoved the spoons into the drawer, hit me on the head, and said, "You should mind your tongue, or the Devil will fork it. You all go into the sitting-room and have a nice game of ludo or something. Or come and help me top and tail the blackcurrants."

But we went up to Red Barn Hill, the rain dripping down our necks, and Angelica wincing along in the chalky mud in a pair of my sister's boots which were a bit too small for her long Catholic feet.

"I don't want awfully to see the witch," she said, stepping round all the puddles she could find. "And in any case I don't believe in them, there is no such thing."

My sister was singing beside me plaiting a bracelet out of water grasses. She stopped singing and said, "Oh yes there are. They nearly all got burned at the stake, but this one got away and lives up there." She nodded her sou'wester towards the mist-shrouded hill ahead. "They were all burned by the Catholics ages ago . . . and then got buried at crossroads with bits of wood in their hearts." She started to sing again. Making very loud "La la-laaaas . . ."

"You are really very silly," said Angelica. "The Catholics didn't do any such thing. It was just People who did it . . . and you've got it muddled up, because if they did burn them how could they put bits of wood in their hearts at the crossroads? They would not have had any heart left would they? Anyway, that was highwaymen," she said happily.

"It was witches and it was crossroads," said my sister.

"You've got it all muddled," said Angelica.

"I have not got it all muddled," said my sister, shaking rain off her face. "It's you who are muddled. All Catholic people are muddled."

"They are not," said Angelica.

My sister went white with rage and brushed her face roughly with her hands as if it was covered in flies.

"My brother was going to be a Catholic once," she said.

"Shut up!" I said.

"You were! You were! You know you were ... you were going to be a Catholic and then you got put off because of all the learning. And he painted a statue of Jesus and gave him black hair and a yellow beard! There you are!" she cried triumphantly. "That's muddled if you like," and she walked ahead in the rain, scoffing, under her breath, nodding and wagging her head like a hen.

"She's boasting and telling lies," I said.

"I think she is a very stupid person indeed," said Angelica, "and I won't believe another single word she says." We walked on in silence. It was awfully difficult trying to talk to her, she was so polite and quiet, and she used words as if they cost her money each time.

* * *

When we went up the lane into the Market Cross my sister was in a happier state of mind because she had suddenly found a penny in the fluff of her raincoat pocket and went clumping into Bakers to spend it, and very kindly she bought us all a present. A farthing humbug each. Two for her, which was fair, it was her penny, and one each for Angelica and me. I shoved mine into my mouth there and then, but I saw Angelica carefully wrap hers in a handkerchief and put it in her bloomers.

Up in the little wood everything was shrouded in mist and raindrops. The mud was chalky white, and there was no sound except our feet slithering among the elder roots; and the scuttering of a rabbit now and then.

And then, quite suddenly, there was the caravan; glistening in the wet. A little wisp of smoke coming from the tin chimney stack: shabby looking and muddy. We squatted down under a bush and watched. I could hear Angelica breathing from the clamber up the hill; her breath hung round her face like a muslin cheese bag. My sister was chewing her humbug very quietly, in case Eggshell should hear anything.

But there was no one about. No cats even. Just an old tin table with a bit of lino stuck on it, some boxes, and a chopping block, and the milk churn, all rusty. The windows were tight shut—and the door. The rain had stopped and we were getting cramp a bit. And cold.

"If we *do* see her," said my sister in a whisper, "let's only wait a minute and then run away quickly. Just so that Angelica can see her Very First Witch." And she settled herself down in the dripping grasses like a broody goose.

Angelica moved a little and slid two inches down the bank. She gave a bit of a cry and hauled herself up to the bush again.

"I told you all about witches and that. I *told* you. It's silly and we'll all take cold," she said miserably.

My sister chewed hard and swallowed quite a large piece of humbug because I heard her do a "squeaking" noise very quietly. I was sucking mine slowly to make it last.

"All you believe in is Angels and Devils and Eternal Damnation and Purgatory and things," she said.

"Are," said Angelica.

My sister loooked at her blankly. "Are what?"

"It's 'are' not 'is'."

"But is *what*?" I asked.

"Are Angels, and the things she said just now."

"I don't know what you mean."

"Angels are plural. You can't be 'is' Angels. You have to say 'are Angels'."

"Potty," said my sister.

And suddenly we saw Eggshell. It was very frightening; she was coming up the hill through the mist on the other side of the caravan dragging a great big piece of a tree; and there were three cats running beside her. She was wet as wet, an old sack round her shoulders and she was muttering away to the cats. You couldn't hear what she was saying, just something like, "Tweedie, tweedie, tweedie." And she was shaking her head from side to side and dragging at the bit of tree.

We were frozen in a little heap under the bushes. No one even breathed. Eggshell was struggling and pulling at the branch, and the cats all came skittering up to the caravan, but the branch seemed to have got caught in something and suddenly, with a cry, Eggshell fell over in the mud; her legs up in the air and the sack and her hat all twisty. We caught our breaths with horror and suddenly Angelica said: "Help her." And before my sister or I could stop her she was slithering down the hill to where old Eggshell was struggling to sit up.

We were very astonished. And suddenly found that we were sliding down the bank too, and the three of us stood awkwardly round the wet and muddy Eggshell, who looked up at us with fury and cried: "What you want then?" Angelica started to try and help her up but got her arm punched for her trouble. "You be off!" cried Eggshell. "Leave me be." Anyway she couldn't get up and Angelica said: "We only want to help you. We'll pull you a bit." And my sister and I started to tug at her soaking old coat and she was pushing us away, and eventually we all got tangled up in a bit of a smelly pile, but at least she was standing on her own two legs. She started to brush herself down and tidy her hat, pulling it right over her eyes, and mumbling away like soup boiling. I started to pull up the branch, which was actually quite heavy, and in a few moments we had got to the caravan and the cats, which were crying about the steps. Eggshell started rummaging about in the pocket of her coat, wiped her nose on the back of her hand, and took out a big iron key from a crumpled piece of rag.

Angelica said, "Where shall we leave the wood?" and Eggshell just mumbled away and pointed under the caravan while she clambered up to the little stable door. Underneath was a big pile of sticks and logs—for her fire, I suppose—and so we lugged the branch underneath, panting and puffing and feeling a bit braver. Nothing terrible seemed to have happened. I mean she hadn't screamed at us or made a spell; anyway not that we could feel. The cats went on crying and rubbing their legs against the caravan steps and Eggshell opened the door and went in. The cats scampered after her. It was dark inside, as far as we could see that is, but there seemed to be a little iron stove-thing on one side with legs, and a bed and an old cupboard painted yellow and blue. Eggshell was rummaging about in the dark and we started to turn and go away. My sister said suddenly, "I've swallowed all my humbug," and we heard Eggshell call us. We turned in terror; we were just a little way down the path and she was standing on the steps with something in her hand.

"Come and look," she said. All wet and muddy and looking

terribly like a witch. "Come 'ere." And she offered a shape in her hands. It was a huge shell. As big as a hat. Brown spotted, with funny opened lips, like someone laughing. We went to the foot of the steps and she pushed the shell at Angelica. "Read what it says then," she said. "You read what it says."

Angelica took the shell in both her hands and we peered at the thing. "It says Bombay," she said politely. Eggshell came down a couple of stairs holding the little railing. "What does it say on t'other side?" We turned it round and there was the word MOTHER.

Angelica said: "On one side it says Bombay and on this side it says Mother." And handed the shell back to the Witch who took it quickly. "That's for the wood," she said, "fer helpin' with the wood. It's from my boy, oh a long time ago. They sent all his things. And this was fer me. It says Mother, don't it?"

We nodded. Eggshell went back up the steps slowly. The mist drifting away through the woods behind, the cats mewing. "Tiddy, tweedie, tweedie," she kept saying, and went into the caravan and closed the lower part of the door.

"That's fer helpin' with the wood. Now you clear off and leave me be." She closed the top half of the door and we couldn't see her.

We turned and started to walk down the winding path through the elders.

*　　*　　*

We didn't talk much until we had got down to Sloop Lane and then my sister said we mustn't forget the paraffin and the bacon. So we went into Wildes the Grocers and got them and started back home. The rain had quite stopped, and a white sun glittered and flickered on the river. The tide was coming in and all the muddy banks were being covered with swirly water. There was a cob swan ducking about slowly and two people we didn't know were fishing.

"It's a funny thing to write on a shell," said my sister. "Mother and wherever it was." She pulled off her sou'wester hat and shook her hair. "I suppose it was a sort of present thing, like we bring our mother when we go to Eastbourne."

"What sort of things do you mean?" said Angelica.

"Well, once we bought her a china lighthouse with 'Eastbourne' written on it and a sort of shield thing. Didn't we?" she asked me. And when I agreed she rattled on skipping over the planks of the white bridge ... "And once we bought her a dear little china shoe, didn't we? With little blue flowers on it and it just had 'Made In England' on it. But we bought it in Seaford."

We crossed the bridge and up the path, over the main road, and through the gate into Great Meadow. The paraffin tin was rather heavy.

"I think you were very brave about the Witch," I said. Angelica opened her mac and pulled up her sock which had slipped down. "She's just a poor old woman with troubles of her own," she said. "She was very pleased we helped her. And it was rather nice to see her shell. I don't suppose many people have seen that." My sister hummed her humming-not-listening song.

the Cottage from Great Meadow —

And there was the house, and the wooden fence and the privy roof and Lally pegging out some washing. She waved and called out something about the sun and trying to dry off a few things— but we weren't really listening. Angelica clambered over the fence and wandered off to help Lally with the laundry basket. My sister sniffed and swung back and forth on the gate. "Hummm," she said. "Well, it's very easy not to worry about witches if you're going to be a Nun. Very easy indeed." The gate squeaked a bit and she slipped off and helped me carry the paraffin. "Very easy indeed it is," she mumbled. And did a snort.

5

I CLONKED the two buckets gently on to the kitchen floor so that the water wouldn't spill over the polished bricks. I was a bit puffed because it was quite a long way from the pump. It was my morning job to fill four buckets "for the morning wash", as we called it . . . and then I had to do four more after lunch. My sister never had to. She just carried the milk in a white enamel can from the dairy down at the Court. It was quite a long way too; but not near as heavy as eight buckets of water.

They were still sitting at the breakfast table. Lally was talking to Angelica about her packing and some washing. My sister was building a spilly hill in the sugar bowl, dribbling sugar all over the tablecloth. Lally hit her and spilled a lot more. "Now look what you've done, Miss Fiddler," she cried, "can't keep still for a minute . . . sugar all over the place, now we'll be smothered in ants. Angelica, tell your mother I couldn't get the stain out of your green cotton. If you'd come to me sooner I might have managed. But damsons is damsons and they stay." She took up the pile of ironing and set it on the dresser. "That's ready for you when you start packing this evening . . . and now," she said, looking at us all, "what are you going to do with yourselves? Angelica? What would you like to do on your Last Day?"

Angelica looked a bit startled, I suppose that Last Day sounded a bit deathly or something, but as she was the guest it was up to her to decide.

"I really don't mind," she said helpfully.

Lally started sweeping up the breakfast things and clattering them on to a tray. "Well make up your minds and get out from under my feet, all of you," she said.

The sun was hot even though it was early. There was still dew on the big spikes of larkspur outside the kitchen door. We sat under the apple tree to decide. "We could go grass sledging up at Wilmington," said my sister. "We make a sledge out of a big old tin tray, and put some rope on it and then we take it up to the very top of the Long Man and slide all the way down . . . right down to the Royal Oak almost . . . it's very exciting."

The Pump.

Angelica didn't say anything. She was busy plaiting three grasses together.

"Sometimes you fall off," said my sister. "Once He fell off and cut His knee to the bone . . . show Angelica where you cut your knee to the bone," she said. But Angelica didn't seem interested.

She stared up into the apple tree as if there was an angel there. "It bled terribly. Or we could go to the cave or the dew pond. Only you could fall in the dew pond and if you do no one can ever get you out because it's very deep and goes to a point in the middle. We saw a drowned sheep there once. And the cave is a bit frightening. There are bats."

Angelica said, "I don't like bats, thank you."

We were quite silent for a minute and then I had a good idea. "Let's go to the church, then, and show her the altar and where the murder was. Shall we?"

My sister was on her feet in a minute and so was I and Angelica rather scrambled up and followed us down the garden path to the lane. I thought it was best just to go, otherwise we should have been there all day or something silly. And we were both rather longing for Angelica Chesterfield to go home to London and stop bothering us. We had to keep on thinking of things to amuse her. She never thought of anything herself. Only reading. And that was very dull and selfish of her.

We turned left into the lane and clambered up to the top where there was a great field of corn growing. And a little path waggling through it. And in the middle of the field, with great, huge trees all round it, was the Smallest Church In Sussex. Our house was the rectory. But all we had to do was change the water and the flowers in the vases once or twice a week. On the altar. Well, they weren't vases for the flowers. Jam jars. But we put white and blue crêpe paper round them so they looked rather pretty. And my sister always picked the flowers and arranged them herself. Sitting in the sun on a gravestone singing a hymn-sounding-song.

There was a little wooden fence all round the church, with a squeaky iron gate and inside the gate was the churchyard. All the tombs and gravestones were squinty, like people standing on a ship in a storm. Leaning in all directions and covered with moss. There was no one buried there who was new. The newest one was called Anne Stacie Departed This Life 1778 aged 78. We thought that was very interesting, but Angelica didn't. The door was always open and inside there was a lovely cool feeling and a smell of floor polish and candles. It was very, very small. Sometimes the Rector, Mr Eric Bentley, came up and preached a sermon. One Sunday in the month. And we all went. And there was another for the Harvest. And then lots of people came with sheaves of corn and apples and bread and things. And it was lovely. Usually there were only about twelve or fifteen people there: it only had room for twenty anyway. And hikers used to come and people from as far away as Lewes or Polegate. It was

too small inside for an organ so there was just a piano at the back and Winnie Maltravers playing hymns and singing very loudly, shaking her bun, so that we waited for it to start falling down round her shoulders, which it always did—in long grey wisps like a horse's tail.

On these days Lally wore her Best Brown and a hat with ivy

leaves on it which she bought one day in Seaford. It was a bit like a pudding basin and came right down to her eyes so that she had to tilt her head backwards to read the hymn book . . . only she never wore glasses so she just sang "la la la la" all the time, pretending she could see the tiny printing. Which, of course, with that hat, she couldn't.

Our mother gave us a penny each for the collection when it came round during "The Lord is My Shepherd" and it was interesting to see how much was in the plate to send to the African Orphans somewhere. Never very much. Because the hikers were a poor looking lot and no one ever gave more than a sixpence or a threepenny-bit. But Mr Bentley sent it all off to Africa once a month or so, with the collection from his big church in the village.

"This is the smallest church in England," said my sister, "and that's the altar where the murder was." She was speaking in a rather whispery way, not because of the murder but because you do whisper in church . . . even if it is very small. Angelica had made the sign of a cross and done her bob in the aisle and then we went and sat in one of the wooden pews. There were lots of little humpty cushions covered in carpet and some rather old hymn books. Angelica picked through one but didn't seem to take any notice of the word Murder at all. My sister got a bit irritated.

"About the murder," she said in the whispery voice, leaning very close to Angelica and putting her hand on the hymn book to stop her looking, ". . . about the murder. Well . . . it was ages ago and there was this Vicar, you see, and he had a very pretty wife and she was much younger than he was and didn't like churches and that sort of thing very much. And they were always having terrible rows and things. And one day he came into the church and found her kissing a man. Here. Right where we are sitting." She stopped for breath and stared at Angelica. Who didn't say anything at all. Just looked back. My sister started piling the hymn books on top of each other. "The church was much bigger in those days of course . . . huge they say."

Angelica said, "Who said so?"

"The people in the village. Mrs Fluke and Miss Maltravers and people. But the vicar took a candlestick from the altar and hit the man who was kissing his wife and killed him. And then he set fire to the church with the candles and they were burned to death. And that's why the church is so small. Only this bit was left."

The pile of hymn books fell down and they scattered all over the floor so we had to grovel about looking for them and putting them back on the pew shelves. It seemed a silly way to spend a Last Day . . . with the sun outside and Angelica not caring anyway. She was on her hands and knees under a bench and I heard her say she didn't believe it anyway. Not a word. And she crawled out and brushed down her skirt. My sister was red in the face and rather angry.

"Oh! Look! How sweet!" she said. "I've got a holy picture, it must have come out of the books. It's so pretty, it's a lady with some roses and a heart with red spokes pointing out." She slid it into a book and went off to look at the flowers on the altar which were looking a bit mouldy because we hadn't changed them since Angelica had come to stay. I wandered out and sat on one of the stones and peeled some moss off the word "resteth" with a bit of twig and Angelica did her cross and bob and came out too and squinted into the sunlight.

"I don't think it's really true, that story," she said, sitting down beside me. "I expect it is just a legend or something, don't you?"

I said I didn't know but it was true anyway, and we'd heard it lots of times and that when they got the bodies out of the church they were just ashes and they put them into a box together and took them down in a cart to the village, all mixed together like Hundreds and Thousands, and Angelica laughed a barking laugh meaning I was silly. So I shut up. But my sister came out and lay in the grass. "Now what shall we do?" she asked crossly. No one spoke. The day was very still. Not even a little breeze to make the poppies nod. Grasshoppers were clicking away and a pigeon was cooing up in one of the elms. It was the sort of morning for doing nothing on . . . so we just sat still. I went on picking away at "resteth" and found "in" under a lump of yellow lichen. My sister sat up, put her face to the sun.

"Lally said the murder was just passion. The vicar was so angry, he just hit the man with the candlestick without even thinking. He was so angry. Like when He . . .," nodding her closed eyes towards me, "stuck a knife in my back last Easter."

Angelica looked at me with her mouth open, and her eyebrows went up into her fringe.

"You didn't!"

"He jolly well did. Ask him."

"You didn't?"

I went on scratching at "in" and moved on to "for".

"Yes he did. You tell her or I'll show her the place."

"Yes I did," I said. "I did and I'm glad. It taught her a lesson."

"Humph," said my sister and opened her eyes.

"But why did you?" said Angelica.

"Because I was reading his silly old 'Larks' before he did."

"And it was brand new and no one had looked at it before," I said.

"But that wasn't a terrible thing to do."

"It was to him," said my sister. "He stuck the knife right in, just here," and she twisted about to show the place on her back.

"Only *I* can look at my 'Larks' for the first time. I saved it up all the way from Bakers and then when we got home I had to go and get some water and while I was gone she pinched it from the table and started to read it, and she scrunched it all up." I was shaking with anger at the thought of it and the bit of twig snapped in two.

My sister snorted with laughter and lay down on her back.

"He ran away, didn't you?" she said. "He just ran away and hid all night under the bridge down by the river while I was practically dying."

"You were not dying, it was a titchy little scratch. I've seen it," I said.

Angelica suddenly got up and stood looking at us with her beaky nose. "My mother said that you can't believe a word you say in your family. You all tell terrible stories because you are too romantic. She says it's because your mother was an actress and your father is a journalist and you just don't know what is real and what isn't."

We both looked at her very slowly. My sister sat up. And I said, "Well this part is true, and she has got a scar and you can ask Lally and I got a thrashing with a paint brush from my father, because actually he is an Artist, and the story about the murder is true because everyone knows it is . . . and so that's that."

My sister got up and pulled her socks out of her sandals where they had got all ruckled. "It's all true," she said. "And if you don't watch out, he might stick a knife into you too. He can do anything! . . . He once made Betty Engles climb a ladder and lit a bonfire at the bottom of it so she couldn't get down. And that's true too." And she tossed her hair to get the grass out of it and went off down the path to the gate.

Angelica and I followed her slowly. There wasn't much to do any more. The day seemed rotten. "I wouldn't really do anything like that," I said. "Only you aren't much like us, and you don't like the country much do you . . . I mean honestly?"

Angelica pushed the iron gate open and squeezed through into the lane. "It's not the same as Hampstead," she said. "It's all right I suppose. But there's nothing to do."

"But you don't like doing anything!" I said. "You just like to read or sew or read."

"Well, I like reading and sewing. But I don't like murders and witches and rain and all the funny things in the grass. You know . . ." She meant grasshoppers and burnet-moths and chalk blues and ladybirds and things. I really think she was more frightened of them than witches.

"Well, anyway," I said, "I wouldn't put a knife in you for that. God's honour."

She winced a little bit when I said God's honour but smiled a thank-you smile, and we just went back to the cottage in silence. People are funny.

The dew had long ago left the larkspur and the sun was beating down on the fields . . . all the grasses seemed to be silver and gold . . . and far away, past High and Over, you could just see a little line of blue which was the sea at Cuckmere Haven, and just as we got to the house Lally came out with a big stone jug of ginger beer and a bowl of biscuits. "Mademoiselle from Armentiers has been telling me you've been up to the Church and shocked the wits out of Angelica," she said, setting the jug in the grass by the step. "I just hope," she said to Angelica, "that they told you he got such a thrashing from his father that he couldn't sit down for a month of Sundays. Sticking knives in people's backs. I ask you!" she exclaimed to the sky. "He had a very nasty evening under the old bridge, didn't you? Very nasty indeed with half the village looking for him and his sister almost bleeding to death in the kitchen. What a day. What a family. It's a wonder I keep sane at all with this lot around me." And she stumped back into the house singing her John Boles song. Once, on her half-day,

50

she and Mrs Jane, who was staying with us, went to the cinema in Seaford and saw somebody called John Boles singing a song called "The Song Of The Dawn" or something . . . and that's about the only song she ever knew. But she only knew about three or four words, and like the hymn she "la laa-ed" the rest. And we listened to her Dawn Song while she banged about in the kitchen; we drank the ginger beer in the sun.

Presently Angelica said very thoughtfully, "I am sorry if I have been a nuisance to you."

"You haven't at all," I said, hoping she'd believe it.

"Well, I expect you'll be glad when I get on the bus this afternoon. You'll be glad to see the last of me. Good riddance to bad rubbish you'll say," and she started to cry.

Quickly I put my arm round her shoulders but she shook me off in case I might knife her or something, and stared at me with weepy eyes. "Don't!" she wailed. "Don't touch me." And she fumbled in her knickers for her handkerchief and blew her nose. We were silent for a bit.

"It's because I'm older than you two and I'm not much good at the country and things . . . but I do like you both, really I do. Even if you do set fire to people and knife people and frighten people with witches and murder. I do, honestly I do. I just don't show it very well." And she started to cry again. Before I could do anything, Lally came tearing out of the house, cuffed me on the head and pulled Angelica to her.

"What's he been up to, then?" she cried. "What have you been doing to Angelica? I can't turn my back for a minute without something happens."

Angelica stopped snivelling and said it wasn't my fault and that she was sorry and she'd go in and start her packing before the bus left for Seaford. And so Lally took her away chattering to her like anything and I rubbed my head, it was quite a hard cuff, and went off into the garden to think things over. Just as I was going past the raspberries I heard my sister burst with laughter in the house, and Lally called out something about giving me a good wallop because no doubt I needed it—and then someone rattled a window closed upstairs. And I was alone. And in peace. And ate some raspberries and thought what a rum life it was. Down at the bottom of Great Meadow there were twelve cows all standing with their heads together round the gate in the shade swishing their tails because of the flies, and up on the side of High and Over the big White Horse shone in the sunlight. It was lovely and peaceful. I was looking forward very much indeed to the bus for Seaford.

★   ★   ★

The canary I-didn't-really-win-at-the-fair wasn't very well. Although I had made a proper cage for it out of a Lifebuoy soap box and a real cage front, and had put proper perches and a seed and water pot and things, it just seemed frightened all the time. It just jumped from one perch to another all day long, or fluttered up to the top and banged its head and came fluttering down again to lie gasping in the sand tray. Also, its feathers were a bit moulty, and where the yellow ones came out brownish ones came back. It looked a bit piebald after a time. Lally said it was a linnet and not a canary at all.

"A poor little linnet, that's what it is," she said one evening when we were all sitting round the table trimming the lamp wicks. "I reckon Reg Fluke was right; they just trap them with bird lime and dip them in yellow dye and sell 'em to the fair people." She was polishing a big brass lamp vigorously and there was a nice smell of metal polish and paraffin. I was very carefully cutting round the wicks with an old razor blade and my sister was washing the chimneys in a bowl of soapy water and rinsing them at the sink. It was our Lamp Evening. A Wednesday. The middle of the week.

"I should let it go if I were you. How would you like to be cooped up in a little cage like that?" said Lally, giving the lamp an extra, final, wipe round and carrying it over to the others on the top of the copper. "Tell you what," she said. "If you do, I'll see if we can't get a real canary next time we go up to Twickenham to see Mrs Jane. How would that do?" She set the lamp among the others on the copper. There were quite a lot of them altogether. The one from our bedroom, the one from hers, the three from the sitting-room and the big hanging one with honeysuckle and clover on the shade which hung over the dining-room table. While she and my sister were drying the glass chimneys, I was having a good think about the canary. It was no use to agree with Lally immediately, you had to let it simmer along a bit, otherwise if you said "all right", or even "perhaps" she meant that you had said "Yes", and things got a

52

bit muddly. So I had a bit of a think and trimmed away for a while without saying anything at all.

It was a lovely warm evening. The kitchen windows were wide open and there was a soft breeze coming over from the downs smelling of cut hay and earth, and bats flitted about in the light from the last of the sun which was slipping away behind the elms of the gully, shining red through the branches like the fire in the range at Mrs Jane's house in Twickenham. When I thought of the range and of Twickenham I had a rather nice quick feeling inside. Next to here, I liked there the best in the world. Her house was very small indeed. There was the scullery first, with the sink and the pump in a corner where we all had to wash in the mornings and last thing at night, then the kitchen which was titchy too, but very cosy, with the range and brass gas lamps and Mr Jane's little bamboo table where he had his meals alone by the range itself, and the big table where we all ate from different plates and odd patterned cups and saucers. Mrs Jane said children liked variety. Then through the kitchen was the parlour. Which we only ever went into on Sundays after lunch. The parlour was a lovely room. There was a real marble mantelpiece and a little iron fire burning and three armchairs and a settee with only one curvy end, and a big sideboard where the bowls with the eggs were kept. One bowl had "Fresh Eggs" and the other just had "Yesterdays". In the middle of the sideboard there was a huge glass case with a whole family of stuffed partridges: the mother was looking very worried with her wings partly open and all the little chicks sitting underneath, and the father was standing at the back with his neck out and his beak open giving a warning. It was very pretty with lots of dried grasses and ferns and on the bottom of the case, in gold letters, it said "Wheelers Copse 1886. G. N. Jane", which was Mr Jane's name and the place where he had shot them somewhere quite near Richmond. It was my favourite thing, apart from the giant pike in the kitchen which he caught near Teddington, and the two big jars on the mantel which were covered with bobbly blackberries and brown and red leaves.

Upstairs there were three little bedrooms. One for us, one for Lally, and one for Mr and Mrs Jane. We never went in that one though. Our room had a window over the back garden and the pear trees, two beds and a po cupboard with a candlestick. And there was one picture of a big dog looking out of a kennel with rain pouring down and it was called "No Walkies Today". We rather liked that.

Outside there was a little front garden with a rockery made from lumps of clinker from the gas works and a pretty little star-shaped bed in the middle full of London Pride; and at the back there was a huge, long garden full of pear and apple trees and a big greenhouse against the wall which had a vine which came

1/2 Walnut Cottages. Twickenham.

from Hampton Court; and outside the back door a big walnut tree which is why the cottage was called "Walnut Cottage". Or rather Cottages, because there were actually two cottages joined together. Mrs Jane lived in one half and Mr and Mrs Poulter and their daughter Gooze lived in the other.

We didn't see much of Mr and Mrs Poulter, they were quite old, and just now and then I would see him pottering about in his vegetables next door, or perhaps Mrs Poulter would peg out a bit of washing. Sometimes they'd wave at us. But usually they were very quiet. I don't think that they ever spoke to Mrs Jane or Lally over the little fence which ran down the middle of the gardens, but Gooze did quite often. Gooze was older than Lally and wore glasses and a slide in her hair which was rather short and had a fringe in front. She wore plimsolls, black and white speckles, just the same as the ones we wore for Gym at school, and a long droopy woolly with a belt. She was very pale and smiled all the time. And she hadn't got many teeth. But she was very nice, and once she called us over to the fence to show us an Oxo tin with a dead mouse in it. "Found it in the wash-house dead," she said. "Now I'm going to bury 'im, Mrs Poulter can't abide mice," and she went away laughing a lot. We thought she was rather odd. Lally said she was "a bit thin up on top, but no harm in her", and told us that when she had asked her mother and father where she came from they told her from under a goose-berry bush. And that's why she was called Gooze.

Thinking about it all I began to hum a bit and feel happy and looking forward to something. "When would we go to Twicken-ham?" I asked. Lally was just passing me, carrying the lamps on a tray into the sitting-room and she gave quite a jump. "Goodness, you startled me. I thought you were in one of your sulks," she said and went on into the room. "We could go when I have my two weeks in September," she called. "If your mother and father say yes you could come up with me then. September for the Victoria Plums." I collected the wicks and took the chimneys from my sister, who was busy breathing on them and polishing them up with a yellow duster. I heard Lally climbing the stairs to the bedrooms with our lamps and so I called out to her, "All right. I'll let the canary go tomorrow morning if we can go to Twickenham in September." My sister looked very astonished. "Don't forget to remind her about the other canary, the one she said you could have if you go there," she hissed. "She might forget." I went to the stairs and called up into the darkening rooms, "You won't forget the canary, tho', will you?"

Lally was in her room and the door was closed so that her voice sounded far away. "We'll see about that when the time comes. If you've done those wicks and the chimneys you'd better set the table for supper. The Prince of Wales will be here presently . . ." I went back to the kitchen and started smoothing out the table-cloth. "She hasn't forgotten about the bird, she's just not going to say anything definite," I said.

My sister scattered some plates about and got the pickles down and the butter and the cocoa jug. "Well, let's let the other one go first thing in the morning, that'll remind her of her promise," she said and smiled a smug looking smile. "Perhaps we could get two canaries next time . . . real ones I mean. And then we could build an aviary place and have a real tree and things inside so that they could have a nest and eggs and everything. And we could sell the babies and make a lot of money, that would be nice, wouldn't it?" But I was too busy thinking about Twickenham to answer her.

★   ★   ★

Very early the next morning we took the cage out into the garden under the apple tree and I opened the door. The canary just skittered and fluttered and banged itself against the wires and Lally told us to come away and leave it alone. Which we did. And when we turned round it had gone! Just like that. It didn't fly away over the fields singing and singing for joy. Just vanished. There was nothing in the cage except a few crumbly feathers.

"I never saw it go!" said my sister. "It must have been in a terrific hurry to escape."

I felt quite miserable really. I had been so proud of it. But of course if it was really a dyed linnet it was better to let it go because it would never have got tame; wild birds never do in cages. My sister tried to cheer me up; she could be quite nice sometimes when she was feeling in the mood, which wasn't often; and sometimes it was because she wanted me to do something for her which she knew she couldn't do for herself. And she was in one of those moods this morning, I could feel it.

"Come on," she said, taking my arm, "let's go down to the gully, I've got something marvellous to show you. You will be surprised. Come on." And because I hadn't anything else to do at that moment I went with her. We clambered up the hill outside the fence, to the top, and reached the big wood where the gully was hidden. It was cool and green and damp smelling under the trees; the sides of the gully were all big lumps of chalk with funny roots tangling about and long trails of ivy and deadly nightshade. It was very quiet in there; you could just hear the wind moving about in the tops of the trees and the noise of our feet slithering in the muddy ruts of the floor.

There were voles down there, and hedgehogs too. We used to hear them at dusk squeaking and rustling about in the leaves

looking for slugs. Which we thought rather disgusting. And once we found a great toad with golden eyes bulging in a little cave place in the chalk. It was almost as big as a plate and when we carried it back to the house and showed Lally she covered her face with her hands and threw the darning at us. "Take the horrible thing away!" she cried. "It'll give you warts you'll see. Take it out this instant." She was really awfully silly about toads. She didn't mind anything else almost, except cows, but she was scared out of her wits by a humble, nice looking old toad.

But there weren't any toads down in the gully this morning. And we twisted along through the old cart ruts and brambles until my sister told me to stop, and there in front of me was a great pile of old tin cans and bits of bedsteads and rusty wire. It was just an old rubbish dump. Nothing exciting at all.

"I can't possibly be surprised by an old rubbish dump," I said. "And anyway, I've seen it before. It's been here for years and years."

My sister was rooting about in the tins and bits of old iron bedsteads, there were tangles of old chicken wire and an oil stove with a broken door lying in a clutter of pram wheels and shards of a broken plough.

Suddenly, amidst all the clanking and clonking my sister gave a cry and called out: "Shut your eyes. This is the surprise!" So I shut my eyes and heard her breathing and bonking and then she said I could open them and I did and there she was holding up a silly old tin box. There was nothing surprising about it at all. Just a biggish sort of biscuit tin with "Huntley and Palmers" written on it, that's all.

"Look!" she said. "Isn't it sweet, though?"

"It's a biscuit tin. I've seen hundreds and hundreds of them and I don't think it's a bit of a surprise."

She came clambering over the pile of old junk holding her rotten old tin. "But it's practically new!" she said. "There's almost no rust on it. And it's got a nice lid which fits. It's just what I want to make my scent with." And she set it down carefully in the muddy chalk.

"What do you mean, your scent?" I asked. She really could be very dotty sometimes, and I knew that somewhere she was getting me to do something for her. She was singing away and opening and closing the lid of her tin and tearing off the remains of the paper label.

"It's such a marvellous find. I discovered it yesterday all by myself. I was down here and I just saw it glinting in the sun, so I came all the way down, not a bit frightened really, and when I saw it I was *so* happy. Because now I can make my scent if you'll help me just a bit. All you have to do," she said quickly in case I started to clamber up the gully and leave her in the junk heap, "all you have to do is to knock some lovely holes in the sides, and a few on top, and then I will have a wonderful stove thing to boil up the rose petals and so on." She sat there looking up at me, her eyes wide with pleasure. I think she could almost smell her beastly scent already.

"Then what do you do? If I do knock holes in it?" I asked.

She crossed her legs importantly and hugged herself with her skinny brown arms. "Well," she said thoughtfully. "Well then when you do, I'll put it on some big stones, and then I'll make a fire inside with some logs, and put on the lid and then I'll have a stove. See? And the draught will come down through the holes and make the fire burn . . . and then it'll go up and heat the can of water and rose petals on top. And when it's all boiled it'll be scent."

I thought about this for a time. It seemed a bit dense really; but I had nothing else to do and no money to spend down at Bakers and I was still feeling a bit miserable about the canary linnet and the empty cage. So I agreed to help her and we knocked holes in the tin with a hammer and a quite big nail. I made a sort of ring pattern on each side and a bigger one on the lid. She went off collecting the stones to set it on so that we could get a good draught under it, and gathered some dead sticks and bits of bark to start the fire. And then came the boring part really; collecting the rose petals and the flowers to boil up. We got quite a lot. And some nasturtiums and a few sweet-peas which were growing all round the privy. And then she filled a cleanish tin can with water, poured in the petals and set it on the stove.

I must say that her idea worked a bit better than I thought. But it did take rather a long time to get the fire alight and we wasted hundreds of matches and used two pages of an old comic before it started to burn, and when it did there was so much smoke that my sister started coughing and groaning with her eyes pouring with tears; she looked just like a dreadful old witch. If Angelica had been there she really would have had to believe it, Catholic or not, because she was just like one. I got fed up with the smoke, and after all it wasn't my scent and I had helped her, so after a while when the smoke was rather thick and she was still spluttering and coughing away, I went off on my own under the trees and soon reached the end of the gully which came out at the very bottom of Great Meadow near the road to the village. People said that the gully was once part of an old smugglers' road which led from a tunnel under our house and right down to the Magpie Public House in the village. Some people said that it went on from there all the way to the cliffs at Birling Gap where they landed all the rum and stuff on the beach and brought it up on ponies to our house where they hid it in the tunnel under our hall.

Once our mother was crossing the hall with a bowl of flowers to set on the sitting-room table and there was an awful crash and a screech and when we all ran into the hall there was no sign of our mother at all. Just a big hole in the floor-boards. Our father was very shocked, indeed. We all were.

"Margaret!" he yelled out, "Margaret, what's happened, where are you?" And then far away under the hole, or so it seemed, we heard our mother's voice calling up, "I've fallen through the floor. I'm in a hole down here."

Our father was peering over the edge of the hole and Lally was wringing her hands and saying, "Oh poor Lady! Poor soul! O! What'll we do?" My sister was too terrified to cry, but hearing our mother's voice was a bit reassuring.

"Margaret, are you hurt?" called our father, starting to struggle down the edge of the hole.

"No, just bruised, I think," came our mother's voice. "Try and get a torch or a light, it's terribly dark down here."

Lally ran off for a torch and our father threw down a box of matches and started scrambling through the hole calling out to her all the time, "I'm coming down, dear, I'm coming down." It was all very exciting once we knew she wasn't dead or covered in blood. At last he was hanging by his hands and I heard our mother saying in a very muffled sort of voice, "I've got your legs, darling," or something and then he disappeared too. Just then Lally came back with the torch from the kitchen and gave a great cry when she saw no father and just the empty hole.

"Where's he gone?" she cried. "Oh Lord have mercy."

"He's down the hole with our mother." I explained he just climbed down. We passed the torch to him, it was so deep down in the hole that just his hand came through the floor. "Your mother's all right," he said and took the torch and disappeared into the dark. We were a bit worried; the three of us just sat round the hole and waited. Lally was fanning herself with her hands. "I can't take these shocks," she said. "They get my heart quick as a dart," and puffed away. My sister was kneeling down, peering over the floor. All the boards were broken round the edge where our mother had gone through.

"This house is too old," said Lally, getting some of her breath back. "Those boards are rotten through and through, it's a wonder she wasn't killed I declare. Like bits of sponge cake they are, and covered with that rug you'd never see a sign. Too old. The whole place is too old."

After a while we got ladders and things and helped them up

again; our mother was very stiff but all right except for a big bump on her head, but she kissed us both and said there was nothing to worry about, and then our father came up looking quite excited and said the hole was a sort of tunnel all lined with bricks . . . but that it was blocked up with rubble at one end. He seemed more excited about the brick walls of the tunnel which he said were all made of very thin bricks which meant that they were Tudor, or something, or earlier. Then Lally made our mother have a lay-down, as she called it; and when there were really no bones broken and everything was tidied up we were allowed to go down ourselves.

It was very creepy. It was dark and damp and there were little puddles on the muddy floor . . . and it was quite round, like a railway tunnel, but very much smaller . . . only wide enough for two to walk side by side. It went quite a long way until the rubble started and our father said we must be beyond the cottage by now and in the Great Meadow, or nearly. Lally didn't like it much at all. She didn't even like going down the ladder to start with, and when she found an old muddy wellington boot lying in the slime of the floor she nearly had a turn and our father helped her out again and up the ladder. But it was just an old wellington, I mean nothing to do with smugglers or anything exciting like that.

After a while we had all the floor-boards mended, and people came and examined the tunnel and said that it probably started in the middle of the little church and came down under our house and then went on down the hill under the meadow to the village. But we never really found out. And in time we all forgot about it, except on winters nights when I thought we heard ghostly rumbling noises of barrels being rolled under the house. But it was only ever the wind in the elms. Anyway it was quite exciting to have a part of a real smugglers' tunnel under your own hall. Except of course that our mother could have been killed or broken her legs or something, and afterwards Lally used to walk on tiptoe crossing the hall to the sitting-room in case it all fell down again. But it never did.

6

A T TWICKENHAM, after Walnut Cottage, there were three
other favourite places; although Walnut, with its garden and
the greenhouse and a great long shed which Mr Jane used for
"pottering" in, was really the most favourite. I did like the toy
shop in Church Street, the boat-yard near the bridge where we
used to get punts from, Eel Pie Island, and Marble Hill.

Marble Hill was lovely. It was a big white house, not as big as
Hampton Court, but white and gleaming in the sun. There was
a great park all about it, and real hills which you could run up,
and trees and, best of all, a lake-thing full of lilies and goldfish.
Not many people used to go there. Perhaps because of the White
Ladies in the lake. They were huge. Bigger than me or even
bigger than our father—and they were all sitting on white rocks
combing their hair, or pulling their friends out of the water. It
really was very strange to look at. These big ladies, and some
were gentlemen, were sort of all having a day by the seaside, only
in the lake. The ones in the water, well, the parts of the ones
which were in the water, were all green with slime, and they
reached their hands up to the ones who were all busy combing
their hair, for help.

My sister thought they were all drowning, or had fallen in
among the lilies and fishes; she liked them as much as I did. But
she said they were rather rude, simply because they hadn't got
any clothes on, and she was worried about the gentlemen ones
who wore a sort of leaf thing and were all trying to climb the
white rocks. Lally said that it was a fountain and made from
marble in Italy and was very famous and beautiful if you liked
that sort of thing. But Mrs Jane didn't, and wouldn't really look
at them, when she came sometimes with us, and just went on
with her knitting in a chair.

We used to go there quite often, to get a breath of air, as Lally
said, and also to meet some of her other friends who also had
children with them, but much younger than we were . . . usually
in prams. It was quite a long way from Twickenham and we
took a bus from The Green and clambered up on the top deck
and sat on the slatty seats looking over the side. It was rather like

being on a boat. And sometimes, in wet weather, we had a canvas apron thing which we pulled over our knees, which made us feel very snug and safe.

From the top of the bus you could look down on people in the street, and they never knew, and also, which was more fun, you could see into people's gardens all along the way, and sometimes into their rooms. Which was very private, rather like spying. You could see people washing up, or sewing things at a machine, or having their teas, and they never ever knew that we were both watching them all. Mrs Jane said they ought to have curtains up, but that would have spoiled the fun really. It was just that they didn't know we were watching that was so interesting. Once we saw a very fat man dancing all by himself; he twirled round and round, and had his arms up in the air. I think that he was singing too, because his mouth kept on opening and shutting like a fish. We were always told it was rude to stare, but on top of a bus it was hard not to. You couldn't just look ahead all the time like Mrs Jane who was terrified that the wind would take her hat off, even though it was pinned hard into her bun. She used to get quite cross with Lally for letting us spit on the people in the street. Well, not actually spit *on* them, rather we used to drop a bit of a gobbit on the ones who had hats on. Never on people who hadn't.

"They really are getting out of hand," she used to say to Lally. "Why don't you stop them? It's disgusting what they're doing."

"It's only a bit of spittle, Mother," said Lally. "Your hat won't blow off, you know . . . you'll have arm-ache if you go on holding on to it like that."

"And if it does blow off? What then? It's my best you know. We aren't all made of money like some I wouldn't like to mention not half an hour from Twickenham Green. You've got spoiled in your ways, my girl. When I was in Service it took me a year to save up for a new hat . . . I am not about to forget that, my girl." When she said My Girl to Lally we knew that she was really a bit vexed. And Lally knew it too, because she shook a fist at us and told us to stop, or else we'd get a good hiding.

Going home was rather nice too, nearly as exciting as going to Marble Hill. We got off at The Green and walked down under the chestnut trees, across the main road, and then down the street to the Cottages. They were right down at the bottom; you could see them from a long way off because of the big walnut tree and the little white fence round the clinker rockery in the front garden full of London Pride. Sometimes Mr Jane would be home first; we always knew because his bicycle was propped up against the shed in the little yard at the back through the green door.

"Father's home," said Mrs Jane, pulling out her hat-pin and smoothing her bun, and went into the kitchen. We washed our hands at the scullery sink, a big yellow stone one, with a pump and a tin bowl and a pink cake of soap which smelled of disinfectant, combed our hair, and went into the kitchen for tea.

The kitchen was really quite small with a little window which looked out into the garden but which was so full of geraniums and wandering sailor that you could hardly see out. There was a range with a brass tap and knobs on the oven doors, a big table where we all ate, beside the staircase, and a small cross-legged bamboo table where Mr Jane ate alone by the fire. He was very deaf and didn't like having to make conversation. He hardly ever spoke at all, actually. Sometimes he said in a very rumbling voice, "Thank you, Mother," or "I think I'll be going up then," or sometimes when he found something interesting in the local paper he'd say, "I see they're at it again." But you never knew who they were or what they were up to. So you couldn't answer him even to be polite. No one ever seemed to talk to him really. But, sometimes, when we were in bed, we could hear Mrs Jane's voice telling him what we had all been doing during the day. We never heard him, only her, because she had to talk very loudly. Their room was next door to ours so we were able to hear everything pretty clearly. I felt rather uncomfortable and tried to make coughing noises so that she'd perhaps hear that we were awake. But she never did, and after a while I didn't bother any longer.

Over the range there was a stuffed pike and a very brown picture of two people praying in a sunset, and above our table there was a much bigger picture of ladies in night dresses lying all over a staircase with bowls of fruit and flowers scattered every-where. The one I liked best was next to the scullery door. It was very sad. A man in a kilt with a bandaged arm was crying on a lady's shoulder, and she looked awfully pale. Or glad. Or some-thing. But my sister and I both thought it was dreadfully sad except that there was a rather silly looking baby in it too, and we felt that rather spoiled it all. But the room, with the gas lamps flickering and the range glowing all red, was very cosy indeed and if there had to be a winter it was better to have it in the kitchen at Walnut than anywhere else.

Lally was setting the table, laying out the plates and the white cups with the gold clover leaf on them. Not Best today, because we were Family. I took down our plates; my sister had a picture of a bunch of roses on hers, and mine had a view of the pier at Worthing. We always had these special plates and washed them up ourselves afterwards.

"Your favourites today!" said Lally, bringing in a china bowl filled with freshly boiled winkles, which she placed on the table with a brown loaf of bread, butter and a scatter of hat-pins to eat the winkles with. Mrs Jane was busy filling the big blue teapot.

"I can't abide those silly little things," she said, indicating the winkles with a nod of her head, "too fiddly and nothing on them to fill a person. Give me a nice fat bloater any day." She swung the kettle back over the fire and stood the teapot in the hearth to "draw" as she called it, and set a large plate of bloaters before Mr Jane. He looked up from his paper slowly.

"What's that then?" he asked.

"It's your tea, what else," shouted Mrs Jane kindly.

"Bloater is it?"

"That's what it is. You know you like them so don't make a fuss."

"It's the bones," he mumbled.

"You trim your moustache and you wouldn't have trouble with bones," said Mrs Jane, cutting him three large slices of bread. "Now, you be a dear soul and get them behind you and never you mind the bones. The children wanted winkles and you can't manage them with the pins and all. A bloater's filling and good," she finished briskly. "Won't go to the barber and won't let me use the scissors on him," she said to Lally, ". . . and now he complains about the bones because his whiskers are too long. He's a stubborn man. Always was, and always will be, please God."

After the winkles, which took quite a long time to eat because you had to pull them out of their shells with the hat-pins and sprinkle them with vinegar, we had home-made raspberry jam and a large piece of seedcake, and that was tea. Afterwards we all helped with the washing up in the scullery and set the crockery back on its shelves again and Lally cleared the table so that she could do some mending while Mr Jane snored quietly in his big chair, his paper over his face to keep out the light.

"When he wakes up after his nap," said Mrs Jane, "you can ask him to show you his bit of Zeppelin if you like. He may not feel up to it, on the other hand he may, there's no telling. But keep a sharp eye open for when he starts to stir and if he *doesn't* start to read his paper, you can ask him."

A little while later the paper slid off his face, he rubbed his eyes, shook his head a bit, and folded his arms on his rather large stomach.

"Dropped off," he said.

"Yes, dear soul, you did. Snoring like a grampus you were."

"Snoring was I?" He looked vaguely curious.

"Like a grampus," cried Mrs Jane, folding up the newspaper and putting it under a cushion. "Now why don't you take the children out to see your bit of Zeppelin? Do you good to get a breath of fresh air . . . it isn't dark yet and it's not that far to the shed." She was being very bossy and almost pulled him out of his chair which he clearly didn't want to leave. Muttering under his breath he took his keys off the mantelshelf, pulled his red and white spotted handkerchief tight round his neck and, pulling me gently by the hair, he went to the scullery door. He smelled nicely of cough-drops, as he always did.

"Not far to the shed!" he said grumpily.

"No it's not! You need a bit of exercise," called Mrs Jane, stacking up his cup and saucer and plate.

"Not far to the Palace either," he said, "and I been there twice today on my bike. Once there and once back. I have had all the exercise I need for one day."

"You haven't been twice to the Palace, Father, you've been there once. The next time you were coming *from* the Palace home. So it stands to reason you only *went* once. Unless you forgot something and had to go back?"

"Whether I went twice or not doesn't matter. It's the same journey whichever way. You try it, my girl," he grumbled out of the door and I followed him out into the yard. "Women," he mumbled, fiddling with his keys and finding the right one he opened the shed door and the familiar smell of dust and varnish and winter onions filled the air.

The shed was long and low and dark. It was stacked with old boxes, piles of sacking, fishing nets, fishing rods, ropes of onions and shallots and sacks of corn for the hens. On one side ran a long wooden work bench with shelves above cluttered with boxes marked in white painted letters "Screws", "Nails", "Washers", "Tin Tacks" and so on, and all with their sizes after them. He was very methodical. Above the shelves hung a fox's head with its mouth open, and glassy eyes staring. He had shot it many years ago near Richmond which was where he used to do all his shooting when he was a young man. He fumbled about with some matches and lit the hanging lamp above the bench and suddenly the shed was filled with leaping shadows which came and went with the swinging of the lamp while he searched for the biscuit tin of Treasures. I knew where it was, but was much too polite to say, and anyway he liked to make it all a bit more exciting before finding it, which he did presently, and set before me on the rough wooden top of the bench. It was a fairly large tin with a scratched picture of Windsor Castle on one side and the King's mother and father on the lid.

Carefully he opened it and gently shook everything out. Brass buttons, cigarette cards in neat little bundles, a tusk from a wild pig, a tooth from a shark, a set of dominoes, a bullet, some old coins, and best of all these, the bit of the Zeppelin. A small ragged cross of aluminium, with bolts stuck on it. I took it in my hand reverently. Although I had done this many times with him, I knew he liked me to be pleased each time.

"Potters Bar, that was. I'll never forget the night that came down."

"All in flames?"

"Yers. Burning like a beacon . . . like a great big burning fish in the sky." He put his fingers to his moustache to find, I thought, a lost bone from the bloater.

"Young Bert Taylor and me got pretty near to it after it was cool, and pulled this bit off as a sort of memento. It gave them Jerries a bit of a fright, that did, and they'd been dropping their bombs all over just anywhere and it served them right. Zeppelin they called it . . . a great big thing it was. You never saw such a blaze." And then he lost interest and started pottering about in the shed. I asked him if I could take it and show my sister and he said I could but to bring it back as soon as she had seen it, he said otherwise he'd catch his death because the shed was damp, but he didn't seem to be in much of a hurry.

My sister had stayed in the kitchen because the shed gave her the creeps and once she had seen the fox snap its jaws at her, so she said, and its eyes followed her everywhere she moved. Which was silly seeing that they were glass eyes and it was only a head anyway, not a whole fox. Anyway she wasn't interested in the bit of Zeppelin.

"It's only a silly bit of twisty tin," she said. "How can you tell it's from a whatever it's called? It might just be a bit off an old cart or something."

"It's from a Zeppelin and it got shot down at Potters Bar all on fire. Everyone was burned up too. It's famous," I said.

"Well, it served them right, getting burned up, if they were Germans, and it's not the sort of thing girls like anyway. Wars and things like that. Now if it had been a dear little mouse, or a baby rabbit . . . or something *sweet* like that, well, it would be different. But it's just a soppy old bit of tin that's all and there's nothing interesting in that." She was helping Lally to sort out some eggs to go in the bowls in the parlour next door. "Todays" and "Yesterdays". Lally was marking some with a "T" and others with a "Y" and there was a separate little bowl with six Bantam eggs in it. These were for my sister and me. We had two each for breakfast every morning if we were lucky, with fried bread and bacon. Mrs Jane collected them all up and took them into the parlour.

"You'd better take it back to Father," she called. "He'll catch his death in that old shed, it's full of dust and rubbish, it'll bring on his cough again. Be a good boy and take it back, do. And tell him to come in while you're at it. Tell him I said so."

Together, he and I shovelled all the bits and pieces back in the tin box, the buttons and the dominoes and the bit of Zeppelin. He doused the lamp, and we made our way back to the glowing kitchen and the little scullery lit by one wavering candle where we had to, both, wash our hands before we were allowed into the house again.

"There's no knowing what you have handled in that old shed," said Mrs Jane, ". . . full of rats and mice and the dear knows what else. And Father must be tired if he *was* twice to the Palace today, although I very much doubt that, I'm sure. I'll ask him in bed later."

"Did he go to see the King and Queen?" said my sister in a silly way, not really meaning it but just being irritating.

Lally gave a sort of sniff of laughter. "I'll give you King and

Queen, my girl. Father's been to Hampton Court . . . not the one in London . . . he goes there every day of his life and you know it, Madam. He tends the clocks and sees that they all tell the same time as each other. It's a very responsible job, you know One day the Prince of Wales will pop in, and ask him the time and he'll be able to say, right out, 'Half-past eleven', or whatever it will be, 'Your Highness, and its exactly right'!" She poked away at the fire in the range, stuck on another lump of coal, fixed the slide in her hair, and took down the box of Games which sat on top of the green wooden cupboard.

"Come along now . . . we have time for one good game of Snakes and Ladders before cocoa." And spread the board out on the table.

⋆　⋆　⋆

It was lovely and peaceful lying on the grass under the great pear tree. If you looked up through the hundreds of leaves you could just see little specks of blue sky and sometimes bits of white cloud drifting far above. It was just like being in the country and not at all in a town like Twickenham. Just across the grass was the hen run, and on the other side the place where the ducks lived, which was muddy and sploshy with water that they spilled out of the old tin bath which Mr Jane had sunk into the the ground to make a little pond for them. And past, quite a long way past, them was the greenhouse with the vine. All over one wall, great glossy leaves and bunches and bunches of fat blue grapes in October. It really was like the country; and even seeing old Mrs Poulter hanging out her washing over the fence didn't spoil anything, because she was so quiet she hardly got noticed. But Mrs Jane said that it was all changing:

"Not like it was, mark my words. I remember, not so long ago, walking all the way to the Village through the fields . . . from here to Church Street . . . and now they're building rows and rows of houses all round Pope's Grove, and The Lodge is sold and they do say it's going to be a hotel or something. I never thought I'd see the day. I hope Father and I don't live to see the time when all this has to go, as go it will, mark my words, everything goes too fast nowadays . . . much too fast." She jabbed her knitting needles into a ball of wool and started to tidy up her old straw work basket.

Lally was sewing buttons on one of my shirts when she suddenly said: "Mother, the boy here wants a canary bird. He won one at the fair, remember, but it was a wild bird so we let it go. I promised him a real canary." My heart leapt. She *had* remembered! I looked at her with such delight that she scowled at me and said: "Don't you get too uppity, Sir . . . nothing settled yet. I'm only asking, that's all." I rolled back on to the grass and closed my eyes. My heart thumping. Listening to the talking, crossing my fingers. Mrs Jane sounded a bit distant, I think she had started to walk up to the house but I heard her say: "You better have a talk to Father . . . he knows what's what in this place. Bert Batt had some a while ago, but I don't know now, ask your Father." I opened my eyes and stared up into the pear tree . . . she *had* remembered after all. Now all I had to do was pray.

When we were washing our hands for lunch I whispered the news to my sister who was so impressed that she wiped her hands on her shorts instead of the towel.

"I wonder if we can have *two*? One for me and one for you like I said and we can have babies and sell them and all that sort of thing? Wouldn't it be marvellous if we could?"

I said I didn't care about two as long as there was one for me because it was, after all, my canary; I had let the wild one go free so it was my reward.

"You don't get rewarded for doing kind things," said my sister. "Everyone knows that. But I'd help you to look after it, I promise. Oh! wouldn't it be *lovely* to have babies and nests and all that sort of thing? But wouldn't it?"

The next evening when Mr Jane came back from the Palace on his bike, had had his tea, read his paper and slept a little, Lally shouted at him about the canary and Mr Batt, and he said, yes, Mr Batt had some . . . this year's hatchings and five shillings each.

My sister covered her face with her hands and cried, "Oh! Oh! He's only got one shilling and four coppers left." She looked, when she took her hands away from her poky face, quite pleased. I wanted to hit her but I was too shocked by the price. I only got sixpence a week pocket money and this I had saved up for three weeks to come to Twickenham. The canary seemed a long way beyond my reach now. But I didn't let anyone see, I just went on writing in my little red note-book. I was busy writing a new play and I had to put my thoughts together so that no one could really guess what I was thinking. And the play had to be finished before we all left at the end of the week, because we were going to "do" it on our last night as a Thank You to Mrs Jane for having us there.

"I don't think he really wants a canary now, do you?" said Lally, cheerfully cutting up a long green bean. "I think he's got it out of his system, Mother." I hadn't but she couldn't know that. My sister sat staring at me, Lally went on with her beans, and Mrs Jane was busy ironing. There was a nice smell of damp linen and starch, and only the clock ticking and Mr Jane snoring gently. I went on writing busily. It was all rubbish because I was only really thinking of five shillings, so I just wrote boggly boggly boggly all the time and hoped that none of them would notice.

"Got it out of your system," said Lally, brushing all the tops and tails off the beans into a paper bag and taking the full bowl into the scullery. "It's nice to see you with your books for a change is all I can say." I heard the pump going and the water running in the sink and my sister calling out,

"He's writing his play for Sunday night, you see."

"A play?" said Mrs Jane, smoothing away. "That's nice."

"Not this one," said my sister, "this one is all about bats and ghosts and things."

"It isn't at all," I said. She didn't know.

"I like a nice play," said Mrs Jane. "I haven't been to a theatre since before the Flood. Well, since a very long time ago. And I do like a nice play, especially if it's got a tune or two."

Lally came bumbling back in with a saucepan of water and the beans and started to set them on the range with a clonk. "Last play you went to my dear was a couple of years back when we all went up to see 'Bitter Sweet', the time when Brother Harold and Ruby got married."

Mrs Jane put down her iron and folded her arms across her pinafore. "Of course we did," she said. "I'd quite forgot. Harold and Ruby got married that Thursday and then we went to His Majesty's and saw that pretty play when Mrs Williams dropped her bag of plums all over the Dress Circle! I laughed fit to burst my stays, I must say . . . what a thing to do! Still, it was a pretty play . . . and very sad too . . . wasn't it sad then, Lally? As far as I can remember it was *very* sad . . . but we were all so taken with Mrs Williams' plums I can't recall very much I do admit."

"There were some lovely tunes in that," said Lally, "really

71

pretty. But what Mrs Williams was doing with plums in the Dress Circle I never shall know. A box of Cadburys yes: plums no. I was really cross, wasn't I, Mother? Remember? Cross."

Mrs Jane sighed deeply and went on smoothing away. "Yes, you were, very cross as I recall, but I had to laugh . . . it was just like your father playing skittles down at the Flagstaff, the noise they made clattering everywhere."

For a little while there was silence and then I suddenly said: "I suppose I could go and work or something, couldn't I?"

"What for?" said Lally sharply.

"To get the money for the canary."

"Oh! The canary . . . well . . . odd jobs do you mean?"

"Yes . . . anything."

"You *could* I suppose . . ." She sounded vague and looked at Mrs Jane. "He *could* do odd jobs about the place to earn a bit for his canary, couldn't he, Mother?"

"There's quite a lot to get on with here," said Mrs Jane. "The shed needs a good clean out, there's weeding to be done in the vegetable garden . . . I daresay we could keep you busy for three-pence an hour if that's what you want?" She folded up some shirts and put the iron on a little brass stand by the range. "Next Door said they wanted someone to whitewash the chicken shed. . . . He's a bit stiff with his back, and Gooze can't hardly hold her head up let alone a whitewash brush . . . I reckon if you offered they'd be pleased to pay you for your canary."

It was settled quite easily. I started work the next morning in our shed, carting all the boxes and sacks and bits and pieces out into the yard and getting down to a good sweep. My sister helped a bit too: she had a feeling that if she didn't she wouldn't be able to claim any of the canary when it finally came, and she hated the idea of that. But after I had made her carry down the fox's head, and some old fly papers, and lug a big bag full of rotten windfalls she pretty soon gave up, and I got on with things on my own. It was much easier, and I could still think about the play while I worked.

After the shed, which took quite a long time actually, there was the vegetable garden and all the weeds, and after that I washed up eighty flower pots, and cleaned them carefully ready for Mr Jane's seedlings and cuttings for the winter. And then I went over to the Poulters and they said I could whitewash the chicken shed; which took so long to do that I managed to earn a shilling, and Gooze gave me two pennies which she said were really for the Collection on Sunday but she thought that the Africans wouldn't miss two pennies just for one week. Which was very kind of her. She was very shy, and kept twisting the belt of her long droopy woolly cardigan, and scuffing a little hole in the grass where we were standing. But she pushed the two warm pennies into my hand and scurried off to her back door so that I couldn't really thank her.

On the Friday we all set off to Mr Batt's house across the Green. Lally in her summer frock-for-Town, which was different to the one she wore in Sussex because it had red squares all over it and she wore white ankle strap shoes and carried a purse. But she didn't wear her hat. Because Mr Batt was a "neighbour" and she didn't want him to think she was just putting on airs when she came to visit.

No. 14 Sumatra Road was not as pretty as Walnut Cottage. It was all red brick with a pointed roof, a bay window, and a thick laurel hedge all round. Over the green front door there was a stone lady's face, staring down with wide eyes, surrounded by yellow brick. We didn't go into the house, but through a side gate into the yard and then down the long garden path to the sheds at the bottom. It really wasn't much of a garden. Not like ours at Walnut. There were lots of old boxes and tins, a broken pram, and some washing hanging on a line. No flowers, or trees, just some rather dead looking Michaelmas daisies and a few rows of yellow cabbages.

Mr Batt was thin and friendly and didn't wear a collar. He took us into the sheds through a little door—and then the magic started! The sheds were full of cages, row upon row of them, filled with birds of all kinds. It was all very clean and tidy, not a bit like his back garden, and he had to talk quite loudly because of the tweeting of all the birds who were hopping about on their perches and twittering and feeding away.

I selected a canary, bright yellow, with pink legs, who seemed to be very cheerful and singing a lot.

"Good choice," said Mr Batt. "He's a bright little feller, sings like a clockwork dickie bird. You'd think all you had to do was wind him up and let him be. But no! Oh no! You got to look after 'im . . . feed him proper, twice a day you fill up his seed bowl, clean water, lots of grit and a nice bit of lettuce, some chickweed, a piece of prime apple, and a nice bit of old cuttlefish

. . . then he'll sing for you to show his thanks . . . but he ain't no clockwork dickie. . . . You *sure* you'll take care of him, otherwise I'd have to say No?"

Walking back down Sumatra Road, holding the little travelling cage, with my real canary, after all this time, was almost more than I could bear. I daren't speak I was so happy, and when my sister pointed out how big the conkers all were, coming across the Green, I didn't even look. Just went walking straight on longing to get to Walnut so that I could take him up to my room and just gaze at him in silence. But first we had to get a packet of seed and some grit and a bit of cuttlefish from Mrs Hicks at the Corner Shop, and then when I had paid for all that I had only the two pence which Gooze had given me. But it was worth it.

Mrs Jane sighed a bit and said she couldn't abide birds in cages. "It isn't natural," she said sadly. "He ought to be out there flying about free."

"Wouldn't last a minute out there, Mother. Cats 'ud get him in no time, and anyway he comes from a foreign country, he couldn't get the proper food in the garden . . . and think of the winter."

"Makes no difference. Shouldn't be in a cage. Where does it come from then?"

"Madeira," said Lally, finally as if she knew.

"That's where the cake comes from," said my sister, showing off.

"Well, it's a long way off . . . and very hot there. So you keep him warm and don't take him up to your bedroom. He stays here in the kitchen. Where it's warm. And you can put him in the window as long as you don't knock Mrs Jane's geraniums about."

"You mind my geraniums . . . very brittle they are . . . it's a good thing Father is deaf, though I shouldn't say it, for that twittering would drive him out of his wits . . . and me out of mine I shouldn't wonder, though I'm a patient woman, God knows . . . and don't go scattering seed about or we shall have mice."

But really, in spite of them all being a bit difficult, people were really very nice about him, and after tea we all had a talk about what to call him, and finally decided on Madeira because that's where he came from, and Lally said it would help me with my geography if I went and looked it up on a map. Which I did:

but it was very hard to find, and very small indeed when we saw it in a big bit of blue sea, just about as big as a fly-blow. And it can't have been important because it wasn't red, like India and Africa and Great Britain. But we called him that, anyway, to please Lally.

Mrs Jane didn't say much about the name. I could see she didn't think it very good for a bird.

"It's too cumbersome," she said. "You ought to give it a nice name like Joey or Bobby or something pretty." She closed up the big Atlas and stuck it back on the shelf beside the Bible and three bound volumes of The Family Circle. Lally came back from the scullery with the tray of tea things and started setting them up on the shelves by the range.

"Bobby is a dog's name, and Joey is for a parrot, Mother. Madeira is *very* nice I think. Unusual."

"Doesn't trip off the tongue," said Mrs Jane, setting up her folding red and blue carpet chair by the fire opposite Mr Jane, who was reading his paper by the light of the gas lamp above.

"What do you think, Father?" she shouted at him, sitting into her chair and sorting through a pile of clean socks in her lap. He looked up vaguely from the paper.

"Eh?" he said.

Mrs Jane leaned towards him and shouted again. "About Madeira. They're going to call the bird Madeira!" He looked at her in surprise and then slowly round us all.

"I don't think so, Mother," he said eventually. "Perhaps at Christmas. I'd rather have a nice jug of ale," and he went back to his paper. Mrs Jane looked perplexed.

"He didn't understand me, oh dear! I wonder what he thought I'd said?" She went on sorting the socks, rolling them into neat little bundles when they hadn't got a hole or something. "And we never got to see your play did we?" she asked. "I expect the bird quite put it out of your mind, that's it."

Lally said that that was it and that anyway the cottage was really too small to make a stage in, and we couldn't hang a curtain up, and anyway I hadn't written the words so we couldn't learn them but perhaps next time, and in the meanwhile we had all better start thinking about packing tomorrow for the day after we had to leave. Which filled me with sadness because we hated leaving Walnut even though it only meant going back to The Cottage and our father and mother.

"I wanted to do the play just as a sort of Thank You . . . I did forget because of the bird!" I said.

"And you would have liked it too," said my sister sadly. "It was all about this Lady who goes to a haunted house and gets scared out of her wits by a huge big bat and . . ." Lally cut her short:

"Don't give the story away, silly! Fancy spoiling the surprise. We'll all do it next time and that'll be fine."

Mrs Jane sat back in her chair and started to thread a needle:

"We don't need no thanking, bless you. It's a pleasure to have you here. Oh dear! That reminds me . . . we've got Brother Harold and Ruby coming down *next* Sunday for tea with that child." She heaved a great sigh, and Lally put an arm on her shoulder and laughed:

"Cheer up, Mother, do . . . it's only for tea and they are your flesh and blood after all."

Mrs Jane was cross looking: "It's just the way that Baby Dennis *will* break all my eggs so that I have to hide them in a cupboard and then he starts kicking your father! It's not natural in a child of three . . . kicks your father on the shins who has done him no harm in all the world! I don't know why Ruby doesn't take the back of her hand to him I'm sure. And my eggs . . ." She was really quite vexed and, pushing her wooden mushroom into the heel of a sock, she started darning very fast.

Mr Jane suddenly folded his paper, gave a big yawn, scratched his head and looked for a few moments at his wife in front of him, stitching away.

"Mother!" he said, searching for his handkerchief in a trouser pocket. "Since you're on your feet, hand me down the tin of humbugs will yer . . . I just fancy one this evening." Mrs Jane gave him a look and asked me to get the tin off the mantelpiece where it always stood under the picture of the people praying in the fields, and I handed it to him for him to choose one which always took him quite a long time although they were all exactly the same size and colour; when he found the one he wanted he sniffed it, held it to the light, and then, very carefully, put it in his mouth as if it was the first humbug he had ever tasted. Sucking at it, he offered me the tin and my sister and I had one each and then I put it up on the shelf again.

"I don't know, really I don't," said Mrs Jane. "He really lives in a world of his own does Father. It comes of working in the silence and winding too many clocks. He doesn't pay no heed to anyone else."

But just as I was about to get the old piece of sheet which she had given me to put over Madeira's cage at nights, I heard Mr Jane say with a mouth full of humbug: "I think there's some old wire fronts hanging up in the shed you know. Give the boy one so he can make a cage for his bird when he gets back, be better'n that silly little box from Bert Batt."

I was very happy and shouted, "Thank You!" to him but he only smiled and waved his hand in the air.

"Nice little bird," he said. "He don't worry me because I can't hear him . . . that twittering would drive me out of my wits all day long, wouldn't it, Mother?" But he didn't wait for an answer, just closed his eyes and rolled his humbug comfortably round his mouth. Mrs Jane bit off the thread and started to roll the socks into a ball.

"He likes you two but he can't *abide* Baby Dennis . . . and no more can I, God forgive me. If only he wouldn't kick so! You go and look for that cage front tomorrow, young man, don't do it tonight with all the dust and that lying about out there. And you . . ." she said, pointing at my sister, "when you have to leave on Sunday, don't go hiding behind his chair . . . we know you don't want to leave, and it's very kind of you, but it does upset him so. He feels sorry for a week of Sundays . . ."

But she smiled very kindly when she said it, and closed her basket.

7

IN the train from Calais to Wimereux we had the whole compartment to ourselves, which was very nice indeed. There
really wasn't much room for anybody else anyway. On one side
sat Lally and myself and my sister . . . that was three; and opposite, sitting in a gloomy row and looking very white and rotten,
were the three Chesterfield children, Angelica, Beth and Paul,
and their nanny who was called Amy O'Shea and who was older
than Lally and wore a grey two-piece suit and a white straw hat
with a black ribbon like a man's. She was pretty ugly too. And
skinny. And sat there clutching her huge handbag as if it had all
their money in it. Which it didn't. Our fathers and mothers had
all that. And they were coming by motor-car to Wimereux
because it was more comfortable and in any case there wasn't
room for us all in the O.M.

They were all looking so white and gloomy because they had
all been terribly sick on the boat, which was really a bit funny
because none of us were. And that made us feel very good. We
had been to Wimereux quite often for holidays so we knew what
to expect. Every time we got on the boat Lally would make us
sit up on the deck and eat lemons. It wasn't a very nice thing to
do but we did it because she said it stopped you being seasick,
and the air was good for us.

So we did that. And we were never sick although Lally once
said she felt queasy and hoped no one would speak to us because
she'd have a terrible turn and what would we do then?

But this day everything had been lovely. Sunny, with a wind
and the sea all glossy and pale and foamy like ginger beer; and
gulls swinging over the funnels, and the flags streaming in the
breeze. The Chesterfields all went down below to a cabin, which
Lally told Amy was a Silly Thing To Do. And it was. Almost as
soon as we left Folkestone Paul Chesterfield came up on deck
with a white face and said that Amy had fallen down in a heap
and had knocked her hat off.

When we got to the cabin she was sitting on the edge of a bunk
holding her head, her hat all squint, and her pince-nez, hanging
from her lapel by a little gold chain, were glinting in the sun.

"I'm taken bad!" she moaned. "If only it would keep still for a minute I'd be all right, I'm sure. It's the floor swaying about so. Oh! What will become of us all if I'm taken queer?" Lally was very brisk indeed and ordered Angelica and Paul and Beth up on the deck, and told Amy to put her feet up and cover her eyes with a handkerchief.

Amy moaned and rolled from side to side and said No. No! Nothing would make her move and the children were to stay within her sight for she was Responsible. Angelica was sitting bolt upright like a white rabbit, and Beth just crouched in a corner holding on to the handle of the little door which led to the lavatory.

"Oh! Make it stop, dear God!" cried Amy, which made my sister and me giggle. Lally hit us sharply and said, "What a silly thing to say, Miss O'Shea! If the good Lord stopped the boat now for you, we'd all be swinging about here for dear knows how long . . . soon as we get on the sooner we'll be on dry land."

"I'll never see the land again. God help us all," moaned Amy O'Shea and gave a dreadful gasp and covered her face with her handkerchief which smelled of lavender water. Suddenly Beth made a strangling sort of noise and Lally spun us both round and sent us up the stairs. We heard a splashing noise and then the door slammed shut.

We had a very nice time looking at all the people lying on the deck with big white enamel bowls beside them. They all looked very green and sad, only the sailors looked cheerful, and they were dashing about the sloping decks laughing and eating big ham rolls and sloshing water everywhere. We called out "Bonjour!" to them all, and they all waved back and said "Bonjour" also. It was a *very* nice feeling, as if we had always been travelling which was very good for you because, as Lally said, it broadened your mind.

In a little while we could see the long flat line of land ahead . . . and the sunshine sparkling on white sailing boats and the windows of houses in France where we were going to spend four weeks at the Hôtel d'Angleterre. Lally joined us by the rail pulling on her gloves and snapping her handbag shut, she tucked a bit of hair under her hat with the ivy leaves on it, and said: "Miss O'Shea's in a poor way, I'm afraid. They've all been sick. But what can you expect all cooped up in that little room with no air and no lemons?"

We felt sorry for them in a vague way, but quite glad about Angelica who was really so prim that a bit of seasick would do her good. Beth, who was two years younger than Angelica, was rather a nice girl and we quite liked her. She had a freckly face and gaps in her teeth but she liked doing nearly all the things we liked doing, so she wasn't a Drawback. Paul was the youngest and Not Very Well because he had something wrong with his chest which made him very pale and quiet and he spent most of his time reading. So we didn't pay any attention to him much except to say "Good morning, Paul," or "Hello, Paul," or "Are you having a nice day?" just things like that which he only had to say "Yes" or "No" to, which is what he did. And nothing more.

We watched France get nearer and nearer, and heard the boat make slowing-down noises, and the water thrashing and churning about under the propellers . . . and then we could see the great clock at Calais swing into view, and all the crooked houses; and cranes striking up into the sky, like schoolteachers' fingers. The gulls wheeled and screeched and scattered over the ginger-beery water like handfuls of rice at a wedding. And the sun glinted on the slimy green seaweedy walls of the piers while men in blue rushed all alongside throwing ropes at us, shouting and whistling. It was very exciting to feel the big ship slide slowly into her place, nudging and bumping gently at the high stone walls, and watching all the ropes growing taut to stretching point as they made us fast.

Then in a flash the gangplanks were up and we all wobbled down to stand on the cobbled road of the docks. We stood there among piles of wooden boxes smelling of fish, and still felt the land swaying a little after the movement of the ship. Lally went off into the crowd of people, looking for Amy and the Chester-fields who wouldn't leave their cabin until the ship had really stopped and everything was quite still. And then they had a terrible job getting down the gangplank because it was steep and Amy's bag, Angelica's books, and the travelling rugs seemed to all get mixed up. But eventually, pale and exhausted, they were all among the fish, and we started to make our way over to the station. It took quite a while to sort out all our luggage, find the tickets, and say "merci" to everyone in sight: Lally said we had to because you never knew who was driving the train.

In the end we all clambered into one compartment together in

1 My sister and I sitting on the back stairs, July 1927.

2(a) My sister and I in the village. She wearing her "hate". 1932.

2(b) Aleford's stallion (Dobbin) in Great Meadow. Self and sister.

the middle, just in case anything hit us in the front, or from the back, and then we were assured by Lally, we'd be completely safe and not get squashed which was often the case On French Railways.

"I do think it's exciting!" said my sister happily, but no one answered her because, with a terrific shriek of the whistle and three big jig-joggy-jerks, the train started to steam out of the station into the sunlit town.

Amy O'Shea sat bolt upright looking fearfully out of the windows to see how fast we were going, and Angelica and Beth just stared ahead. Paul went to sleep.

"He's just like the Dormouse in Alice," whispered my sister.

Lally took off her gloves and started to count all the bits of luggage on the racks, nodding her head and counting under her breath, and suddenly we roared into a tunnel and everything was black and I heard Amy O'Shea cry out in fright but we were soon through and out into the fields and woods running quietly through lovely flat fields full of streams and little clumps of willows. There were men and women working in the fields with horses, and a girl of our age, with a flock of sheep, waved to us and we waved back like anything. Except the Chesterfields, who just sat.

★　★　★

The Hôtel d'Angleterre was very nice and on the promenade looking straight on to the sea. We had stayed there before so the fat lady in black, with pearls and a rose, knew us right away and kissed my sister who didn't like it much because she always used to shout at her, "O! La belle poupée!" which Lally said meant what a pretty doll; and my sister didn't like the doll part. She didn't look like one so it was a bit silly, but kind, I suppose.

Our room was the same one we always had, tall windows over the sea, with a balcony, a big bed for Lally and two smaller ones for us. In one corner there was a screen, and behind it was a place to wash your face and hands and another, on the floor, which was for washing your feet—which seemed a good idea because ours were always so sandy. The wallpaper was very pretty, covered in roses and lilac and there was a huge wardrobe and an armchair and a little table with three chairs for us to have our meals at.

Looking over the balcony you could see all the people on the beach, the waves flapping along the sand, and the blinds of the hotel right below. We were only on the first floor in case of a fire happening. Lally said she wasn't going to risk being any higher thank-you-very-much, which is why we always had to book the same room well in advance. If you looked to the right you could see down to the canal bridge and the spire of the church, and if you looked left you could see more hotels and then the lovely big green hump of the cliffs. There were no motors on the promenade, only bicycles, so that you could run out of the hotel down the steps, across the road, and on to the beach. It really was the nicest place in the world. Abroad.

The first thing Lally unpacked, before our suitcases even, or the big trunk, was her little wicker basket. In it she had a titchy teapot, three cups, a little tin kettle, and a very small stove-thing which she stood on a tin tray by the washbowl, with a bottle of milk and a spoon. Then she lit it, and the whole room started to smell of methylated spirits. There was a curious pale blue flame, and in almost no time at all, the tin kettle was boiling and steaming the mirror over the washplace. And then we all had a "good strong cup of tea" on the balcony before we did anything else. Not that my sister and I wanted tea at all: but it was the rule, and we had to stick to it with Lally.

After we had unpacked almost completely, Lally went off to the W.C. across the corridor and emptied the teapot and cups down the lav while we were changing into our summer things. Sandals, shorts, and our rather silly white cotton hats which we both hated. Lally was sure that we would get sunstroke while we were shrimping, so we had to wear these awful white cotton "hates", we called them, which pulled down right over our ears.

"With all this sun burning down on your heads they'll be boiled like a couple of eggs, sure as sure. You wear them until your mother says not. Then it's out of my hands."

After a day or two we managed to lose them somewhere, but for the first day it was The Rule.

The Chesterfields seemed better and more cheerful, although Amy was still dressed in her two-piece with a veil round her hat to keep it in place. We all went shrimping and I caught three baby flounders and about a dozen shrimps which we kept in a bucket until we had to go back to the hotel to meet Our Parents. Lally made us throw the shrimps and the flounders back into the sea, because last year we had taken them all back to the room and filled the thing for washing your feet with sea water, some pretty seaweed, a lot of shrimps and some more baby flounders. One of us left the tap running just a little bit so that they could get oxygen, and during lunch in the big restaurant under our room, quite a large part of the ceiling fell down on some people at a table near us. There was a lot of fuss and water and plaster everywhere and it was all because the rather stupid feet-washing basin thing had overflowed and gone through the floor.

Our room was a bit of a mess too, with sand and seaweed and the flounders all plopping away on the floor gasping, poor things. I got a terrific walloping from our father and lost my Saturday franc for two weeks to help pay for the damage to the floor and the ceiling of the restaurant. Which seemed a bit unfair really, because two francs can't have been nearly enough to pay for *all* the mess. And we had to say we were sorry, in French, to the people who had got wet and covered in plaster, and also to the Lady who owned the hotel in black and pearls and a rose. And she wasn't very smiling either. At least, my sister said, she didn't grab her and call her a "belle poupée" any more for that holiday and that it was almost worth all the punishments we had to have in order not to be frightened out of her wits on the staircase every morning. Anyway. Back we had to throw them under Lally's firm gaze, and back we all trooped to the hotel.

Our parents were very handsome we thought. More handsome than Mr and Mrs Chesterfield by far. Our father was very brown and cheerful in white trousers with a tie round his waist and a very French shirt all stripy like a sailor's, and our mother was looking very beautiful in beach-pyjams with a funny white hat called a Dough-Boy hat because it was what American sailors wore in the war and they were called dough-boys. I don't know why.

Aunt Freda had a pointed nose just like Angelica, and wore a hat with a rose and a huge brim which came so far down that all you could see was her nose sticking out and her pointed chin; she had to hold her head quite high up and backwards to see where she was going. Uncle John was rather jolly with a big belly and a pipe and always laughed a good deal. They weren't really our Aunt and Uncle but we had always known them, ever since before we were born, and so they got to be almost Family.

We all had dinner together at a huge table in one corner of the restaurant, and we were allowed a wine glass of beer or a glass of red wine with mineral water while we ate. This was a special treat this holiday for it was a sign that we were "growing up" and should be allowed to get accustomed to it. Lally was terribly shocked but kept herself to herself and only said how awful it was when we were getting ready for bed later. "Starting the Rot," she said.

Our mother said we should have an early night after such a tiring day and that tomorrow we would all go on a lovely trip to the oyster beds outside the town, and that we could go in a real coach with a horse pulling it. Which sounded very interesting.

"I thought that wine was very nice, didn't you?" said my sister from her bed in the corner, and I agreed although I thought that tomorrow I'd probably try the beer instead in spite of what Lally said about it starting the Rot.

"I don't feel a bit homesick yet, do you?" asked my sister.

"We've only been here today . . . it's too soon. It comes on later."

"I don't think I'll *ever* be homesick here. I think it's lovely."

"I wonder if the Chesterfields will be sick in the coach tomorrow?"

"I wonder. Fains we don't sit beside them."

Lally called out and told us to be quiet and get to sleep or we'd all be sick in the coach with a good hiding. So we went to sleep; it seemed the best thing to do.

* * *

The Chesterfields were all sitting at the breakfast table when we got down. Amy was in a green frock but still wore her hat. She had a little book in her hand and was reading it very carefully through her shining glasses.

"Reading at table indeed!" said Lally in a pretending-stern voice and setting us all round the big table. Amy closed the book and took off her glasses.

"Not actually reading, just glancing through. The tea's fresh, they just brought it in, although it's as weak as dishwater to me."

Lally poured us all a cup and helped herself to sugar.

"I have to agree with you, Amy, dishwater it is . . . however, remember that I've always got my little supply upstairs if you ever feel the need. Nice strong Mazawattee, and a ginger snap, makes a great difference to the afternoon, I always say. What is your little book then?" You could tell she was very curious about the book because she had offered Amy her precious tea before she asked the question.

Amy picked up the book and put on her glasses again. "It's a French phrase book. It once belonged to my father, God rest his soul, and I thought it would be useful for the children if we learned a few things to say . . . like where is the Church please? Or can you direct me to the cemeteries . . . things like that, you know? Otherwise we'd be at the mercy of foreigners wouldn't we?"

"Well for dear-knows-whose-sake!" cried Lally. "You aren't going to take the children round all the churches and cemeteries of France, are you, Amy? There are lots of nice things to see! It's morbid."

"It's what?" said Amy.

"Morbid."

"Morbid to learn a few phrases, is it?"

"No . . . that's all right. But morbid to dwell on cemeteries and such."

"I'm not *dwelling* on them, I assure you. It just so happens that I have a very dear brother in one of them." She looked rather pink in the face. "And I've a notion to go and find him."

Lally looked very uncomfortable and told my sister to take her elbows off the table which they weren't on. So we knew she was a bit flustered about the brother in the cemetery.

"I'm very sorry, I'm sure," she said. "I didn't realise that at all. Is it here?"

"It's here," said Amy. "Not a few miles away from this very town . . . he was hit in '17 and I just feel that I'd like to find him."

Lally was spreading marmalade on a piece of toast. "Well, we'll just have to ask the Porter at the desk and he'll know and then maybe we could all go and help you. That is if you'd not object I mean to say?"

Amy seemed pleased at the idea and said she didn't relish the idea of going on her own and that one day soon perhaps we could make an excursion, it wasn't very far away and she also believed that Miss Cavell was buried in the same place and that would be very interesting for us all. We didn't know who Miss Cavell was so I didn't really see that it could be so very interesting to go and look for two people we didn't know and had never heard about

85

and who were dead. It was much better to be on the beach. But if Lally had offered then we had to go, for nothing would put her off once she had made up her mind or given her word.

"Fancy having to go and look at dead people when you are on holiday," grumbled my sister when we were all standing in the lobby waiting for The Parents to come down and start the morning by going to the oyster beds. "I think it's very silly indeed. And we don't even know them so it won't even be interesting." But she said it in a whisper to me so no one else heard and she knew I agreed because I nodded. But it wasn't going to be today, and with any luck they might forget all about it in time.

★　★　★

The oyster beds were quite a way from Wimereux, along a very pretty road running straight as an arrow through lovely flat fields which rolled away for miles and miles to the sky. It was a very hot morning, and sitting up on the top of the coach-thing I could see all round me as we clip-clopped slowly along behind a bony white horse. The coach was black, and the old lady driving the horse was all in black, with a floppy bonnet on her head. Angelica and I, being the eldest and tallest, had to sit on the top beside her, one on each side, while Amy, Lally, and the other three all sat squashed up inside. Our parents had gone on ahead in our father's big silver O.M. motor-car, all laughing and talking.

The sun shone down on the little streams and woods, and sent long black shadows from the tall trees along the road, across us like black bars. We could hear the birds singing, and the clip clop of the horses hooves and that's all, except for the creaking of the carriage which swayed about a bit and made Amy feel rather giddy.

Angelica sat staring ahead, holding onto the little iron rail round the seat, as if she was on a rather nasty thing at a fairground. I wished my sister was there instead because she would have much preferred it—she was very fond of horses, even the back part of them which was, sometimes, rather rude. Swaying about on top of the carriage, and feeling so happy in the sun and being so high up and looking forward to the oyster beds, I asked Angelica who the dead lady was with Amy's brother. Angelica gave me a pitying smile and pushed her pigtails over her shoulder with the hand that wasn't holding on to the iron rail.

"Miss Cavell is nothing to do with Amy's brother. She's just been laid to rest in the same place as he has. That's all."

"But who was she? I mean why does Amy want to go and see her grave?"

"She was a very brave lady who was a nurse and a spy and got shot by the Germans," she said, all in one breath so that I could hardly understand her, what with the swaying about and the clip clopping and creaking and the old black lady wobbling about between us. "Was she really a spy?" I called out, wondering if I had heard her correctly.

"Yes. Yes, she was a sort of spy but she was a nice one because she was British, and the Germans hated her and shot her at dawn."

The coach joggled about over a large pot-hole in the road and she grabbed the iron rail with both her hands and didn't seem inclined to say anything more on the subject. So I didn't say anything else either.

Suddenly the old lady made some noises to the horse, and pulled at the reins and we turned off the main road down a little rutted lane, which made the coach wobble about very alarmingly and even I had to grab the iron rail at my side lest I slipped off or fell into the old woman's lap. And then we were rolling along a quite high dyke which ran in a straight line down to the sea. On either side of us were huge square ponds, almost as big as tennis courts, and they shone and glinted in the bright sunlight like mirrors lying flat in the fields.

"The oyster beds! The oyster beds!" I cried but no one heard me inside the coach and Angelica had gone pale from the rutted road and didn't seem a bit interested.

It was very beautiful indeed. At the far end of the dyke there was a little clump of buildings like a farm, and I could see the sun shining on the silver of our father's motor-car, and streaking the sea with long lines of gold. It was very hot, and for once I was quite glad to be wearing my white cotton "hate".

It was a farm, an oyster farm, and as we clattered into the yard the Parents, who were all sitting at a long wooden table drinking out of little glasses, waved and cheered as if we had arrived from Africa or somewhere. They were all very jolly and helped everyone out of the coach while Angelica and I started to clamber down the sides. Angelica said she must go first and I was to wait until she got to the ground. She was just frightened that I'd see her bloomers or something. I was much too excited to see the oyster beds to bother about her old bloomers anyway.

We had a very nice time at the oyster beds, and were allowed to go with an old man who only spoke French to catch our own in a thing like a big wire shrimping net. The water in the beds was so clear, and so shallow, that you could see the oysters quite plainly, lying all over the sandy bottom, like fat buns. Some had green seaweed growing on them, some were very small indeed, and some were really very big. We carried them back to the table in a wooden bucket and the Parents cheered and seemed delighted and made us sit down together as if it was a sort of a party. Which in a way it was, all of us together and in the sunshine and so happy. Our father said that as it would be our first oysters we should be allowed a little glass of wine to have with them, and when Lally looked a bit put out, he said that it was a Celebration to have your first oyster and it was like launching a ship: you couldn't do it without a little wine.

So the glass jugs of wine arrived at the table, and lemonade for Paul, who was the youngest and didn't have wine or oysters yet, and then the big plates arrived surrounded with seaweed and piled high with the oysters all opened and sparkling in the sun. My sister went white when she saw them.

"They're raw," she hissed.

"I know. That's how you eat them."

"Raw?"

"Yes. Sometimes they get cooked."

"Alive?" Her voice was almost a wail and Angelica and Beth looked at her with a start and then at the great plates of oysters before them.

"They can't be alive!" said Angelica. "It's like being a cannibal!" Then big bowls of cut lemons and bottles of vinegar were plonked on the wooden table and all the parents started to stretch out for the food. My sister sat shocked into silence while everyone except Lally and Amy raised their glasses in a toast and cried "Bon appetit!" No one took any notice after that, on purpose, and just got on with the eating part. Our father said to me to watch how he did it, with a fork, while Uncle John just took up the whole shell and emptied everything into his mouth.

"You don't swallow them like your Uncle," said our father. "You just chump them up . . . that's the right way!"

88

Uncle John winked at me across the table. "All a matter of personal taste, my boy . . . you swaller them or you chew them up. Aren't any rules, just personal taste!" He quickly swallowed another one. "Food of the Gods!" he said. "Food of the Gods!"

Lally took her fork and speared an oyster from its shell which she politely offered to my horrified sister who shook her head from side to side and covered her mouth with both her hands, watching, with wide eyes, as Lally put it into her mouth and chewed it up happily.

Seeing Lally looking so cheerful I said, "It's the same as winkles, that's all."

"Winkles are *boiled.*"

"Well, even if they are . . . they don't feel anything."

"No, but I will! All crawling about inside me alive."

"You just chew them up and then they won't."

"Poor little things . . . that would be killing them then."

"If our father does it it can't possibly hurt them." She really was very silly. She stuck her fork hard into the wooden table and said: "You haven't even *tried* one yet so how can you possibly know?"

I grabbed a fork from the pile beside me, took an oyster, put it in my mouth and ate it. Her face fell open like an old cupboard door.

"There!" I said.

"Oh, poor little thing . . . poor little thing," she wailed; but it was the most lovely taste I had ever had. Salt, sea, slippery, sweet and cool. I chewed it with pleasure so that she would see and also so that it really would not flop about inside me. Because she had put me off a bit with that. But not off enough.

"It's lovely!" I cried to everyone as if they didn't know. "It's lovely . . . you must eat them, it's easy and they are beautiful."

Our father was very pleased and raised his glass to me and so did our mother who was laughing and looking pretty and happy. I could have eaten the whole plate but Lally counted out five more and that was that, but I ate them as slowly as possible to make them last, and sipped my glass of wine just like our father. I felt it was a very important day.

★ ★ ★

Later there was a big fish and then cheese and fruit, and after it was all over the Parents all got into the O.M. with many waves and kisses and drove away and we were to follow, when we felt like it, in the carriage after we had had a "bit of a paddle" on the long sandy beach beyond the farm.

The Chesterfields went off shrimping along the edge of the sea which seemed to be feeling as lazy as we were because it just nudged the sand gently and hardly moved at all, but far away out where it ended against the sky, some big white clouds started growing into the hot blue like enormous cauliflowers. Lally was helping us with our sand castle which had a tower at each corner and a moat all round and a very big tower in the middle which we were decorating with razor-shells and little round pink ones. She stood up and dusted the sand off her hands against her skirt and looked out to sea.

"Shouldn't wonder we had a bit of a storm presently. Those clouds don't look too good to me," and she tramped slowly up the beach to where Amy was sitting on her folding stool, which she always carried with her everywhere, reading her phrase book under a parasol.

"Did you really like those dreadful oysters?" said my sister.

"They were marvellous."

"But I mean what did they taste like, all alive and squirmy?"

"It wasn't a bit squirmy."

"Well . . . you know what I mean. All alive."

"It tasted just like the smell of rock-pools."

"How could it? Silly. You can't taste a smell!"

"You can. And they did. Exactly."

"Tasting like a smell. I've never heard of anything so soppy." She started to dig out a bit more of the moat under the draw-bridge and a lump of wall fell down and we had to splash more water on it to hold it up, and she said: "Well, perhaps next time I'll try one and see for myself . . . just to try, that's all, and if I don't like it I can always just spit it out, can't I?" and Lally called us to come on and start getting ready to go back, because the carriage was waiting and the clouds were getting a bit big.

"We don't want to get stuck in a storm here," she called. "So make haste all of you and get ready or we shall have the Prince of Wales waiting about in the hotel, and we don't want that, do we?"

While we were all drying ourselves and putting on sandals and shorts and things, and pushing each other over on the sand while we stood on one leg, Lally picked up Amy's little brown book and was rifling through it interestedly. "Humph!" she cried "I don't think that this is going to be much good to us, Amy . . . whatever would I want muslin for, I ask you?"

Amy was combing Paul's hair and looked rather cross. "I don't know, I'm sure," she said. "My father, God rest his soul, said it was a very useful book to have with you when you were Abroad." Lally went on rifling through the pages.

"I've no doubt it was when he came, but this is 1898 and what would I be doing in a draper's shop saying, 'This muslin is too thin, have you something thicker?' . . . Goodness me! What *would* I be wanting muslin for, I ask you?"

Amy started to look rather red in the face and huffy and she pulled Paul's hair so hard that he yelled and fell over in the sand, and she had to say she was sorry and try to find the parting again. "Oh! do hold still!" she cried. "You really are a flibbertigibbet and no mistake." But really she knew it was her fault because Lally had flustered her. "You might want to use it for jelly-bags," she said, tucking Paul's shirt into his shorts and trying to fix his snake-belt which had got stuck.

"I might," agreed Lally. "And then I might not. But I grant you that . . . although I can't for the life of me see why."

Amy fixed the belt and told Paul to get on his sandals and sat down rather heavily on her stool. "There are a lot of very useful things if you look under 'Travelling' and 'Hospital' and 'At The Station'," she said, trying to close her parasol, because a hot wind was beginning to blow and the sand was scattering all over the place and stinging our faces.

"At The Hospital," read Lally in a laughing voice, "my leg, arm, foot, head, elbow, nose, finger is broken! It doesn't say anything about neck, I notice, so where would that get you?"

"If your neck was broken, the dear God knows, you'd not be able to speak so that's why they left the word out . . . it stands to reason surely."

The big clouds were starting to cover the sun, and the sands were growing dark, the sea was flat and grey looking in spite of the hot wind which was now really starting, tumbling the folded towels across the beach so that we had to run after them while Lally was still holding the book open and reading bits from it while the pages blew and flapped in her hands. "Travelling! 'The Postillion Has Been Struck By Lightning'—well!" she cried laughing. "That wouldn't get us far today, would it?"

Amy got up off her stool and started to fold it.

"It might, my dear," she said, "considering the weather. We had all better be off before the Heavens open and it's a long journey back." And she called about like an old hen for the Chesterfields and they started wandering up to the farm. We followed behind with towels and baskets and buckets and spades and a knotted handkerchief full of shells which my sister had collected, and a long wet strip of bobbly seaweed which was a present for our mother.

As we plodded up through the hot, sliding sand, I said, "What's a postillion?" and Lally said it was a man who sat on top of the coaches in the olden days and blew a horn to tell people it was coming. "I'm afraid we'll have to find something a bit newer for the cemetery or the dear knows where we'll all end up."

At the farm the old lady who drove the coach was waving her arms and holding a big black umbrella and pointing to the sky. It was getting darker and darker, and the big cauliflower clouds were almost right over our heads, and were heavy and purple-coloured with golden edges. As we started clambering into the coach the first plip-plops of rain fell, as big as threepenny pieces, splattering into the dusty road and pattering on the windows.

"Surely we can squeeze poor Angelica inside with us!" cried Amy; but there wasn't an inch of room with all the baskets, and buckets, and towels, and shrimping nets, so we both had to climb on to the top of the coach with the old lady, who was covering herself with bits of macintosh and shoved the umbrella at me to hold over us while she pulled the reins and started off down the long dyke, through the oyster beds now all potted and spotted with fat raindrops.

It wasn't a very comfortable journey, and when we got to the rutted lane which led to the main road, the coach rolled about like a fishing boat, and everyone screamed out from inside. But the old lady was not going to wait for anyone, and she hit the horse quite hard so that we rattled and rumbled and swayed along like anything, and Angelica called out and hung on to the iron rails and the rain came pouring down, so that I couldn't hold the umbrella *and* hold on at the same time, what with the wind roaring and jiggling everything. When we reached the main road and turned on to it, the old lady slowed down a bit and the wheels went a bit smoother, and she started to try and put the old bits of macintosh round Angelica and myself, while I tried to hold the umbrella over all our heads. But it wasn't much use because I kept sticking the spokes in her eyes or hitting her on the head with the thing, so she was getting wetter and wetter and looking very cross. Suddenly there was a flash and a zig-zag of forked lightning which stabbed into the fields beside us. Angelica flung herself into the old lady's lap and I threw the umbrella on to the floor and held on to her as well; she just walloped the horse a bit harder and on we went, splashing through the rain and the great crash of thunder which roared down over us and which so frightened the horse that he galloped down the road with his ears flat to his head and the old lady waving her whip in the air.

On we rattled, with the wheels all going wobbly so that I feared one of them would presently fall off and go winging out into the ditches on either side. There was another great zig-zag of lightning just behind us and then a terrific crash of thunder. The rain was streaming down so hard that I could hardly see, but I clung on to the old lady and just hoped that if I didn't hold the iron rail I wouldn't get struck the next time there was a flash. All I could see of Angelica was one arm and a flying pigtail with a ragged red ribbon streaming in the wind. I wondered if she had been struck and was dead. But she wasn't.

And then the first houses came, and a bus, and the road got smoother and the rain became gentler and in a short time we rumbled down the Promenade towards the hotel. There was no one about. And the beaches were quite empty except for lots of tumbled deck-chairs and tents which had blown down in the storm, and now the sea was really rough and swirling and crashing round the wooden breakwaters.

In front of the hotel, under the big glass blind, we all got off the dripping coach, the horse was steaming as if he had been boiled, and Angelica didn't bother about whether I could see her knickers or not, she just scrambled down off the top looking like a drowned rat, her hair all straggly and the red ribbons untied and squiggling like red worms. Lally got out first and pulled my sister from inside, looking very red and rather cross.

"Beth and Paul have been sick," she said flatly. "And all over my floral. And Amy's in a bad way, too, I'm afraid. Run inside and get the keys and open the rooms, there's a good boy. We'll be up directly, just take your own things with you," she added, shoving towels and shrimping nets and seaweed into my arms.

"A fine postillion you made," she said. "You didn't blow your horn once!"

"And I didn't get struck by lightning either," I said.

"You get on up there," said Lally, "or you'll get struck by lightning from another direction!"

And as I hurried off up the steps with my sister hard behind me, she called out to put on the kettle and to ask the maid for an extra cup for Amy who would need it.

★　★　★

It was quite a long climb up the white, chalky road to the cemetery. On either side there were fields full of standing corn, green as green, and rolling away into the distance. The sky was clear and blue, with one or two little fat clouds gently drifting towards the sea which sparkled in the brilliant sunlight. A lark went whirling up like a spinning top as we passed, singing very loudly to keep us away from his nest somewhere, but there was no other sound except the whispers in the corn and Lally puffing a bit behind us.

"Don't scuff your feet!" she called out between puffs. "There's enough dust without you making more. I'm white as Lot's wife as it is."

Amy was walking behind with her veil pulled down all round her straw man's hat to keep off the flies, she said, and the dust of the road. She had her stool, and her big bag and a small bunch of flowers which we had stopped to buy outside the hotel when we left for the bus to the town where the cemetery was. My sister and I were a bit worried that we hadn't got any flowers to put on Amy's Brother's Grave ... if we found him ... but we picked quite a big bunch of poppies which were growing all along the road, to put on the grave of the Miss Cavell.

"She'll like that," said Lally with assurance. "She'd think it very nice of two English children to remember her and pick her some flowers."

The gates of the cemetery were very white and tall, and made of stone. There was a big cross over them and a wall all the way round. Amy was rather pale and nervous, and we were quiet so as not to disturb her because it was a very sad thing she was doing and we did not want to get in the way. When we got inside the cemetery we all stopped. It was the biggest one we had ever seen,

94

much bigger than the one at Teddington or even the one in our own village where we used to have the fair. It was huge. Miles and miles of little white crosses, and long green-grassy paths between them all with little black pointed trees every now and then. There weren't any flowers on many of the graves. Some had little jam jars with a few wilting daisies which looked very sad. And some had rose bushes growing beside them—which was rather nice. Here and there we could see little groups of people in black walking down the grassy paths, or a single person kneeling by a grave all alone.

"Oh dear!" said Lally, in a very low voice. "So many; so many poor souls." She took us both by a hand and we started to walk slowly among the white crosses looking at the names; just things like F. J. Jones, and a number and the name of the regiment and sometimes the date. But what was awful was just where it had Unknown written. Just one word. And we all wondered who they were and of course no one would ever come to see them, because they were unknown, and no one put flowers there.

Amy had a handkerchief to her face but she was peering about her and for once she looked quite nice and not irritating.

"I wonder what to do?" she said worriedly. "There are so many, so many, and I don't know where I'd begin."

Lally said: "You go over to that fellow who's weeding there, I expect he belongs to the place and he'll tell you. I imagine you have to look under the O's", she said, giving Amy a little push.

Amy looked doubtful, but she opened her bag and took out her phrase book where she had marked some pages for "Asking Directions", which she had shown us in the bus, and nervously walked up to the man who was busy weeding and when he looked up at her we all got quite a start because he only had half a face. She started to read from her book and then we heard him speak to her in real Cockney and he laughed and said he was English and what could he do for her? Well, it was a big relief, and presently, scratching his head, he took her off up one of the long grassy paths far away from us. My sister was very silent. The bunch of poppies was getting a bit droopy, and we both felt rather miserable in that quiet place with so many white crosses shining in the sun.

Lally cleared her throat and told us to cheer up. "Goodness me! You look a couple of miseries I must say! You ought to be very happy that you're both here on such a lovely day as this, because all these poor men here died just so that you could be walking about in the sun without a care in the world. They wouldn't think you were very grateful if they could see your miserable faces, now would they? You see what it says on top of that big stone cross there? Their Sacrifice Was Not In Vain. So just you remember that. And show your manners." She was really quite bossy, but it was only because she was feeling sad too, and didn't want to show it.

"What shall we do about Amy?" said my sister for something to say, and Lally said we were to leave her be so that she could find her brother in peace. "It's a private thing," she said firmly. "So now let's go and see if we can find Miss Cavell."

Just then, another wounded man came along and was very nice and said that he came from Herne Bay, where Lally had once spent a holiday, but he shook his head and said he didn't know a Miss Cavell. She wasn't here, he said, not as far as he knew, which was a bit disappointing. He took us all over the place and we saw some quite big graves with weeping angels and stone pots on them, but there was no one called Miss Cavell. So Lally suggested that my sister should put her flowers on one of the "unknown" graves, just as a sign of respect for the dead. And before they died themselves.

"Amy must have got it all a bit muddled," said Lally. "And no one could really blame her because this was a very Trying Day for her."

My sister put the poppies on the grave rather nervously as if someone would tell her not to, but the man from Herne Bay was very nice and said that quite a lot of people came and did that and that later on he'd try and find a little jar to put them in; he said there was probably one in his shed. Then he asked me if I would like to see something very fine, and when I said I would, he limped away up a long grassy path to a big box thing. Well, it looked like a box. It was standing at the head of a very tidy grave, and it had a glass cover. Inside the box was a beautiful uniform jacket and a cap with gold braid all over it, and the jacket had a lot of medals and buttons. It was all a bit faded by the sun, but even so it sparkled. But it looked sadder even than the crosses, all empty, and the man from Herne Bay said that it belonged to a French General or someone and that his wife had asked for it to be like this.

"Won't last long," said Lally cheerfully. "The moths have been at it already, not to mention the wet."

The man agreed and said the winters there were really cruel but he thought that I'd be interested. And in a way I was. But I didn't feel particularly happy about any part of the day really. It all had a Holy and sad feeling and it was so quiet and still that not even a bird sang. Suddenly we saw Amy walking alone down the little sloping path. I think she had had a good cry, for her eyes were rather red and so was her nose, but she was making a little wavering smile as she came across the rows of crosses to us, and had put her phrase book in her bag. The man with the wounded face wasn't there any longer, so I suppose she'd found the grave and he'd left her to be private too. We all sat down on a stone seat, and waited for her to reach us, after we had said goodbye and thank you to the Herne Bay man.

It was quite nice to sit down, and the stone seat was hot in the sun, but Amy was soon standing beside us pushing her handkerchief into her pocket.

"Do you want to come and see him?" she asked.

It was just another grave like all the rest. A white cross and his name, Peter Eric O'Shea, and a number after it.

"What does Cpl mean?" asked my sister, and Amy said that he was a Corporal and very clever. "Is he really under there?" said my sister, and Amy said she hoped so. "As long as I know *where* he is, it doesn't feel so bad," she said with a sigh. She stood for a long minute looking out over all the crosses which surrounded us like a white sea. "Oh the grief, dear God," she said sadly. "Oh the grief and the terrible waste of it all."

And then we started off silently down the path towards the gates with the cross on the top. We kept a bit behind the two of them, looking at the names and numbers and regiments, but just as we got near the bottom, I saw Amy's head bow down and Lally slipped her hand into Amy's arm and lifted her own head high. We walked down the road quite far behind them, scuffing the dust into white clouds all round us.

There was no one to tell us not to.

8

I WAS sitting under the elderberry bush up by the privy, which was where I always went when I wanted to have a good "think" with no one to disturb me, and Lally stuck her head out of a window, shook a rug very hard over the sill, and called down: "Don't sit there like yesterday's loaf, with a shopping list as long as my arm on top of the copper and a ten shilling note, and don't forget the change. Also take the milk-can, should you see Mr Mitchell and get me a pint and a half and a small pot of cream which we'll have with the gooseberries." She slapped the rug a few more times against the flint wall, covered the garden in dust, and went back in. She always seemed to know exactly where I'd be when she wanted me, which was very aggravating.

"I'll come too," said my sister, pulling on her Hate. "I'll bring a bit of sugar for the pony if we do see Mr Mitchell, and if we don't I'll eat it myself."

We collected the milk-can, the list, the ten shilling note, and started off down the field to the gully. It was quite a long way to the village, easily two miles, so I was pretty sure that I wasn't going to have much of a "think" that morning, which was a pity. Because something was just beginning in my head when Lally called me.

The poppies were nearly all over, and so were the buttercups; the long high hedge running down the field beside the gully was thick with Queen Anne's lace and Campion. Summer, as Herbert Fluke would say, was getting a move on. But the sun was still high and hot, and the Downs fat and green, like the bellies of horses, rounded against the sky, glossy and rippling where the wind ruffled through the thick summer grasses.

"You've got a mood on," said my sister after a bit of a silence.

"I was just having a 'think' when Lally yelled about this, and now I can't remember what it was that I was thinking, that's all."

She was skiffling along in the white dust of the path kicking empty snail shells about.

"Was it about something lovely?"

"No. Actually. It was about a Play."

"Oh! That!" and she lost interest. She always did. The moment

I even said the very word she lost interest and went off on her own. This time she started picking a spot on her chin. I slapped her hand and she got such a shock that she dropped the milk-can and it rolled and clattered down the path and the lid flew into the hedge.

"Look what you've done! Just look! You stupid fool!" She was furious because I had shocked her, not because she'd dropped the can, and she went scrabbling about in the grasses collecting all the bits together. I went on down the hill and heard her clonking along behind me.

"It's all full of dust and leaves and things, and you could have hurt me doing that! Hitting a person and giving them a fright. I might get something terrible on my chin now and it'll be all your fault."

"You're not supposed to pick spots, you know that."

"I wasn't picking it. I was feeling it."

"Same thing."

"It's not the same thing. Now I might get ringworm just because you're in a mood."

I didn't answer her, but started to run a bit so that she had to hurry to keep up with me. As I got to the old iron gate into the main road she suddenly made a terrible noise and I thought she might have been bitten or something because she was standing quite still just clutching her skirt with her face all screwed up.

"What's the matter?" I called.

"You're vile! You're vile!" She dropped the can into the grass and started patting her stupid skirt with both her hands. "The sugar lumps!" she wailed. "I've lost them . . . you made me . . . you made me when you hit me. They've gone. Now I can't feed Daisy. You're vile!"

I slammed the gate and crossed the road and left her there yowling away. But by the time I had reached the little bridge over the stream where we caught roach, she had got to me, all puffing and breathy, mumbling away about her rotten old sugar. I was glad she hadn't been bitten because I really did like her very much when she was being all right, but when she wasn't, like now about the sugar, I didn't at all. So I just started whistling and took no notice. It was the only thing to do, because I had completely forgotten what it was I was thinking about up there under the elderberry.

Mitchell's cart was standing in the shade just as we got to

Sloop Lane. It had two big wheels and was painted yellow and black, and had a big silver milk churn on top with brass letters spelling out MITCHELLS DAIRY—NEW MILK all round it, and silver ladles hanging in different sizes to measure the milk. We got the pint and a half and the cream, and my sister told the stupid fat pony all about the sugar, and Mr Mitchell said he

The Market Square & the Grocers.

couldn't change a ten shilling note, and what did I think he was, the Bank of England? and he'd get it next time around. So we went on into the Market Square and over the cobbled road to the grocers.

Wildes was in the middle of the square, next door to the Magpie Inn and opposite Woods the Butchers. It had two bulgy windows with lots of little panes of glass, and a front door painted black with golden letters over the top spelling the name.

Inside it was cool, and dim, and smelled of bacon and paraffin, and fresh bread. On one side was a counter with tins of tea behind and barrels of apples and dried peas and corn and walnuts in front of it. On the ceiling hung dustpans and brushes with wooden handles, rat traps, lavatory rolls threaded like beads on loops of string, and bunches of enamel mugs and saucepans which jingled and jangled in the wind when you opened the door.

On the other side was another counter with the scales, big brass ones with all the weights sparkling in a row from very big to very small like the Three Bears; and there were big blocks of butter, and white tubs of lard, and slabs of bacon and legs of ham hanging from the beams just above your head. It really was a very nice place indeed, and there was always such a lot to see that we never minded waiting about while Mr Wilde checked off the things on the list and stuffed them all into the shopping bag. At the very end of the shop, past all the barrels of apples and dog biscuits and things, there was another counter with a wire cage thing over it. This was the Post Office and Miss Maltravers, who played the organ, sat behind it looking like a ghost-lady with her wispy hair and white sleeves over her frock to keep it clean. She was always scribbling away at something, or weighing a parcel, or licking a stamp. She was very busy indeed.

"There is some post for you if you don't mind taking it up and saving the van a journey," she called, and slid something under the cage at us. "One's a postcard from your mother in France, says she's having a lovely time and they'll be home on Sunday, God willing, and the other's something for Miss Jane from Debenham & Freebody, a catalogue by the look of it, which seems a long way to go for a coat when Seaford is on the doorstep."

She really was cheeky. But we didn't like to say so because she was a good friend of the Vicar's and was very churchy, what with her organ and doing the flowers and reciting poems at the Church Teas. So we just didn't say anything; except behind her back.

When we were crossing the river by the wooden bridge my sister said: "She really is the nosiest woman in the world. She spoiled our postcard! Fancy reading someone's postcard and telling them everything in the middle of the shop! Like that time when she told Lally there was some sad news for her in a telegram and Lally went all white and she said, 'I'm afraid your brother's had a little operation and he's quite poorly.' Do you remember? Right in front of everyone else and Lally nearly had a turn there and then. And anyway it was only his appendicitis or something. I think she's nosy and mean."

The postcard was of a big white church and it said: "Having a lovely time. Home on Sunday evening. Hope you are being good. Love from Daddy and Mummy," and that was all, but it was very nice, or would have been if Miss Maltravers hadn't spoiled it.

"I know what we should do," said my sister, trying not to spill the milk as we scrambled on to the main road and across it up to the iron gate. "We should send her a postcard from Eastbourne or somewhere, and say on it 'Miss Maltravers has dandruff and that's why her hair falls down all the time.' That would teach her a really good lesson. It would frighten her to bits, I bet."

It was cool in the kitchen and the table was all laid for lunch with a big jug of ginger beer waiting. Lally was very indignant.

"Jerusalem! She is a nosy parker, what's it got to do with her if I get a catalogue from Debenhams, I'd like to know? I'd like to give her a piece of my mind, I really would. Drat the woman, she really gives me the pip!" But she took her catalogue and went off up to her room to have a look at it, and presently we could hear her singing away "It Happened In Monterey" at the top of her voice, so we felt that she must have found something she liked, because she only sang songs like that when she was particularly pleased. That song was her next favourite one after "The Song Of The Dawn" and she only liked them because this John Boles sang them and she thought he had nice legs or something funny like that. We thought he was a bit soft-looking really, and rather like Fred Brooks, the bus conductor, when she took us to Eastbourne to see a Talkie at the Palace. It was very much forbidden to go to the Pictures and our Parents always said No, but this time, while they were away, Lally had longed to go and see John Boles singing and she had taken us as a treat.

"It's deceitful, I know," she said in the bus, "and I shall get punished for my sins, but what else do I do? I can't leave you both outside, can I? And I've set my heart on it and it is Perfectly Suitable because it's all music and dancing and there is nothing in it to give you a fright. And it's all in colour and you can hear it too. So we'll pretend it's a treat, but if you mention it by so much as a whisper, I'll be sent packing and you'll have someone else to run errands for."

It was very curious to sit in the dark and see all the colours and the lovely costumes, and even funnier to hear it like the wireless only much louder. But we didn't think much of John Thingummy —except he was just like Fred Brooks which annoyed Lally very much.

"If young Fred Brooks had legs like those and a voice like that he could carry me off tomorrow and I wouldn't raise a whimper!" she said, putting her hand on her hip and doing her Haughty Look.

A long time ago she had taken me to see a film in a Picture Palace in London, and it was all about a little boy who got stuck on a sinking ship in a storm. It was very thrilling and I was enjoying it very much until someone locked him in a cabin trunk just as the ship began to go down, and I got so frightened that I ate half the skip off my school cap and swallowed it. And was very sick later. "The child is bringing up tweed and cardboard! I wonder why?" said our mother. And then Lally confessed and got a ticking off. So our mother said Never Again because I was too impressionable or something. So Lally had to go alone on her days off, except this time at Eastbourne when we were deceitful. We never told of course, and we had rather a difficult time not talking about John Whatsisname and Mexico and how they got the colours on the screen to move and sing and all at the same time. But we managed in the end, although we all felt a bit guilty about having been anyway. It didn't matter so much about the songs, I mean we could sing them quite easily all over the place because Lally had records of them which she used to play on her little black portable gramophone. So that was quite easy, and we knew all the words backwards because she only had eight records and we got very used to them.

Sometimes, in the evenings if she didn't feel like reading to us from *A Peep Behind the Scenes*, which was a terribly sad book and made us all sob like anything when it got to the part where the little girl's mother dies in the caravan in the circus and only the clown is there to hold her hand, we used to have a Little Concert. We wound up the black portable and started off always with "It Happened In Monterey" and then "The Song Of The Dawn" and then one or two more and always finished off with "Spread A Little Happiness" which made us all feel cheerful. While we were listening to the concert, of course, there was a job to do. That was the trouble. You always knew when Lally said, "What about a little cheer up, a Little Concert?" And then we had to clean the lamps, cut the rhubarb for the rhubarb and ginger jam, shell peas or something like that. I mean you never just sat there and thought about nothing or anything like that. But it was very nice and sometimes, not always, we were allowed a special treat and we put on a record called "Laughing Gas" which was all about a man reading a Will and someone turns on the laughing gas and they all start laughing. It was terribly funny and we almost made ourselves ill. Sometimes we used to roll on the floor, it was so funny, and Lally said that we'd do ourselves a mischief but we only got hiccups. She didn't let us play it too much for that reason.

But whatever the concert was, we always ended with "Spread A Little Happiness" and that put us all in a thoughtful mood—until we both started remembering the Gas song, and started to giggle and got sent to bed sniggering and hiccuping.

★ ★ ★

Having supper with our parents in the big room was very good. We all sat down together at the big round table. Our father did the carving and Lally served the vegetables or I did, or my sister did, and everyone was very happy and said what we had each been doing during the day.

The room was whitewashed, like the kitchen, with an ingle-nook fireplace which had two big wooden seats in it on each side of the fire, a polished brick floor and lots of fat wickerwork armchairs with feathery cushions. The lamp with the honey-suckle hung over the table, and there was another one near our father's chair where he could read more easily. There were lots of old jugs full of flowers, even in winter, and a clock with a boat in a storm on it and a slow swinging pendulum. This was really our Parents' private place to be, and we were only allowed there really if there were friends to tea or something, or if they had dinner with us all, otherwise we all spent our time in the big white kitchen, with the copper-fire and Minnehaha, the cat, for company. We liked it better there because we could do what we liked and it was difficult in the big room because people were reading or talking.

When our parents came back from Paris we had a chicken from The Court, and stuffing and new potatoes from the garden, and our father had brought back two big bottles of wine, and some rather smelly cheese, which he liked especially, and some mustard. So it was quite French and even Lally had a little sip of wine and everyone was very pleased to be together again.

"Hope you both behaved yourselves," said our mother, not meaning it, and Lally said that we had been Treasures and very helpful, which always made us pleased although we knew she didn't mean that either.

"Because if not," said our mother, "it'll be a dreadful waste of two lovely presents from Paris." And after dinner, when we had cleared away and helped with the washing up, we went back into the big room and there were the packages on the table, almost like Christmas.

My sister's package was, I noticed, a bit bigger than mine, but I had two to her one. And Lally had two as well. So it was all going to be fair. Lally got some stockings and a bottle of something which smelled of lemons and would make a bit of a change from Devonshire Violets; my sister had furniture for her dolls' house, and I got a wind-up racing car, blue and red, with a driver sitting inside and a paperweight thing which was a glass ball full of water and the Eiffel Tower with a little flag on top, and when you shook it hard it made a terrific snowstorm. It had "Paris" written in blue writing on the base.

It was very nice in the big room with them both back. Even though it was very nice too with Lally and the cat, and going to the Picture Palace, which we had promised not to mention, and making jam and even having to go shopping every day almost. But it was a good comfortable feeling all being together again, and even Minnehaha came in and jumped on to my father's lap while he was reading his letters. Lally was having a very nice time talking like anything to our mother. She said she didn't count talking to children much, and missed the real Grown Ups, but all she was talking about was rotten old Miss Maltravers and being so nosy so it really wasn't different conversation, just the same as with us, but to someone else.

"She quite spoiled the children's postcard, you know. Reading it out like that."

"I don't think she meant to be nosy," said our mother. "After all, anyone can read a postcard if they want to. They aren't supposed to be private, otherwise you would put them in an envelope, surely?"

Lally sniffed a bit and wouldn't give in. "And telling everyone about my catalogue from Debenhams. *That's* cheeky, I must say!"

"But I expect that had the name printed on the outside, didn't it? So she wasn't really being nosy. After all, it is a small village, she doesn't get much fun, I imagine, or excitement for that matter." Our mother was always very reasonable, and put like that, Miss Maltravers didn't seem to be so awful, especially if anyone could read anyone's postcard if they liked. I didn't know about that bit. But Lally was not best pleased.

"Well," she said, gathering up all the wrapping paper from the gifts and making a neat little pile on the table, "if she thinks it's exciting to read other people's letters, that's her business I suppose. But the next time I write off for anything, I'll tell them to put it in a plain envelope. I don't want the whole of Sussex to know I have it in mind to get a new coat for the winter, that's MY business. Come along you two . . ." she said, "give your parents a bit of a rest and get up the wooden hill to Bedfordshire toot-sweet, it's well past time."

★　★　★

The O.M. glimmered in the shade under the trees. It was beautiful, and we were all very proud of it. Our father most of all. It was his favourite thing, our mother said, next to *The Times* which is where he worked. She said he liked it better than us all put together, but we knew that wasn't true. It's just that she got a bit fed up having her hair blown all over the place when she had just had it "done", and getting cold in the winter, and wet in the rain. The O.M. was all made of aluminium and was, our father said, an Open Tourer. It went very fast indeed, at least when he was driving it it did, and we got quite cold and wet sometimes when he couldn't be bothered to stop to put up the hood and the side windows.

My sister, Lally and I sat in the back together, under a black leather cover thing, with a separate windshield which had three sides and didn't keep the wind off us at all. We were quite warm under the black cover, but our heads poked out and got very cold, and red, so our father bought us each a leather helmet which covered us almost completely, with ear-muff things and goggles. Lally grumbled a bit about getting her hair in a mess and one day had it all cut off, like a boy's, to save the trouble.

Our mother sat in front wrapped up in a moleskin rug, with scarves and things, but she still got terribly blown about and didn't like the car as much as we did. We all felt very swanky whizzing along in it, all silver with a lovely flying eagle on the bonnet and a very loud horn to frighten the wits out of people who were being slow, or getting in our father's way.

Sometimes, as a treat, we used to pack a big wicker hamper, load up with cups and kettles and bottles of water and a stove, travelling rugs and our father's paint-box, his easel, his stool, and his canvases and Minnehaha, and go off on a picnic somewhere far. Like Arundel, or Ashdown Forest, or Chichester: we used to leave the cottage quite early, after breakfast, and he never said where we were going, just that it was going to be a lovely place; and that was half the fun. But not for our mother. I mean she liked going on a picnic and making the sandwiches and the cold pies and things, but it was the getting there she didn't much like. Because our father would never stop if he could help it, until he wanted a little refreshment. And that could be hours and hours later. Well, nearly.

"Ulric! You really will have to stop soon."

"Why, dear? We have just started off."

"The children are starting to fidget."

She could see us in her little side mirror. We couldn't do much ourselves because of our windscreen, and we couldn't shout because of the wind and the speed, and so we had to make signs so that she would see, which she nearly always did. If she didn't, Lally used to hold a big handkerchief up, so that it fluttered in the wind; she called it our Distress Signal. But still our father wouldn't stop.

"Ulric dear, please!" she would cry. We couldn't hear because of the screen, but we could jolly well tell what she was saying. And then we would reach an inn, usually one our father had chosen from a map long before we started out. It was usually the prettiest, with a garden or a lovely view, and where the beer was specially good. And we'd swerve into the courtyard and people would come out to look at the beautiful silver car from Italy, and we would all feel very pleased. Especially Lally who was longing to "go" as much as we were.

"I do wish," our mother would say, "I do wish you'd listen to me."

Our father would be very smiling and cheerful because he loved driving more than anything it seemed, especially on these picnic days, with the wind and the sun and a big glass of beer beside him.

"I do listen to you, darling, you know I do."

"The children are not camels!"

"Well . . . it hasn't been *so* long. And now everything's all right."

It usually was. Just. We had a packet of potato chips and American Ice Cream Sodas . . . and Lally had a shandy and we all sat in the sun and wondered where the next stop would be. Minnehaha had a collar and a lead and sat beside us spitting at any dog that was silly enough to come near.

Then off we went again, eating Rowntrees Clear Gums which our father always bought for us as a surprise, even though we knew he would do it, and he never forgot; we always pretended it was the first time. And it seemed like that on these days.

And then we had to find somewhere to stop for lunch, which was always very difficult because once our father got behind his wheel again he wanted to go almost to India before he would stop. We all used to shout and point out lovely places, with trees, and grass, and streams or woods, but he simply wouldn't listen.

"I can't stop here, it's on a corner," he would shout over the windscreen. Or else it was on a hill going up, a hill going down, too muddy, or else we didn't see the place in time and he whizzed right past. Our mother got more and more cross, and sometimes it was nearly afternoon when we bumped on to a dusty bit of track and he found a place which was covered in old tin cans, bits of paper, or the remains of an old firesite. It was always a beastly place he chose, but he didn't seem to mind, and we all piled out and got the baskets and stove and things, and spread out the travelling rugs and cushions and tied Minnehaha to a tree or a stick or something.

It didn't really matter in the end. Especially when we had our slices of cold chicken pie, or meat loaf or whatever it was our mother had made for the day. She was a bit grumpy of course: because the ground was dirty and she usually had on a pretty white frock and had to sit carefully on the travelling rug. But our father was very happy, making a little fire from twigs and bits of log, which we didn't need because we had the stove, or going off to find somewhere he could sit and do a painting.

"Why we have to come fifty miles to sit in a rubbish heap to eat, I shall never know," said our mother, laying out the mugs and packets of things to eat.

"We passed so *many* pretty places," said Lally cheerfully. "You'll never change him though, not now you won't. Give him his car and we're off no matter where. Anyway, the sun's out, and what we all need is a bit of something nice in our insides and then we'll all feel much better, and after lunch we can clear up the old tins and things and stick them in the bushes and everything will look a treat, you see."

Going home, after tea which always tasted horrid out of Thermos flasks, in the golden light of the late afternoon we were all very happy because the day, as always, had been happy too. Sometimes we stopped again at an inn for more lemonade and chips, but never more than one glass because of the Not Stopping Bit . . . but crunching up the chalky lane to the Cottage was really always the very best part. Our father drove the O.M. into a very small chalk quarry where it lived, just at the bottom of

The Court Farm & Piggy Corner

the long path up to the garden. And loaded with the baskets and hampers and rugs and the stove, we clambered up under the big elms to the wooden gate and then through the vegetable garden smelling warm in the early dusk.

Sometimes there were glow-worms glinting greenishly in the long grasses, and slow snails sliding gently across the path in the light of the torch. And the bitter-sweet scent of blackcurrant leaves filled the still summer evening as we brushed past them on the way to the kitchen door.

After the lamps were lit, the unpacking done and everything put away, and the table laid for supper in the big room, it was pleasant to slip outside and sit under the apple tree and look right down Great Meadow to the lamps sparkling in the dairy at the Court at Piggy Corner and think how nice our house must look from down there, like a ship on a hill, with the windows glowing golden and smoke wisping from the tall chimney stack.

The dairy of the Court was right on a corner of the road, next door to the pigsties, and when we were coming back from anywhere in the O.M. we always knew just how near home we were by the smell, which is why we called it Piggy Corner. It wasn't a beastly smell, just a Farm Smell, and it always meant that we were going to turn left up the white road to the quarry and the house. And truly, coming home was about the nicest part of ever going out on a picnic.

★   ★   ★

Reg Fluke said that there was a pike in the river Ouse at Itford almost a yard long, and very fierce. He said no one had ever caught it although people had been trying and trying for years and years.

"Too wily . . . 'e knows a thing or two after all this time, I reckon. Old Hallam up at Selmeston said as 'ow once he did get 'im on his line but he fought so hard he broke it and dived away. Hallam reckons he's got about as many 'ooks in 'is jaws as he's got teeth, and I wouldn't wonder."

It was decided that we would go and have a try ourselves. At least, he would go and try with his friend Percy Brooks, because they both had real fishing rods with reels and floats and all sorts of hooks and things, but they kindly said I could come with them as long as I brought some grub. So in a way I was quite included in the party, and I felt that it was all right to tell my sister and Lally that We were going to try for the Giant Pike in the Ouse. At first Lally was a bit put out and I was worried that she'd say No.

"Whereabouts in the Ouse, I'd like to know? It's miles away and you could fall in and then what?"

"Well . . . it's over near Bellingham, across the railway, and if I fell in Reg or Percy would get me out and it would be very exciting if we did catch it."

I was laying the table for lunch, and she was basting a leg of lamb in the oven, kneeling on the floor with a red face, from the heat, and spooning the juice over the crackling top.

"And pray how will you get there? Bellingham's nearly at Lewes! There is no money for bus fares, you know . . . it'll take you half a day to walk."

"We are going to go over the Downs, up past Red Barn and along the top to the Beacon and then down to the Brooks. We'll have to start early in the morning, and I've got to take the grub."

"The what?" She looked up from the oven with raised eyebrows, the spoon in her hand, her apron all bumfley from kneeling.

"The food, I mean."

She slammed the oven door and took the ladle over to the sink. "They'll spoil your ways those two, you mark my words. Grub indeed! What sort of *grub*, may I ask, do you envisage?"

She was being cross, I could feel that, and she was trying to find a way of saying no without really saying no. She never wanted to actually refuse if she could help it, but it was useful if something difficult came along which was putting off a bit. Like food.

"I'll make some sandwiches, and perhaps an egg or something. I don't want much," I said quickly, and so that she couldn't interrupt me I went on very fast and said that I would make them myself the night before, if she would let me have the egg to boil, and that I had three pence saved and could use that for some lemonade or something. I could see that she really wasn't best pleased because she banged the steamer quite hard on top of the copper, and the lid fell off and all the steam went up in the air and she cried out angrily: "Drat the thing! What do you want to come and ask me difficult things for when I'm steaming cauliflower!"

But in the end it was all right and she said I could go, and gave me some cold lamb for the sandwiches and a new egg to boil and I did them all myself without any trouble, and with no mess. No mess was very important with Lally.

Next morning, very early, while the sun was making long thin shadows across the gully and the dew was like silver beads everywhere, I went down the brick path to meet Reg and Perce with my satchel full of sandwiches and a bottle of home-made ginger beer.

The Market Place was very quiet and still at that time in the morning; not even Mitchells Dairy was about. The shops were all closed and there was only a sleepy-looking girl sweeping the steps of the Magpie Inn. By the time we had climbed up to the top of Long Burgh Hill I was pretty well puffed out but I couldn't say much because the other two had rods and baskets and things, and I only had my satchel with the sandwiches and my bottle of ginger beer. Walking along the grassy track behind Reg and Perce up on the top there, made me feel very good. The air was still, not yet hot, and all about us lay the whole of Sussex. On the right was all the weald fading away into the misty morning in pale blue and green ridges; on the left you looked down to the sea, sparkling and winking in the sun, and Newhaven, like a toy town with red and grey roofs all jumbled together and the church spire sticking up, and beyond that the long quay poking a bent finger into the sea.

There was no sound at all, just our feet through the dew-silvered grasses and the larks; now and then sheep bleating, because this was all sheep land. And every so often we came to one of the dew ponds which people said were so deep that you got drowned in them if you slid down the sides, but Reg said that was all My Eye and that there was nothing in them except a few efts and water-boatmen, and if they were that deep why did the shepherds let the sheep drink from them, which is what they were for? Which seemed reasonable.

When we got to Firle Beacon we had a bit of a sit down. It was halfway, and Reg and Perce had an apple and I drank some of my ginger beer, and we lay in the sun listening to the sheep bells and the larks singing and the wind withering about in the gorse. At least I did. They were talking about bait and hooks and just where the exact place to find the pike was. Reg had taken off his wellingtons and I noticed that he was wearing grey socks with holes in them, but I didn't say anything and presently we packed up and started on the path again to Bellingham Hill.

By the time we reached it, and could look down over the valley below to Lewes and the castle sitting on top of the town like a piece of broken pumice stone, and Mount Caburn like a volcano, the sun was getting high and it was already warm. But they seemed very pleased because they could see the Ouse winding up the valley like a tin snake, and Reg said the tide would be in by the time we got down there. As we slithered down the steep slope to Itford Farm, Perce said that whatever I did I wasn't to come near the edge of the river bank, because the least shadow,

3(a) Jane Newbold (a friend of my parents), my mother, sister and self, Lally on right. Cuckmere Haven, 1931.

3(b) Family picnic with the Renault. Ashdown Forest, 1929.

4(a) My mother, Elizabeth, Rogan, 1938.

4(b) Family group by the pond. I am wearing the Green Suit from the Fire Sale (see p. 194). Gareth and Rogan. Taken in November 1940.

or movement, would scare the pike away and they'd clobber me one. But since they had let me go with them, and were older than me anyway, I just held my tongue and followed them bumpily over the mole hills to the road and then across the high railway line to the river.

The pike wasn't actually *in* the river; he lived, they said, in a sort of pond thing which ran off the river and was very deep, which is why he was there at all. Because he had grown so big eating all the other fishes in the pond-bit that he had grown too big to swim out again, so he was trapped until someone hooked him.

The pond was quite large, and very weedy. The tide was coming in, rippling the clear water up towards Lewes, and the ground all round was very wet and marshy—which is why they were wearing wellingtons, I realised, because I was sopping wet already; but it didn't matter because it was so warm. Perce gave me a small jam jar with a paper lid and told me to start hunting for grasshoppers because he was going to try them on the pike.

"Get the big 'uns," he said, starting to put his bamboo rod together. "Don't go for the little ones, I want them big and jumping. 'E won't take 'em if they's little and not all wriggling. You can bait the hook if you like."

I got quite a few poor old grasshoppers and a couple of beetles as well in case they would come in handy, and then I sat down, not too far away from the bank, and watched.

Well, there really wasn't very much to watch in the end. Just Reg and Perce sitting hunched up in the rushes not moving. So I opened my satchel and started to unwrap my sandwiches because I hadn't had any breakfast and I was getting quite hungry, but Reg shook a fist at me in the air, and Perce turned round and scowled, because the paper was a bit rustly and they looked very cross. So I lay back in the wettish grass and looked up at the sun and the clear shining sky. It was rather boring, I thought, and I was quite pleased when a lady came slowly walking across the field. She was tall and thin, with a long woolly, and fairish hair which looked rather wispy as if she had just washed it. She was carrying a walking stick and a bunch of wild flowers. When she saw us she stopped and shaded her eyes with her hand to see us better against the white light of the river. Reg looked very grumpily at her and went on fishing. Perce just hunched his shoulders up and didn't move, which was very rude because she was smiling a little and looked quite kind.

"Fishing?" she said in a silly way. Because what else could they be doing? Reg just looked at her and nodded his head, and Perce didn't do anything. She looked vaguely round her and said: "I think I'm lost, I can't find the bridge."

Reg swung his rod into the air and looked sullen. "Up behind you, on the road," he said gruffly, and re-cast his line so that I heard the bait plop into the still morning water.

"Thank you," said the lady and then she held up the bunch of flowers for us all to see. No one said anything, so she turned and started walking back the way she had come, towards the bridge, stepping carefully over the mole hills and tussocks. She didn't look back and I was glad, because we had been very rude, but she hadn't spoken to me so I didn't feel I was quite to blame, and I didn't dare speak or move because of the pike and Perce's face, which was very red and cross.

"Bloomin' nuisance her. She's always about when I get here. Always up and down the river she is, like a bloomin' witch." He reeled in his line and told me to give him another grasshopper because the one he had was drowned and not jerking any longer. While he baited the hook again we all watched her scramble up the bank to the road and then walk across the bridge swinging the stick in her hand; she was smelling her bunch of flowers and didn't look back at us again.

"A foreigner, isn't she?" said Reg.

"Londoner. From over there at Rodmell," said Perce, skewering the biggest grasshopper onto his hook. "They say she's a bit do-lally-tap . . . she writes books." He swung the wriggling bait out into the still pond-like water and muttered something about never getting any peace and quiet. As the float plopped into the water and bobbed gently on the ripples from the tide, we all settled down again to fish. Which was pretty boring I was beginning to think.

So I just lay back quietly in the grasses, and watched the sky and wondered why there were so many witches in Sussex.

* * *

The bus from Seaford had just rumbled up to the Market Cross when we got back to the village, so I knew it was pretty late and that Lally would be fidgeting if I didn't hurry on up the hill to the cottage.

We hadn't caught the pike. Of course. No one really believed that we would, it was just a "try". Perce said that it was the pale-faced lady who put him off the whole day.

"Every time I sets meself down by that little pond-place along she comes wagging her stick and talking away to herself. Potty she is, so would anyone be living right next to a graveyard." He was grumpy, but Reg said it was the bait we had used; next time we went, he said, we should take a bit of fresh liver or something really tempting. But Fred Brooks from the bus said that the pike was just a "rumour", never mind what old Hallam over at Selmeston said, and that he'd been trying for the same pike ever since he was knee high to a duck, and had never had any luck, and that you'd have more luck trying to win the Irish Sweepstake than trying for the pike at Bellingham.

And that seemed to be that: so I just ambled home through the village and across the river and up the hill to the house. The sun was starting to set away behind the gully, and the shadows of the ash and oak were already quite long across the rutted path. The sun was orange-glinting on the diamond panes of glass in the cottage windows, and when I threw my arms up in the air, and stood with my legs apart, my own shadow looked very long and thin, with a tiny little head at the top, like the Long Man of Wilmington.

At the top of the gully, almost where our orchard started, a small white dog came skittering out of the bushes, barking and squealing and then dashed back again, and I knew that it was probably Mr Aleford and his brothers ferreting. And then they all came up through the hedgerow from the gully, with sacks, and a long pole with five rabbits hanging by their legs from it, and the little white dog, Tiger, leaping and jumping for pleasure. We all waved cheerfully and they went on down the hill laughing and talking. Suddenly Mr Ben turned round and called up to me, "Hey? You lost this then?" and he threw something like a ball up in the air towards me. I couldn't catch it because I was carrying my shoes and the satchel, so it rolled rustling into the grass at my feet.

"Butterfingers!" called Mr Ben. "Found it down the warren there, thought it must have belonged to you, reckon it got stuck in a hole and the badgers got it. Been there all summer by the look of it. Cheerio!" and he turned and went after his brothers.

It was George.

Even though it hadn't got a head or a tail or legs or anything, it was clearly George—but now he was just an empty shell looking like someone's old hat, with four holes in it. I took him up and went on up the hill.

★　　★　　★

"Will you dig a grave?" said my sister kindly, knowing I was miserable and trying to be nice. But I shook my head and finished the last bit of my gooseberry fool. Lally poured herself another cup of tea and clonked the spoon about.

"Not much point in having a funeral for just a shell," she said cheerfully. "It's like making a grave for a suit of clothes, isn't it? And no one would want to do that. George has been all eaten up by badgers and ants and that's that: you should have put a string on him like young Fluke told you in the first place. You should always put a string on everything you want to keep, from buttons to tortoises."

She really seemed not to know how miserable I was, but my sister did; anyway part of it, even if it wasn't the part she liked, had been hers too . . . so she understood better.

After supper, she came down to the pump with me, and we started to wash the shell so that all the mud and chalk swirled away. But it wasn't very much good because it was all scratched and chewed up looking and made me even sadder, so I just filled the two buckets for the washing-up and we humped them, slopping water, back to the kitchen. Lally took one, and set it on the copper to boil, and took the other with her to the sink for the rinsing.

"Cheer up, you two! You'd think you'd lost a shilling and found a farthing! It's a lovely summer evening, go out and enjoy it before bedtime."

I started to dry up a cup rather slowly while she swirled the suds about and clinked and clonked the plates and saucers onto the draining board.

"I think it feels like the end of summer now," I said.

"Aren't we the little actor then!" said Lally, drying up a bundle of forks. "All summers have to end sometime you know . . . can't have a summer without a good winter, can you? It stands to reason. It has to to get the land ready for the next time.

Can't be summer all the time." She stacked the forks in a neat pile and started on the knives, wiping them hard against her apron before she polished them on the drying cloth.

My sister hung the cups on the dresser hooks and arranged the plates back on the little shelves.

"I mean to say!" she said suddenly. "If there wasn't a winter whatever would happen to Christmas! Wouldn't it be simply awful with no Christmas! And you can't have a Christmas without a winter, can you? You couldn't have one in summer . . . not possibly."

"They do in Australia," I said grumpily but pleased I knew.

"Oh, Australia! They do everything upside down there, because they are upside down from us, everyone knows that. I expect they even play cricket on Christmas day with nuts or something."

Lally bundled the knives and forks into a drawer, took up the tablecloth, shook it out of the window, and started to fold it, singing happily away as if she had no cares at all in the world.

Of course it didn't matter to her, really, about George; she didn't really know that I was feeling so miserable because I had been careless and let him wander and go off on his own and get eaten by badgers and so on. That was, anyway, all my fault. She just went on singing away "Dawn With Thine Rosy Mantle" as if nothing awful had happened at all.

She even slammed the drawer shut hard, with a bang, when she put the cloth away, and sang even louder. No one cared. Not even my sister: she was mucking about with a jug of flowers on the table, so I just decided to go out into the garden and have a bit of a think, and be on my own.

It was cooler outside. The sky was flat and almost mauve-coloured. Bats swooped like little kites over the wigwams of runner beans in the vegetable garden as I wandered up to the iron gate and out into Great Meadow, holding George's shell in my hands, and wondering why everything had suddenly gone so beastly and sad-feeling.

I heard my sister rustling through the raspberry canes behind me, and the iron fence squeak as she clambered over it and lumped into the meadow. And then she was walking, quite quietly, just behind me, not saying anything, and I knew that she really was a bit sorry for me in her own peculiar way.

Up at the top of the gully, where they had all been ferreting, the grass was trodden and muddy, and there was a bit of rabbit's fur caught on a clump of thistles. But there was no sign, this evening, of any rabbits as there usually was: they had all gone.

"Is this where they found him?" said my sister in a low voice.

"Yes. They were after the rabbits."

"Poor little things . . . what are you going to do with that then?"

I looked down at the chewed-up old shell.

"Just chuck it away, I think."

"Into the gully?"

"Yes . . . into the gully."

We walked slowly over to the chalky edge and looked down into the shadowing little path which ran along the bottom among all the roots and tree trunks. It looked very cold and lonely there. A blackbird blundered away worriedly into the hawthorns and then I suddenly threw the shell high up into the air: we both watched it as it made a wide arc against the fading sky and then fell swiftly into the dark branches over the gully.

For a moment there was silence and then we heard it clitter-clatter-clotter down among the leaves and stones, then everything was still again.

And that was that.

PART 2

WINTER

9

IN my school report for the Lent Term of 1933 Miss Polyphemus, my Housemistress, thought it necessary to observe that "He has still to learn that life is not all cushions and barley sugar." An odd combination of delights, one might think. However, she was right.

A small, eager, middle-aged woman, rather like a Jack Russell, she dragged me unwillingly through Mathematics, applauded wanly from a deck-chair when I muffed a catch at Cricket, and sloshed about in muddy wellingtons with a whistle in her mouth while I stood shivering with cold on the touch line during Football. I know that I tried her patience to the limits.

I hated all three. Mathematics, Cricket and, above all, Football. I found them totally illogical pursuits. I could never, and still cannot, understand why anyone should want to hit a very hard ball with a non-resilient bat high into the air so that someone else could run up and down a scrubby bit of grass until the ball is retrieved. Nor could I see, and I still cannot, the delights in kicking and hacking, and pushing, and shoving, about in mud and wet so that a small leather sphere should reach some designated area of space between two wooden poles shrouded in mist or freezing fog. As for Mathematics I simply didn't believe them.

It was no good telling me that some wise Arab, scrabbling about in the sand decided, all by himself, that Five should be Five and that twice that number should be called Ten. I couldn't accept that at all.

Miss Garlick, who took us for Botany, was marginally kinder in giving me two "Goods" for Diligence and Apprehension, although she had to add that she wished I was "More accurate, both in drawing and writing" and Dr Chanter, predictably Music, was glowing with two "V. Goods" and a genial comment in a flourishing pen that I was "Working very well indeed." It was difficult, even for me, not to be able to learn the words of "The Vicar of Bray" or "Hark Hark the Lark". The tune took a little longer.

The remainder of the report was grey. Dr Lake's final comment, in crimson ink at the bottom of the page, betrayed a good deal of suppressed irritation and weariness. "He makes me impatient. But I am trying to be more philosophical about him. Only time will tell." Trying, was underlined.

It just did not occur to me that what Miss Polyphemus said was not so: although I might have chosen other words than "cushions and barley sugar". I thought life was simply splendid. I had no reason to think otherwise. My days revolved about two pivots, if one can have two pivots. The Cottage in Sussex, and Twickenham.

Not counting my home and family which was, of course, the centre anyway. My life, as far as I could make it, was a total splendour of Summer and Constant Sunshine in which nothing unpleasant was ever allowed to happen. The fact that I was not God, and that unpleasant things *did* occur from time to time, was simply not my affair at all. I had an amazing way of setting those aside, and obliterating from my mind, and being, the things which were boring, dull or distressing. Like my father, I managed, quite skilfully, to set aside the disagreeable parts of life so that I coasted, cheerfully enough, from the Cottage to Twickenham without taking a great deal of notice of the things which littered that happy road. Things which, from time to time, did crack my shins or cause me a bothersome, not to say painful, stumble from my happy Seat of Grace. School, and all those who served within it, from Pupil to Teacher, was a bore and a place where one marked time until the doors opened again and one was released into Pleasures. School was Outside. And most people were Outside. And anything which was Outside was simply that. And did not affect me so far as I could help.

My family, the Cottage and Twickenham were all that mattered to me. Beyond them all else was a blank.

A sad state of affairs.

It was not that I was shielded, or cosseted, really. In fact I was not. My sister Elizabeth and I were both brought up from a very early age to fend for ourselves, to be quite self-sufficient, to work for our pleasures and physically to earn our weekly pocket money. Nothing came too easily. We were members of a young family, and they had to work hard for all they had, and we had to do the same. We lived in a world which was almost completely Grown Up. We delighted in our parents' friends who were mostly painters, writers and journalists, and found most children dull, retarded or childish. So we didn't bother with them. We didn't need them, we felt, and they got in the way. We never made close friends, or stayed at their houses ever; and seldom asked them back to ours. Unless forced by adult politeness. We liked each other better, and our father and mother and Lally provided us with all the pleasure, excitements, and delights we felt we could possibly wish for.

A very smug attitude indeed.

A rather insular life? A little ingrowing? We didn't think so. Nor do I now. It harmed no one: beyond ourselves. And it was about to change.

The Report, quoted above, was alas! only one of a number. They grew very slightly better as the terms went by; but not much. I finally "made it" in Botany, Bookbinding, Metalwork and Drawing. Everything else was just "V. Fair".

My father, who had distant ideas of sending me to Fettes and then watching me proudly follow him dutifully along the dusty corridors of *The Times* until I eventually took over his chair as Art Editor in the Art Department, began, reluctantly but clearly, to realise that his dreams were just that.

The chances of my getting into the Gas, Light and Coke Company were brighter than the possibilities of my even reaching the gates of Fettes. Let alone Printing House Square.

My idleness, my backwardness, my apparent inability to grasp the fundamentals of scholastic life were blamed, possibly correctly, on the fact that I had not been sent off to a Boarding School from the start. It had been a constant battle between my parents, she refusing, he begging. I waged a neutral war. And stayed.

Time which had now been lost for twelve years had to be regained somehow. The visions of Fettes and *The Times*, though dimmed, still gleamed like an afterthought, through my father's disappointment. He did all that he possibly could to redress the wrongs. I was sent, willy nilly, to a very expensive tutor for a year in a grey stucco house in Willow Road, Hampstead.

I can only remember that it was an unpleasant shock and one which I found a little harder than usual to obliterate quite so easily from my existence. I don't, oddly enough, remember very much about it. Obliterating was still at work whatever should befall me. I don't even remember much about the Tutor except that he was very old and wore a celluloid collar and lace-up boots. There were two other boys there with me, one older and one the same age. But they were keener than I so I hardly ever spoke to them, and the eldest one was extremely busy with something rather complicated like Trigonometry. We sat round a green baize table. The Tutor at one end with an empty chair at the other. We vaguely wondered who it was for until one day a silent, elderly lady slid into it and sat there knitting during a long lecture on the Lowest Common Denominator. She only came once. Sensibly.

I spent most of my time gazing out of the window at the trees on the Heath, and the Tutor spent most of his sleeping, or speaking, in a low murmur, to the Trigonometry Boy. It was a lethal, dull, boring year. And did me no good at all. At the time. But as far as I was able I did try, although to little effect. I simply sat there planning books or poems or a new, and usually improbable, plot for a play.

Eventually, and despairingly, I was removed and sent back to the school up the hill. Where I prospered exceedingly after my time away by Producing, Writing, Directing and Acting in my own versions of "Just William" and the other William stories. These were done during the school breaks, and my unfortunate class-mates, bullied, cajoled and sometimes even blackmailed, into playing in them, were forced to relinquish the delights of football, marbles and cigarette card swapping for the doubtful pleasures of giving highly embarrassed performances in smaller roles than mine.

It was quite clear that the entire school staff had now considered my case hopeless, and to my simple, and gratified, astonishment, I was permitted to "do" these plays as long as they didn't interfere with the boys' working life at school.

In fact they became so popular that I even had chairs set up for the staff who actually came and watched some of the performances, thus giving me, if not the others, a first heady whiff of an Audience. Albeit they were pretty stolid and dull, they were there. And the show became For Them. Even the Headmaster vaguely approved. What else could he do?

My father by this time was now thoroughly disillusioned with me. I could sense it very well. He never made jokes any more and always seemed rather preoccupied and distant when I was in the same room with him. Lally, correctly, pointed out that he was "disappointed" in me, that it was entirely my own fault, I had been given every chance and warning, and that if I didn't set to and pull up my socks I'd be in for a very unpleasant surprise one day. She also added that he had a great deal to worry him.

He had. After eleven years my mother suddenly found, to her despair, that she was pregnant, and life shifted imperceptibly, but firmly, into a different gear. My sister and I had noticed that she seemed to be getting rather large, and had, I remember, speculated on the very improbable fact that she might be going to have a baby. But the fact was so abhorrent to us, and we considered her so terribly old anyway, that the idea slipped easily from our narrow little minds and we thought no more about it and merely decided that she was "putting on weight".

She settled all that easily enough one day when we were at the top of the garden picking lilac for the drawing-room.

"I'm going to have a baby," she said. Clearly having rehearsed it for ages.

We showed no surprise, which might have comforted her, because she went on to say that it would be quite soon, that she hoped it would be a boy and that she thought it would because it kicked so much, and that she wanted us to be very, very kind to it and love it and not make it feel that it didn't belong to us all and was loved and welcome.

Later in the Nursery, where my sister now slept alone, since Lally had one day made the disconcerting discovery during Bath Time that I was "growing up", we looked at each other with ashen faces and saw the future, correctly; hideous with crying and Nurses and a stranger in our midst whom we should have to like whether we wanted to or not. This would be no Other Child, no Outsider, but our very own; some eleven years late in joining.

We were bleak.

Everyone was bleak in fact. Eleven years is a long time in which to have forgotten the pattering of those blasted tiny feet. We had, we considered, all got Set In Our Ways. Well: now they were to be shifted a bit, those Ways, things were never to be quite the same again. A new phase was about to start. We all wondered, privately, how we should manage.

* * *

July 1934 was blazing. Roses opened and fell within the day, and the lawns turned rusty beige. My sister was dispatched to our grandmother in Scotland for a while so that her room, the Nursery, could become one again; this time for the Baby. I was allowed to remain at home to welcome this addition. I was, it was pointed out, the eldest and it was right and proper that I should be present in the house when he arrived. The Nursery was stripped out and painted white. A cot and armchair and small table, scales and a bath with ducks on it took the place of our battered toy boxes, book cases and a gabled dolls' house. Then came Nurse Hennessy, a broad, hefty Irish Nurse who crackled like a twig fire and was less friendly.

Lally refused to carry trays up to the Nursery until the Baby was actually born, and so a small, but deep, rift started in the family life. However, Nurse Hennessy seemed not to care and swigged down her Guinness with her lunch as cheerfully as if she had been sitting in her own Nursery sipping champagne, which, she assured us, was what she had been Accustomed to at her Other Places. Lally sipped away at her tea in the kitchen, at her table, and read *Poppies Weekly* slowly from cover to cover without saying a word. I ate with them, my mother, by this time, spending most of the day in her room lying down and feeling wretched. My father was "at *The Times*" and I just sensed that someone had turned my egg-timer upside down and that the sand had started to run the other way. I was not at all comfortable.

One blistering Saturday when strange currents seemed to be racing through the house the brusque Doctor, who was a lady but wore a grey flannel suit with a black tie, had some urgent words with my father and I suddenly found myself walking with him through the careless weekend shoppers of Hampstead. He walked rather quickly, and I was always a little behind him, sweating and bumping into people with prams and baskets and vaguely aware that we had been sent out of the house to await the arrival of the Baby. In a florists near the Heath we spent quite a long time selecting carnations. He bought a vast bunch, choosing them individually, striped pink and white. They were my mother's favourite flower and although they reminded me of Weddings and Death these were destined for a Birth. We then went into a large Stationers and Newsagents where he slowly and thoughtfully chose tubes of oil paint, some tracing paper and a random selection of pen-nibs and bought me a copy of *Boys Own*. This surprised me more than the strange assortment of things he was purchasing for himself. *Boys Own* was very glossy and more expensive than any of the other magazines we were normally able to afford. I realised that he was not, perhaps, being as casual as he seemed. Then we walked back, in silence, down Heath Street to the rather ugly house which was my Centre. It had a high gable, fake beams and two acacia trees in the front garden.

Lally opened the door before we reached it looking rather hot and a little rumpled. But she was half smiling through her anxiety, so I knew immediately that things were more or less all right. Looming behind her in the hall, pulling on her gloves, was Doctor Findlayson, about to leave in her dark green Sunbeam parked at the gate.

"She had a hard time," she said cheerfully. "But she's not a girl any longer. It's a boy by the by and she'd like to see you as soon as she's ready." She gave us both a cold smile, lit a cigarette, and went out to her car.

My father ran up the staircase. I stood and watched the doctor drive away in a hurry. A boy, I thought. Ah well . . . but mother had not died.

I sat in the window seat in the hall and waited. Unconsciously aware that I might be needed or sent for. I rifled through the glossy pages of *Boys Own* and kept one ear cocked for the awaited cry of the Baby. It was Nurse Hennessy, at the top of the stairs, who called me. Not the Baby. She was smiling and carried a white bundle.

"Come up and meet your little brother!" she cried as if we were all at a party.

It looked, from my point of view, like rabbit-offal wrapped in a shawl. I was silent with shock at the sight of this living stranger in our midst. This was the bulge in my mother's belly. This the cause of the vastly disturbed household.

The Nursery smelled of powder and methylated spirit. She unwrapped the offal and laid it in my reluctant arms.

"Hold its neck. Otherwise its head will fall off, and we don't want that, do we!" I was not altogether sure.

Small fists beat helplessly in slow motion at a bloated, scarlet, screwed-up, old man's face. The head weighed tons, the neck seemed delightfully frail. It kicked hard, and I saw the long twisting tube which still trailed from his belly. Nurse Hennessy stuffed a cigarette into her mouth and, taking up some scissors and a reel of white string, showed me how to tie "in" this gristly worm. I was not at all over anxious to do as she suggested, but she said that I was the Eldest and that it was fitting that I should tie up the cord which had attached my brother to his mother all the time that he was growing inside her. She felt, although I rather doubted it myself, that mother would "like this". I didn't think she'd care one way or the other but fiddled with string and gristle and scissors until I had achieved some form of a knot.

"There!" cried Nurse Hennessy. "Now he really is part of this World! All we have to do is wash him thoroughly and that'll rot off in two shakes of a lamb's tail."

In my mother's room the blinds were drawn against the sun; the room was hot and smelled of hospitals. She lay, a large lump, exhausted and overheated, in the great oak bed which she and my father shared. She wore a pretty lace boudoir cap with little bows, and tried to smile in a pale way, reaching out her hand, as I came to the side of the bed.

"I hope you'll be good to him," she said in a whispering voice. "He was a lot of hard work, I can tell you."

I told her, politely, for I was a little afraid of this exhausted, hot, woman who had just had a difficult time and who seemed to be almost in a dream, that I had been shown by Nurse Hennessy how to tie off my brother's cord. She smiled wearily and waved a hand vaguely in the air. "She's a silly bitch!" she said gently. "Brought me a soft boiled egg and toast, can you imagine what an idiot she is. For God's sake take it away and hide it. Give it to Lally and tell her to throw it away." And she seemed to lapse into a troubled sleep and left me standing helplessly looking at the neat little tray and the boiled egg.

Lally snorted and silently stuffed the lot into the sink. "A glass of beer would do her more good, that I can tell you. But you daren't say a thing to these Nurses." She shoved the kettle on to the gas stove and started to lay up a small tray with the best china and a little lace cloth. From somewhere far away it seemed we heard the first cries.

Angry, defiant, furious at being late. We looked at each other with very different thoughts. She shook some sugar lumps into a china bowl. The crying went on. It was not to stop for two years.

*　*　*

"We thought it better," said my mother gently a few weeks later, "than a Boarding School. You really are a bit late for that now, and Aunt Belle adores you and you like her and she has always wanted to have you. She even wanted to adopt you ages ago when you were first born because she thought that I would not be able to bring you up properly. And a Scottish Education is what you need. It's far better than an English one. And you really have had all the chances down here and nothing seems to work. You just can't go on being a duffer, can you?"

She looked beautiful, as she always did, and calm and collected. Obviously this had all been planned before. I was to go to school in Scotland, to stay with her childless sister and her husband, to live near her family, to be brought up by strangers, even if they were Family, and to leave my Centre and my life to which I had happily become accustomed. The shock took some time to hit me. But when it did I was prostrate. Now I was no longer needed. The Baby had become the centre of the Universe. Even my sister had turned traitor and spent hours holding it and kissing it and washing it. Lally, beloved, adored, Lally was preoccupied now with getting rid of the Nurse and restoring the "roses to your mother's cheeks" and my father, after the splendour of the amazing *Boys Own*, had retreated even further away from me than ever.

He was, evidently, putting aside the unpleasant things, as I did, and as he was good at doing. And sending me off, willy nilly, to a strange school in a strange land with strange people could surely be called "unpleasant", even by him.

But, as Lally pointed out, boiling water and steeping great mounds of chrome nappies in a large zinc bath, I had had my chances and had failed them. The Tutor had cost a lot of money, so had the school on the Hill and the uniforms and all the rest of the stuff I had been forced to wear during Term time. Producing plays, however clever, was not going to get me to learn my sums or my spelling and all that sort of thing. What I needed, she said very kindly, was a bit of a "pull on the reins". And this, they all felt sure, was what Scotland and Aunt Belle and Uncle Duff and a very tough school in Glasgow would do for me.

In an emperic state of Self Pity, to which, when things go against my wishes, I am prone, I lay on my bed in my room at the top of the house and, through tear-filled eyes, said most of my farewells to the wallpaper. Blue tits smothered in wisteria. My own deathly choice. The jar of snails by my bed held no delights now. They never had in fact, frightfully boringly they only seemed to eat at night and never moved about in the daylight . . . the small altar which I had made in a corner, looked dusty and un-prayed at. It was. But today it held sudden attractions. I wondered if perhaps a prayer, even so late, would help. But I was too shattered with shock and self pity to move from the bed. I realised that no one wanted me now, and that no one cared about me. The sooner I was removed from this uncaring place the better. It might even, though this did not seem remotely possible at that time, be very interesting in Scotland. I did like my Aunt. I liked the idea of the journey there. I even liked the distant memories of my grandmother's teas and all my uncles and aunts and the odd way they all spoke and eating sticks of Edinburgh Rock. And oat cakes. And even porridge.

I might even like the school. But I felt that I could never really forgive them here for chucking me out without warning. The eldest! Ha! Now that they had a younger one I was to be put aside and dumped "with relations" for God's sake, in a foreign land.

I knew, with savage insight, that I detested that screaming bundle of waving arms and legs on the floor below. I was even being thrown out of My Room so that my sister could have it while Lally shared the Nursery with the howling intruder. They would change the wisteria and the blue tits. Throw away my snails, muddle my books and drawings, even open my desk, and put my clothes in a different place in the house. I was in despair, a mounting wave of dislike and anger rose within me which nearly made me sick. I would never forgive that stinking, smelly, shrieking, little beast who had burst, unwelcome, into my perfect Two Pivot and Centre Life. And I didn't for over twenty years.

* * *

Before she married my father, my very beautiful mother had been an actress. She had reached her peak of success in "Bunty Pulls The Strings" at the Haymarket in 1911. A point in history which we were never to forget. Nor were we ever allowed to forget.

All through childhood we were delighted and saddened with long recitations which she had memorised in order to Entertain The Boys from the Front. They ranged from super Show-Stoppers like "Billy's Rose" which began: "Billy's dead and gone to Heaven, So has Billy's sister Nell" which reduced us all to snivelling sobs long before the final stanzas, to "The Story of Dan Ma'grew" right through Hilaire Belloc and all those "Heartless Tales For Hearthless Homes". We were entranced and delighted. When the War got into its stride she marched all over the country with Concert Parties entertaining the wounded, billed as "Always Applauded", and fondly known to all and sundry as "Little Madge". Finally she went into Munitions when the War got really desperate about 1917 and went back towards London and the Theatre as soon as the Armistice was signed. Life was not easy for young actresses then, no easier than it is today, and to make ends meet she posed for Hands and Head, only, at the Slade, the St Martin's and Chelsea Polytechnic. While awaiting the Call from Cochran; which never came.

In 1920, after a famous Chelsea Arts Ball, she was given a room in someone's studio who was in Paris for three weeks. Without money, with no real roof over her head at that time, and with a group of jolly young artists and actors all in the same boat, she settled happily down to sleep off the delights and exhaustions of the Albert Hall. The young man returned from Paris, with 'flu, two weeks early. That is to say three hours after my mother had comfortably crawled into his vacant bed. She was swiftly ejected by him, and forced, since it was a strange house and she didn't know her way around it having entered it so shortly before, to spend the night huddled in the remains of her Fancy Dress, a Spanish Shawl and a borrowed mantilla, on the mat outside his room. Her anger and rage knew no bounds. However, she discovered that he was ill and stayed to nurse him. Three weeks later they were married. A honeymoon in France and then back to the same tall brick house in St George's Road, West End Lane, which my father owned and let out as rooms to his artist and writer friends. And then came The Call—from Hollywood.

Mother was asked to go to California to join the Lasky Players. Seeing herself thrusting Theda Bara from the confines of the screen, she packed a bag and signed the contract. In that order. My astonished, but cool, father said that it was either Lasky or himself; she could not have both. After days of tearful pleading, sulking, and despair, she stayed, and never ever got further West in her life than New York when she was well over fifty. She never forgot, however, and she never, totally, was able to forgive. But she was a good, properly brought up young woman, and honour was honour and the pact she made with my father lasted happily all their lives together. But the dull pain, and the vague feeling of disappointment, even un-achievement, was to remain buried away inside all her life. And all of ours.

I was born the following March. She was delighted, if vague, about it all. She has always said that I was conceived in Paris, which I do not doubt, for they travelled extensively to France in that first year of marriage, and that she was determined I should be born there. However, she muffed that too through no fault of her own, and though it was touch and go that I should be born in a taxi, they made the nursing home and I arrived at eight-thirty in the morning of March 28th, 1921. From that moment on, loving my father as much as she clearly did, she knew that she was trapped. No longer could Hollywood beckon. Well, it could; but she was never to be able to heed its call. Not that it ever did call again; but she never completely gave up hope.

My mother's background was a large Victorian Ayrshire family. Eleven children in all. She was last but three in the line. My grandfather, once a man of substance, was elegant, handsome, a gifted painter and an indifferent Actor. He was Cartoonist for a Glasgow paper, and was adored by all who met him. He wore cloaks and wide-brimmed hats, and loved my mother most of all his children for she was the "one most like me". Eventually, unable to bear the tremendous constrictions of a tight family life he left home and went out into the world with The Actors, joining the Neilson Terrys, the Forbes Robertsons and the Cyril Maudes and finally, kidnapping my mother from the home, she was ten, pressed her into service as his servant and companion. Together for a number of years, they toured the Provinces, coming, happily, to rest under the elegant portals of the Hay-market Theatre in "Bunty Pulls The Strings".

He had realised, as have done others before him, and since, that though he had a tremendous physical presence and a beautiful voice, he had not got the spark for greatness. He had started in the theatre too late in life and could not adjust, totally, to this glittering world which he so adored but felt a little lost within.

Not so his daughter Margaret. The moment she hit the Stage, at eleven or abouts, she was On. And at the Haymarket, while Grandfather played a tiny part as an old shepherd, his daughter bounced over a canvas wall as the Ingenue. Both their fates were, to some extent, sealed. After "Bunty" closed he went sadly back to Scotland and left his daughter hooked for life. Back to the big family house in Langside, back to his resentful and by now deserted wife, who was rightfully resentful, back to his family of ten who hardly knew him and were so deeply cloaked in their own respectability that they no longer wished to.

Mother was the Lost Sheep. And although they all tried to settle her back among them, she refused to remove her lipstick, and yearned to go back to the South. Which she did pretty quickly, using the Wounded Soldiers, and her charming talent, as an excuse. Her high spirits, her jollity, her very unusual beauty and above all the great warmth of her heart and her adoration for the world at large saw to it that she never failed.

Until the night of the Chelsea Arts Ball in 1920 . . . and that can hardly be called a failure. A change of direction certainly; and I never cease to thank God that she took it.

★   ★   ★

I have said that we, as children, hardly ever made friends. This is not strictly true in the case of about four people, three of whom were at school with me, the other, a girl, who was Italian and lived in a large tumbling Roman family not very far from us. Her name was Giovanna and she was my sister's Best Friend and they went to school together at a large convent, pleasantly set in walled gardens. The other three were, strictly speaking, my Best Friends, although they might not have considered me as such. For they were seldom invited into the walls of my Centre and our friendship existed for most of the time during school.

My nearly closest friend was Jones G. C. He was called Minor to distinguish him from another Jones who was Major and who bullied me without pause, "bumping" me on the Playing Fields, shoving powdered glass down my neck during Physics, and generally behaving in a thoroughly disagreeable way. But Jones G. C. was very quiet, a studious boy who lived in a big house in Finchley Road and kept toads and birds and wore thick hornrimmed glasses. He was as hopeless at Games as I, and was a willing participant in my Plays because he could just read his books until he had to say his lines and no one bothered him. Not even Jones Major.

Foot was very fat. As fat as any boy I ever knew. It was rumoured all over the school that the reason for his weight was not so much that he ate prodigiously, which he did, but that his testicles had failed to drop. This made him rather interesting and a great deal of time was spent at the Showers and in the Changing Rooms to verify this anatomical disaster. No one, it seems, was convinced. And no one ever actually got the chance to clearly find out, for he was as delicate in his undressing and showering as a nun. And even Jones Major didn't do very much about him. Foot ate and read a great deal. He wore thick pebble glasses, and dribbled. He also hated Games, with a dull passion, played all the fat boy parts in my plays and bored a hole with a hat-pin through his mother's bathroom door so that we could all peer at her, with one blurred eye, having her bath. I found this a rather dismal thing to do; she was as fat as he was and just as unattractive.

Trevor Roper was the third and last of my Friends. A tall vibrant boy, who more or less Designed the plays. While I did the writing and directing and casting, and all the acting if I could, he arranged the sets, the seats, the curtains, and lights when needed. He was alive, vivid and busy. Once, as a visitor to our house on a reconnaissance trip to find a suitable stage in which to perform a new play we had written in tandem, he discovered, to his delight, the big bay window in our hall, and with a flourish, which startled my mother, made swift plans to rig curtains, fix lights and turn the place into Drury Lane with a few nails and ten yards of velvet. I pointed out that there was no exiting space left and right of his Proscenium Arch. Merely wall. He airily decided that we should remove all the windows and make our exits and entrances into the garden. It seemed a logical idea to everyone but my mother.

The play was abandoned for the time being.

We made a solid group of four wandering about the grounds of the school in an inseparable block. Discussing plays and stories and who to cast as what. Until my brother was born.

Two days into shock I returned to my friends and told them of the news. They were all suitably amazed. Foot, whom we called Elephant because of his name and not because of his size strangely enough, was horrified. "Your mother's so terribly old. I think it is disgusting. Fancy having a baby as old as that. It might have killed her!" She was, of course, very old. Exactly thirty-three. Trevor Roper found it all unpleasant and decided not to comment beyond saying that it was "jolly hard luck" on me. And Jones G. C. looked very vague and wondered, aloud, how it could have happened.

"I know," said Foot. "It is all too simple, and that's why people should be more careful about where they pee."

We all looked a little surprised; even Trevor Roper was intrigued. Foot explained that all you had to do to have a baby was for the father and mother to pee together into the same chamber pot, and the baby came out of the mixture as a sort of amoeba. It didn't at all convince Jones G. C. who was very good at Botany. And although I knew, because I had been given a small book by my father and looked at the pen and ink drawings, I was not about to tell them. The book was impossible for me to understand from the written point of view, but the diagrams were simple and easy to follow and although it all rather put me off and made my sister scream when I told her up under the lilac one day, I went along with it and obliterated what I could not understand. Or chose not to understand.

★ ★ ★

I tolerated Giovanna Govoni because she was very, very nice and nearly like a boy. And although she was strictly speaking my sister's Best Friend, she was often at the house and kept out of my way so I was not disturbed. On the other hand she seemed to be interested in snails and frogs and stick-insects, and kept goldfish. Which brought her nearer to me than the fact that she spent hours with my sister looking at this absurd baby which had crashed into our midst.

There was another reason for my liking, even accepting, Giovanna as a friend. And that was her mother's cooking. When you went to their house, not unlike our own but a bit bigger with an old chestnut tree in the garden, it was not at all like going to anyone else's house I knew. Although the walls, and rooms, and even the furniture, conformed to the English Style in every conceivable way, the atmosphere within those walls was more Roman than it was London. There was always a most delicious smell of cooking. Of basil, of garlic, of rice and of olive oil. The family, Uncle Gianni and Aunt Isali plus their twin sons, Italo and Mario who were very much younger than we were, filled the house with music, laughter, screaming, and violent conversation which I found both stimulating and exciting. Coupled with the cooking smells, a great bowl of goldfish on the sitting-room mantelpiece, there was also the constant and delightful presence of Madame Chiesi; she was Giovanna's grandmother on her mother's side, a tall elegant woman from the Swiss border, who spoke no English and spent most of her time sitting in a high-backed chair, dressed in black with little white frills, sewing, knitting or making something fragile in threads and silks. I adored her, even though we never spoke a common language, She soothed frayed tempers, found the sweets when needed, scolded and laughed and spread love about her like a bounty.

Giovanna's mother, Isali, was a little younger than our mother, fair and blue-eyed, very strict and correct but always bright and busy in her kitchen making great bowls of pasta and soups filled with as many delights as a Christmas stocking. She very soon took my mother, and her kitchen, in hand and for a long time to come our house was filled with the most delicious aromas, and great cotton sacks of rice and pasta which came from as far away as Milan and Verona. Lally mournfully observed that we all ate more rice than the entire Chinese Nation, and that rice, correctly cooked and prepared, should be served with a bay leaf, honey, and a crisp golden apron. She glumly forked her way through endless Risotto alla Milanese, Risi e Bisi and Risotto Rusticos with a face like thunder and a growing weight problem.

Apart from all the laughing, quarrelling, Italians in the house with the chestnut tree, there was also Bertha.

She was German, blonde, strong, very jolly and came from Hamburg. She spoke dreadful English which delighted us all, for the Govonis spoke fluently, and smelled appallingly. However, she was kind, loved children, especially the twins, Italo and Mario, and never found anything too much for her to do. Every afternoon, wet or fine, she would stand on a rug in the middle of the garden, dressed only in an ugly black and white swimming suit, with a big tin alarm clock ticking away beside her, and do her "Physical Exercises" much to our delight and, at first, astonishment. When the alarm went off she stopped, took three or four deep breaths, picked up the rug and the clock and marched back into the house to start the tea. It was her Strength Through Joy, she said.

We merely thought she was a bit touched in the head, and let it pass. No one else we knew put on a bathing suit and did gymnastics in the back garden with an alarm clock, and no one else we knew went on holiday with a rucksack and a collapsible kayak to canoe round the West Coast of England for their summer holidays. We were aware that she was not joking, or bragging, because she was also an ardent photographer, and one of the special joys of having Bertha home again was to go up to her very smelly little bedroom and sit on the bed amidst the debris of the rucksack and the bits of collapsible kayak, and look through all her "snaps". Views of Swanage, of Bournemouth Pier and Portsmouth, of cheerful groups of brown, sweaty people, waving and laughing at the camera on miles of beaches from Penzance to the Tilly Whimm Caves. She never seemed to miss a trick, and most of them delighted us. Presumably we were not the only ones meant to be delighted.

My father was the only one of us who seemed not to join in our general delight with the Italian Family. He was uncomfortable with Gianni, whom he considered to be a Blackshirt, and found the noise and hurly-burly, which so enchanted us, tiresome and unrelaxing. However, he smothered, as best he was able, these feelings, and we all managed a more or less comfortable relationship. It is unlikely that Gianni, who was a member of the Staff at the Italian Embassy, *was* a Blackshirt, if so an unwilling one. He was an Italian, and deeply proud of his country. However, none of this even remotely concerned me at the time. I had quite enough to worry me.

The resentment of my new brother was compounded by the fact that because of him and his untimely arrival, in the very middle of the summer holidays, we were unable to go, as usual, down to the Cottage. And so the long hot summer was spent sweating away in London, with occasional treks to the Heath or Kenwood for walks and "a breath of air". Although I hated it all, I wished for it not to end, for I knew that with the end of summer came the trip to the North, to a foreign school, to new people and to a new life which, in spite of my Aunt and Uncle's warmth and affection, I dreaded. Wisely, and with great tact, Lally said that it was time we all grew up, things had to change, and we couldn't have it all our own way. Reckoning that MY way was the best way for me I was loth to put it aside. I disliked change of any kind, and I was secretly deeply afraid of having to grow up and go off on my own, a thing I knew was bound to happen one day or another. I preferred another.

I said goodbye to Miss Polyphemus, to Miss Garlick, to Dr Chanter and to weary Dr Lake, gave Jones G. C. all my "Just William" books and left the school on the hill for the last time.

No one seemed very sorry to see me go; they were all pretty busy getting ready for their own holidays to bother about me anyway.

Dr Lake wrote a very pleasant letter to my father saying that I was an "amusing companion and a nice fellow", and that he wished me well. And that was that.

The summer, stuck away in London and far from my beloved gully and Great Meadow, was going to be a long, dull, time. But I realised that I'd better make the most of it.

One morning, very early, before the sun was up, the telephone rang and startled me out of sleep. The telephone was no strange device in our house. We were more than used to it attached as it was to Printing House Square. At all hours of the day or the night it rang with the news that a King had fallen off a rock, a Golden Eagle had hatched near Inverness, a Queen had been killed in a car crash, or a President had jumped out of a window.

We were never surprised by the odd items which filtered into the Nursery, and none of them appeared, at the time, to touch our golden lives. Until this one.

I heard my father answering the machine in his bedroom across the wide landing from mine. I heard him speaking for a long time . . . not hearing the words but being unmistakably aware that whatever he was being told was urgent, worrying and concerned him personally.

I lay looking at my tit-and-wisteria paper and wondered vaguely if it was anything to do with me or school. But nothing was said at breakfast, even though I could see, with a stab of surprise and alarm, that my mother had been crying.

Later, up at the top of the garden where I had built a rather rickety hut in which I painted and wrote my countless plays and stories, she came to see me.

I was making some puppets, I remember, and she vaguely admired a scrap of old brocade which I was using for a costume. "It came from those old curtains you gave me," I said. But she was looking sadly out of the dirty window into the garden and not listening to me.

Presently she turned round and said in a weary voice: "I want

138

you to listen to me very carefully. Daddy and I have to go down to Brighton immediately. It's very sudden and very urgent and we might not be home until tomorrow. You've got a new grandfather."

IO

AIMÉ Emile van den Bogaerde was a tall, dashing, handsome man with great amused eyes and a faded fortune when he met my grandmother Grace some time in the late 1880's.

I don't know very much about him, because my father hardly ever mentioned his name to us as children, and all that we vaguely knew, and it was very vague indeed, pieced together from scraps sought or heard here and there, was that he had gone to South America as an explorer and died there of yellow fever.

He came from an ancient, Catholic family which traced its origins, I am told, to Anne of Cleves, but which finally settled, at the end of the sixteenth century, near Iseghem, a small town in the centre of the orchard country of what was then the Low Countries and is now Belgium. The name, van den Bogaerde, means "of the Orchards" and the coat of arms incorporates three fruit-laden apple trees. That the family was gently noble at its start is not in dispute; however, it apparently slipped towards the Sea (some were to become Admirals) and the Land. From the Land they moved into Law, and my grandfather was born to a famous judge and appears to have lived the life of any other rich gentleman of his time. Part of his education was the traditional Grand Tour which he made with two tutors and an enormous Great Dane. He travelled from Brussels to Paris, Berlin, Munich, Venice, Rome and eventually, London. Liking the English, speaking their language fluently, and being rich and handsome and young, he was attracted to the County Life and spent a great deal of his time in various parts of the shires riding, hunting, shooting and generally enjoying the hospitalities of the larger country houses to which he was invited, or had "letters of reference".

It was while he was in Worcestershire that he met, and fell in love with, Grace Clark of that county and married her. I have always been told that the Clarks were so horrified at the idea of their golden, slender, child marrying a Foreigner that they sent her to a convent. And from there my grandfather kidnapped her and they ran away and got married. But that is legend. And I very much doubt that it happened. However, it well might have for my grandfather was an impetuous, determined man, and Grace a rather timid, gentle, creature who could just about blow her own nose for herself. But she had some will. She firmly refused to live Abroad, embraced the Catholic faith and forced him to buy a large villa in Perry Barr, then a small, pleasant village, just outside Birmingham. To be near her family one supposes. They lived very well. There are photographs of the house, many gabled, with trim lawns and great cedars, coachmen and horses, dogs and maids and my grandmother in vast hats and long silk dresses. My father was born there in 1892 and spent the first few years of his life, a solitary child, happily enough with his little pony cart, his dogs Sherry, Whiskey and Soda, and my grandfather's Great Danes. The favourite of which was called Rosé.

My grandmother, like so many converts, became more Catholic than the Catholics, if that is possible, and made my grandfather's life complicated and tiresome. There was never to be another child apart from my father, because she believed, strictly, that sex should only be accompanied by the birth of a child, and this my grandfather resented. Some time—and here I get vague because I am lost for the facts—some time in the early 1900's he went on a journey to London. He never returned to the sprawling ivy-covered villa in Perry Barr with its cedars and lawns and Converted Catholic mistress, but took ship for South America from whence he was occasionally to write, and send my father photographs of his trips up the Orinoco (he was one of the first white men ever to get as far up it as he apparently did) and from the Amazon and various seedy little villages in Brazil.

He must also have sent presents sometimes, because for many years we had a rather smelly leopard's skin, which crackled and moulted, and the upper and lower jaws of a puma which he apparently shot during one of his expeditions. It is also supposed that he tried to import orchids in abundance to England but that this venture was doomed because of a lack of knowledge of packing and that all the tubers, or bulbs or whatever they are called, were rotted and dead on arrival at Liverpool. If this is true or not I do not know: but that was how we were always told that grandfather lost his fortune. It may well be so, for in 1910 my grandmother was forced to sell up Perry Barr and move, humbly, and in her grief, to a dingy, red-brick house in Bexhill, where she lived a genteel, careful, frugal life bringing up my fatherless parent. She died there alone and bitter, while my father was in Passchendael in 1917. He said that she had died of a broken heart. A lonely, incapable, fragile woman. So, in the middle of a holocaust and at the age of twenty-three, my father to all intents and purposes became an orphan and considered that to be his lot.

It is hardly surprising, therefore, that one hot summer morning, after nearly thirty years of silence, a telephone call from a worried doctor in Brighton informing him that his father was gravely ill and wished to see him before he died, which could be at any moment, should explode like a land-mine within our household.

I have no idea what took place between my father and his own on that fateful day. It was never spoken of and we were certainly not encouraged to ask any questions. It was quite enough for us to know that we had "found" a hitherto dead grandparent whose life, to say the very least, had been a vague shadow lost in the distance of a time unknown to us.

Later I was to find out that all through those many years he had never ever lost track of my father and knew every detail of his existence. He knew of his marriage to my mother, of which he did not approve because she was "foreign", of our births, of his position at *The Times* and, clearly, of his whereabouts at all times. And even though we spent most of our lives living within a few miles of the town in which he had taken up permanent residence, he only got in touch because he feared that, finally, he was dying of pneumonia and asked the doctor, who had been sent for by his daily woman, to inform his son of that fact.

He did not die as it happened. Perhaps the sight of his son and the idea of a large family to gather around him revived him, for he shortly got better and settled back into his dingy house near the West Pier at Brighton.

When it was clear to my father that death was not to ease our new burden, he decided that we had better meet, and some weeks after the telephone call we were driven down to Brighton to see our "dead" grandfather.

It was a faded, grubby house in a faded, grubby square. "To Let" signs hung at every window, and children played hopscotch in the ruined patch of garden in the centre.

Inside it was dark and smelled of stale tobacco and turpentine. The ground-floor room, with a big window, was crammed with canvases, stacks of old newspapers, a huge easel, paints and brushes and a battered couch on a raised platform. The windows were thick with grime, and beside the ugly marble fireplace there were a couple of tables draped in worn American cloth, littered with saucepans and gas rings. Pots of dying herbs stood on the window-sill. We went up some dark, heavily papered, stairs.

He lay, a waxen shrivelled figure with blazing eyes and a small straggly beard, on a vast red lacquer bed in the shape of a swan, the neck and head forming the foot of the bed, the spread tail the head, and the raised wings the sides. It looked like a boat.

He stretched out a thin arm and took our hands, and smiled as we leaned to kiss him. He spoke with a heavy accent, and was delighted that we resembled him as he said.

He had established a pleasant form of rapport with my mother during the weeks, and told her how handsome we were and how handsome she was too.

"She has good eyes, you know, Ulric," he said to my father. "Good eyes. Probably Latin blood, I wouldn't wonder, even if she is Scotch. Remember the Spanish; they swarmed over the west coast of Scotland, and half the population were raped." My mother laughed and he blew her a fragile kiss. "You all probably have Spanish blood as well as Flemish! What a mixture!" He was amused. Turning to me with his fine, gaunt head, he asked me if I was clever. I was forced to admit that I was not.

"How many languages can you speak?" he asked.

"A little French," I said. He laughed and said a little was better than none and that he spoke five fluently, including some South American Indian dialects as well.

"But you must not worry, boy," he said gently. "We are all very slow to develop in our family, so you have time. Do you know the family motto? Does he know it, Ulric? *Semper Viridis* . . . do you know what that means?" And when I shook my head he stroked his little straggly beard and said, "It means Ever Green".

Once a week, until I went to Scotland, we went down to the dirty house and saw him gradually grow stronger, and in time he was pottering, very slowly, about his dusty studio downstairs. On one occasion, swearing that he was strong enough to cook again, he sent me off with a penny to buy him four farthing eggs from a shop up the road.

"Ask for Polish eggs," he said, "they do me very well in an omelette."

The herbs got watered, and my mother replaced chives and

parsley and mint and sought, in vain, for his essential love, tarragon. The gas-rings blazed and he started to smoke endlessly; the smell of cooking now competed with turpentine and tobacco when we went to call.

My father realised that this state of affairs could not go on any longer. It was impossible for us to have him at home, and indeed he flatly refused the idea. So a nursing home where he could furnish his own room was sought and found near Kemp Town, and they told him firmly but gently. His rage knew no bounds. He refused to be moved and demanded to be left alone to his painting and his cooking and his own life. My father, weary of it all, shattered by the additional expense not only of a new son but a new father, gave in and, making him a small allowance which he could ill afford, left him to himself as he demanded.

He was not only impetuous and determined, but a blindingly selfish man. What happened to him in all those long years so near and yet so very far away? When did he return to England? How did he live? Why did he never make the smallest effort to reach my father or his mother, knowing, if one is to believe the facts, that he was well aware all the time of where they were, and what they were doing?

It is impossible to guess. From the moment that the letters stopped coming from South America, about 1908, until the telephone call, all remains lost in a distant past and will never, I suppose, be discovered.

It appears that for some years in England he made a modest living by painting, and selling, copies of Flemish "masterpieces". Usually on leather, or on secondhand canvases. Sometimes he used seamen's wooden chests, or boxes, which he picked up for shillings in the junk markets of Brighton, Worthing and Shoreham. These he covered with leather and jolly Breughel-peasants busy at their weddings, funerals and harvests. Sometimes Princes and Kings, glittering in armour, astride horses slashing at each other with swords or spears. On occasions, to vary the pace, wild groups of dead pheasant or duck hung garlanded in grapes and vines or improbable Coats of Arms.

These he covered with a special varnish which he had invented himself and which in a very short time crackled and "aged" the paint and the leather and gave to all the patina of sepia-antiquity, as long as one didn't look too deeply. Passed off as Early Flemish, or Dutch, two galleries in London kept him gainfully occupied

5 Grandfather Aimé, in the middle, with an unknown friend and their guide. Somewhere on the Amazon about 1907–8 in their base hut. Note orchids everywhere which were, so I was told, the reason for the family's "ruin". The skin survived, smelly and cracking, for many years. The small snapshot, on the shelf, of my father aged 6, stands on my bedside table today.

6(a) My maternal grand-
father as Charles Surface,
"The School for Scandal".

6(b) My mother with Abe
Barker in "Bunty Pulls The
Strings", Haymarket Theatre,
1911.

for some years with these curious works which as often as not ended up in America or Canada.

There still remain some excellent examples of his honesty on the walls of a big pub in Brighton and various smaller establishments along the coast, landlords of which accepted a small canvas for the walls of their private bars in exchange for a few pints of beer. Or, if he was lucky, a bottle of wine.

His "master" was Wouvermaans. And many a second-hand canvas covered by him with rearing horses and falling soldiers may still yet be thundering about in the drawing-rooms of innumerable commercial hotels from Eastbourne to Matlock Spa.

He was, in short, a faker. And a very good one. In spite of all the languages, the travelling, the education and the family background which he had, he seems only to have made his living by deception, but after he came into our lives, or we came into his, whichever way you care to look at it, he stopped painting and scrabbling about in the junk shops and gave it up to live comfortably, if modestly, on the allowance from my unfortunate father.

I, of course, was mesmerised by him. I was happy to sit in a chair beside him in his smelly, crowded studio, looking at his stamp albums, his maps of the Amazon, faded and torn, his piles of old magazines and books, or just listen to him talking in his heavy accent about his journeys into the Andes on a mule or his astonishing voyage on a sailing ship from Lima to Valparaiso; but more than that he would not give away. And the stories had a vague not-quite-true-but-could-be quality about them which in no way diminished their delight.

He sat in a high carved oak armchair, his long bony fingers clasping the arms; his finger-nails were long like a Mandarin's, but always scrupulously clean which constantly amazed me. Sometimes in the middle of a story he would start to crack eggs and flour into a bowl and begin to cook something for his supper, a cake or biscuits: he told me that one of the wobbly tables which supported his gas-rings came from Versailles and probably belonged at one time to Marie Antoinette because there was an "A" worked into the chipped and crumbling gesso. Lifting the tattered American cloth he would make me peer at the fine carved legs and stretchers and ask me if I could see the "A", and sometimes I thought that I did. But I could never be sure. He said that all his Bits and Pieces came from junk shops and sale rooms when he was looking about for his work. The great red lacquer bed was from China and he felt sure that it was brought over after the Boxer Rebellion, and who was I to doubt him? All his Treasures, he said, had cost him nothing but a discerning eye, and he said that one must cultivate such a thing by watching, looking and listening, and also by always asking Why? and What? and Where? "You must be Observant, boy. Always Observe. If you do not understand what you see, ask someone to tell you what it is . . . if they don't know, you must take books and find out. Always seek, always question, always be Interested, otherwise you will perish."

This, strangely enough, was something which my father had inherited from him. We were always told to Look . . . to watch, to see and to listen. Even if it bored us to death at times; like Chamber Music which I hated but had to listen to very often in order to be able, later on I was told, to appreciate the great symphonies. Consequently we were curious children and delighted in finding things out for ourselves even though our frequent questioning must have seemed tremendously irritating to many of our friends. Although I detested any form of Games, and had always managed to avoid Children's Parties for fear that I should be forced to play them, I did enjoy, constantly, my father's Remember Games. In a tube train look and see how many pairs of brown shoes there are on the people opposite. How many bunions, which has a lace untied, who wears spats? And then look away at the faces above and try to fit each one out. This was a simple game to play and fun, but quite often caused offence to the unfortunate victims sitting facing one who twitched and fidgeted and stared about them under the implacable observing eyes of the child opposite.

Other games were looking in shop windows and counting the number of pots or pans with a black lid or a blue lid, how many milk jugs there were on a given row, or plates in a pile, then, making a mental list, one wandered away for a few minutes to return later and check. This caused one to give the impression that one was loitering; however it was all very good training and not easily forgotten. And although I was such a dunce at school, at these games I was more than outstanding, simply because I found detail fascinating. Of course there were never any rewards for being good at these games; it was just expected that you would be, and the reward was getting the lists as correct as possible. And it was rewarding in a strange way. Lastingly so I imagine.

The last time I went to see my grandfather at his smelly old house was just before I went up to Scotland. He was sad that I was leaving for "so far away", as he put it, and made me promise to write to him from time to time and to send him any new stamps which might come out in that strange, to him, country. He was regretful that I was going because he had started to enjoy the family which he had cheerfully denied for so many years and feared the loneliness again. Or at least I suppose that is what it was. Also he was very anxious, suddenly, to tell me about The Family and said that I should know, and be taught, French and German so that I could go back one day to the Estates which he had left and which my unfortunate father never had the chance of seeing until 1921 or '22 when he took my mother back to Iseghem. I say "back" which is incorrect, since he had never ever been there, however "back" is what sounded right. Apart from a tomb in the local church and a street named after my great grandfather, very little remained of the Estates now almost surrounded by factories and urban streets. However, the chateau, which still stands today and looks much as it must have done then, was an imposing place of pale rose brick and grey stone with many shuttered windows, standing on a little hill which sloped down to a long tree-bordered lake spanned by a high, gracefully arching, white iron bridge.

Rooks cawed in the great beeches all around, and there was a screaming baby in a pram on the elegant, many-stepped, terrace. Relations were cool and polite and not about to be welcoming to the English sprig who so suddenly arrived that summer day. And my father left never to return, not to speak of it ever to me at least.

I remember in the war having 48 hours' leave after the catastrophe at Arnhem. I went to the Officers' Leave Hotel, the Palace in Brussels, wanting only to bathe and sleep for the whole two days. A very old porter helped, churlishly, to carry my sleeping-bag and haversack. In the room I fumbled for a tip and saw him looking at my name painted on the canvas of my kit-bag. He asked me, in French, where I came from and what my Christian names were. I told him, and his eyes filled with tears as he pulled off his cap and bowed gently to me, to my embarrassment and surprise. He had been my grandfather's groom at Iseghem and remembered him well.

That was the nearest I ever got to the Estates.

"When you go to this Scottish school you must study your French and German, you must be able to speak them fluently and correctly. It is easy to do, it is in your blood. I speak five, as you know, and I started to learn when I was a very small child, possibly when I was five or six. It is late for you, but you must strive. It will make you less English."

I remember promising that I would try and he gave me a keepsake. A small metal lay figure which he had used for many years to draw from. I was sad at the apparent meanness of the gift, I was hopefully expecting a Delft jar or a rather pleasant jade frog which sat, with a coveted paperweight containing a black and yellow salamander, on the mantelshelf. However, I made do with the tin figure, which is just as well, for it is the only thing I ever received from him beyond the doubtful ability to paint, his good brown eyes, and a vague feeling of failure.

Nearly forty years later, after he had been to see "Death In Venice", my father telephoned me here in France. Something which he had never done before. "I was very moved indeed," he said, "to see my father again."

★　★　★

"Well!" said Lally one evening while she was sewing Cashes labels into all my shirts. "Now we have a new brother and a new grandfather. Whatever next, I wonder! And you mark my words, things always go in threes. They always come in threes, you see if I lie."

Because she absolutely never ever lied to us or evaded any question, we took her very seriously. One never knew when she might be right. Sometimes, like Ilfracombe, we found out that she was wrong, and that instead of Wales on which she insisted, it was in Devon, but those were very slight irregularities. We never got fobbed off with a non-answer. We always got a Fact. Even inaccurate was better than none at all or a "Don't bother me now I'm busy" or "Look it up for yourself, it's in a book." Always an answer. Even if it did mean having to check from time to time, just for safety's sake.

"Does a postillion blow his trumpet on a coach?" I asked my father. We were walking down the lane to the quarry-garage.

"Nonsense. He's the rider on the near horse if you've only got two for the coach; he's the driver."

148

"What happens if he gets struck by lightning then?"

My father laughed. "I wouldn't care to be in the coach, that's all I can say. For God's sake, turn your feet out, you walk like a penguin."

These weren't serious inaccuracies, easily checked after all, and as Lally said, Devon and Wales were both West so we were at least in the right direction.

She had our complete confidence whatever mistakes might be made, and therefore when she said about "coming in threes" I felt uneasy for what next might befall us. I had rather counted on the Scotland Trip as one of the three, but she seemed not to, so I worriedly awaited the final blow.

It came in the form of a letter to my father from the Aleford's Estate Manager. The Alefords owned the Court Farm and all the land around it. They had decided to retire from farming and move away. The Cottage would be up for sale at the auction in December next. The house and one acre. As a separate lot.

We had no idea, Elizabeth and I, that we did not own the Cottage. No idea that we merely rented it by the year from the rather jolly family down at the Court. It was ours completely. We had, it seemed, had it for ever and ever, and every flint and tile belonged to us. The total shock of the truth was far worse than brothers or grandfathers or even a violent change of school. To think that the Cottage was no longer ours, that in fact it never had been except for a weekly payment of seven shillings, was unthinkable. We were struck dumb with horror and grief. A grief which was silent and therefore all the more irritating to our elders. Lally was gentle and patient. She didn't mention anything about "Three" and simply realised that our misery was too great for more than a bit of extra loving and second helpings of pudding.

"They'll find somewhere else, even nicer than the Cottage, you see," she said with tactful ignorance. "Remember what a lot it needs doing to it! That floor in the hall is all rotten; it needs proper sanitation, and water, and light, and the roof's bound to go in the next big storm and really I'm sure it's all for the best. You see if I lie."

But we were listless with despair and all her cheering up was to no avail. My father was patient with our hollow-eyed sullenness and promised that he and our mother would go to the auction in December and try to buy it . . . but I knew as he spoke that it would be only a vague possibility. New brothers and schools and grandfathers cost money, even I began to realise that after a while.

In fact Lally was right about the repairs which the Cottage needed. But somehow without the old pump, without the lamps in the long winter evenings, without those solitary walks to the privy, the Cottage couldn't ever be the same again. The idea of turning on a tap in the big flint kitchen might have been delight for her but was abhorrent to me. I knew, even in my selfish and uncaring way, that things were beginning to change everywhere. Caravans had suddenly sprouted up in the fields at Cuckmere Haven. Beastly little white boxes filled with whey-faced Londoners peering through their "cheery" orange and brown caravan-curtains. Even the Downs behind Friston and East Dean were being ploughed up for the planting of a great pine forest, and there was talk of rows and rows of cheap bungalows being allowed to scab and scar the soft dales and swards of the Seven Sisters themselves. It was all changing all right. And if the Cottage did not belong to us, if it had all been a long, glorious dream and if none of it had ever really happened at all, then, so be it. Life, or rather my own life, for I tended, as usual, to see everything in terms of myself, was starting to shred away like a sail in the wind, and I was very well aware that my little boat was far too frail a craft to weather the storms which were to come. Sail-less I should be sunk or beached. Neither idea pleased me. Staring dully up at my tit-and-wisteria wallpaper, I had realised that Lally's words of some time ago were true. "You can't have a summer without a good winter," she had said. Winter was now.

*   *   *

Bishopbriggs was where the trams from Glasgow ended. Clacketting, racketting, lurching their way from Renfield Street through the black canyons of faceless tenements in Springburn, trundling through acres of blighted wasteland, scabbed with wrecked cars, rubbish tips, blackened clumps of thistle and thorn, they coasted gently into the blank granite square of what once might have been a pleasant country village. Here the small gabled houses, empty-eyed windows, draped in white lace, secret with half drawn blinds, gleamed in misty rain. Beyond slate roofs, the pointed caps of the Tips, like my sister's spilly hills of sugar only black. Dead volcanoes spotting the ruined fields. "The Bingies", relics of a thriving pit closed since the start of the Depression.

From the terminus, the steel rails shining like swords in black granite cobbles, past a scatter of gas lit shops, up a brick alley, through a long dripping tunnel under the railway line, one arrived on "the other side" of the town. A straggling, cold, ugly housing estate, in Avenues, Crescents, Terraces, and Drives; no Streets or Roads for the new middle classes. Flat-faced pebble-dash houses; four windows up, four below, pink-grey asbestos tiled roofs, concrete paths, creosoted picket fences and washing dripping in every back garden. All about one there was nothing to see but row upon row upon row of roofs, backed here and there by the pointed nose of a Tip or a few wind-twisted trees high on an, as yet, untouched hillock. It rained gently.

24 Springburn Terrace was the same as all its neighbours. The only way I could distinguish it for the first few months was by the fact that it stood on a corner and had a slightly larger area of garden around it with a lamp-post at the front gate. The houses were not Houses at all. They were flats. One up and one down. The down one had a front door in the centre, the up one had a front door at the side up a flight of concrete steps. Walls and the floors were made of cardboard. From the front door a long narrow passage. To the right a sitting-room, beyond that a bedroom. At the top of the narrow passage a lavatory and bath together. To the left a dining-room, beyond that the kitchen with a door leading out into the pleasures of a wan garden. Yard more like. A hedge of Golden Elder, a few neat flower-beds, a bit of grass in the middle and in the centre of that a tall iron post for the laundry. A small world for three ill-assorted people.

Aunt Belle, my mother's elder sister, was tall, kind looking, with a patrician face and soft auburn hair flecking with grey. Her husband, Uncle Duff, was slightly shorter than she was, with thin black hair parted in the middle and glued to his head with Yardley's Hair Cream. His small black moustache looked as if it had been smudged on with coal. They welcomed me to this unprepossessing house shyly and warmly with a crackling fire and high tea.

"All boys like to eat," said my aunt, "so I did a Baking for you especially!" There were five different sorts of biscuits, scones, and cup cakes, as well as a Madeira Cake with candy peel on top. Sandwiches, toast, anchovy paste, and strawberry jam.

Also a canary, Joey, who lived in the window in a cage with a yellow silk frill round the base to stop the seed from scattering. Afterwards, in the sitting-room across the hall, we sat by the fire, my aunt sewing, my uncle showing me his bound volumes of Bruce Bairnsfeather's cartoons. I wondered, vaguely, where I should sleep.

About nine o'clock he went out to the kitchen to make the cocoa for supper. My aunt put aside her sewing and said I must be tired after such a long day and so many excitements. I was aware that she meant travelling, and trains and farewells and all that sort of thing. She explained gently that they had moved out of their bedroom next door so that I should have it, and that they would sleep on a Put-U-Up Settee in the dining-room.

"This is a rather small house for the three of us, but I'm sure we'll manage very well," she said. "It's the Depression, you know. Uncle lost everything, I'm afraid, and so we just had to cut our cloth to suit the material. It is not the sort of place we like to live in. But it'll just have to do. I don't suppose you remember the other house, do you?"

I did. Gleaming mahogany furniture, heavy and sombre, shining brass jugs filled with flowers and leaves, a piano scattered with silver frames, high windows velvet-curtained, all looking out over a soft green wooded park. Not at all like this sad, apologetic, squashed little house.

Some of the old stuff had made the swift descent from gentility to near-poverty and looked defiantly out of place in such cramped quarters. The ladder-backed chairs in the dining room, a tall mahogany bookcase, some bold chintz armchairs with anti-macassars pinned to them like maids caps, my grandfather's water-colours in thin gold frames, a set of Nashes Magazine Covers for 1918 framed in black passe-partout, and the black marble mantel-clock which thinly struck the hours and quarters.

My bedroom was a square of pink distemper. Two windows over the bleak square of garden and the dead backs of the houses beyond the ragged hedge. A one-bar electric fire, a yellow oak wardrobe with an oval mirror which reflected the entire room, a dressing chest, a dressing table and a wide yellow oak bed spread with a shining pink satin cover. In the bed a scalding aluminium hot water bottle called a "pig" . . . and a hot brick wrapped in flannel.

I was told to use the bathroom first. A bath, a basin, a lavatory.

His ivory brushes stuck together by their bristles, W.D. entwined in black on the back. The oval tin of Yardley's grease. Toothbrushes huddled in a tumbler like old men at a wedding. Izal on the lavatory paper. We said goodnight, and I lay in the dark of the wide yellow bed listening to them raking out the fire in the sitting-room and setting the china for breakfast. Then bathroom noises and the lavatory flushing twice. Pattering of feet down the corridor to the front door, a chain rattling, a bolt running home, the dining-room door closing. Silence and then the slow, low, murmur of worried conversation through the wall.

The clock struck a quarter. Ting Ting Ting. Light from the lamp-post flickered through leaf shadows on the buff paper blind. A draught waggled the cord and made the little acorn handle tap tap against the glass. In the house upstairs someone else pulled a chain and I heard a soft cataract of water and a pipe beside the wardrobe started to knock gently.

I turned into the pillows and tried to smother my blubbing.

★ ★ ★

I travelled to school every morning with Uncle Duff. We caught the eight-five. The same compartment, the same faces. Three *Glasgow Heralds*, two *Bulletins*, one *Express*. Queen Street station, an enormous inverted iron colander. Black and sooty, rife with pigeons and the smell of urine. Blazes of brilliant light here and there in the gloom from the bookstalls. Farewell to Uncle, he to his office in St Vincent Street, me to George Square and the long haul up the cobbled stone street to The School. Standing isolated in the centre of a vast asphalted playground, surrounded by high iron spikes, its red sandstone blocks rotting in the filth from the city, it resembled a cross between a lunatic asylum and a cotton mill. Faceless windows gazed blankly over the streets below. Electric lights gleamed dully even on the clearest days. A smell of chalk and concrete dust, of sulphur and soot.

Green glazed tiles, ochre distemper, red varnished wood. Cold, unloving, unloved. A Technical School for Technical People. What on earth was I doing here? I who could only just about read and write? Chosen by Uncle Duff for a "good solid background under a progressive teaching staff", it was thoughtfully accepted by my parents as the Final Desperate Measure to try and force some learning into my addled head. They had made a swift tour of the place, dragging me in stupefied horror behind them, had outlined to the Progressive Teaching Staff what was wanted, had shaken hands in a cramped Victorian Headmaster's Study and departed with relief for the South. Leaving me to sort out the road leading to "The Times".

It was only a matter of days before I knew, for certain, that I was in the very worst place for my sort of complaint. I had the technical brain of a newt. Here everyone sat entranced while glum-faced teachers poured one liquid into a flask, and another liquid on to iron filings or something equally inane. They sat with tongues hanging out, and darting eyes crossing the wide blackboards following hieroglyphics which I was told were called logarithms, long division, or agreed, with eager nods, the bold assumption that "if A equals B and C equals D thus E, F, G and X are equal to the sum total Q".

I never knew how many apples a farmer had left in his basket if he gave his wife two-thirds. Or how much water slipped away in an hour if the bath-plug was released and the tap dripped at the rate of fifty drops per minute. What the Hell! I was lost. Notebooks were virginal white. Pencils unblunted. Rubbers un-rubbed. Surrounded by a class of thirty I started to observe them in preference to the impossible messages on the blackboards.

Raw-boned hulks most of them seemed. Red hair and freckles; fair hair and pigs eyes; white faces and acne. Stooped grey-flannel backs, prematurely humped, arms like gorillas stretched out along their desks: booted feet twitching for a football. Or anything to kick.

No vivid Trevor Ropers, no fat kind Foots, no bespectacled Jones G. C.'s here; these were tough, Irish-Scots, one parent away from the Pits, four years or less from the Barricades. Foreigners. And what made things harder was that I couldn't understand a word they said, nor could they understand me. A gulf had started from the very first day with the barrier of our common tongue. I was the odd man out, the Sassenach, posh, weedy, incomprehensible, alien. But I knew that because I was New, this slit-eyed raw-boned herd of bullocks was biding its time until the terror which was growing steadily within me should start to leak away, like blood in a sea of sharks. And when they scented it, they would attack. This I knew.

My desk mate—we sat two to a bench like slaves in the galleys

—was called Tom. He was dark, thin, pleasant looking with round tin glasses. He showed me where to hang my cap and coat, where my locker was, where the lavatories were, the class-rooms I would use, and where to eat our lunch if we didn't go home. Which neither of us did.

A long brick shed, it was pushed into a corner of the Yard almost as an afterthought. It had a tin roof and was euphemistically called the Tuck Shop. Banks of greasy wooden tables, benches on each side, a long counter at one end with tea and coffee urns and racks of soggy hot, or cold, meat pies, sausages, cheese buns, bread and dripping and Mars Bars.

At the other end, two pin tables for the elder boys. We were not allowed to use them until we were sixteen, but everyone did anyway. In one corner a foul, stinking lavatory which was three walls with an open drain round the edges. Sluggish streams of gently steaming urine bubbled along this trough. Cigarette ends and gobs of spittle bobbed about like floats in a stream. On the walls above the slate slabs against which we pissed, a whole holocaust of wild scribbles and obscenities, none of which I understood any better than their language.

In the other corner a cabin with doors like a stable so that one could see the feet and the top of the head of the occupant. Sometimes there were two or three pairs of feet scuffling about below the door, and the knowing shouts and bellows of laughter made me sick with apprehension, not understanding what was going on in there.

Tom used to guide me out of the Tuck Shop as often as the weather allowed and we sat, each with our bottle of Cola, a hot pie and an apple or an orange, on the low wall which ran round the dustbins watching a thousand games of football played with an old tennis ball or a rough block of wood. He talked away from time to time, and I tried to understand him, which made him laugh, and he tried to understand me, which made me laugh too. We were warm together, and I knew that I liked him, but conversation was, of necessity, limited. I did, however, glean that his father was a coal-man and that he, Tom, had won a scholarship to this unenviable school.

I was deeply impressed. Not that his father was a coal-man, but that he had been clever enough to win a scholarship and could still be so gentle, patient and kind. I liked him very much, and he became my mate.

One day when the weather was too wet to go out and eat our lunch on the dustbin wall, some of the Herd started to make muffled, smothered, giggling jokes clearly about me across the greasy tables. They were mostly the elder boys, and the younger ones were sniggering and squirming sycophantically at the jokes.

Tom suddenly stiffened with alarm and mumbled something, but before he was able to say anything more, the Herd had started to move towards me in a slow, undulating wave. With one united lunge they grabbed me and dragged me struggling in nameless terror to the lavatory at the end of the room. I heard Tom shouting, but the doors had swung closed and I was hustled into the cabin, up-ended into the lavatory pan, held firmly by my knees and legs, while someone, as if from a hundred miles down a tunnel, said: "Fuckin' posh twit. Talking so la-di-da need your wee mouth washin' out." Someone pulled the chain and I thought that I had drowned. Gasping and choking, vomiting like a dog on the wet slimy floor, I was told that until I learned to speak correctly this would happen again. Then they left me. I lay for an eternity, retching and gasping in a sea of filth and undigested meat pie. I thought that I would never be able to breathe again. Tears and dribble coursed down my face from the coughing and choking and the retching.

Tom helped me to clean up as best I could in the boiler room under the school. I lay on a pile of coke while he tried to apologise and wiped me down with his handkerchief and some newspaper which we had found. I stayed there hiccuping and heaving until the break bell clanged. Damp, creased and smelly I took my place in Class. No one said anything. They watched over the tops of their books or sideways from the edges of their faces. They were all quietly smiling. Through bleary eyes I looked back at them. And decided to learn to speak correctly.

For days I was in terror that I should catch some disease from my Lavatory Drowning. With some of my luncheon money—I got one and sixpence a day from Uncle Duff each morning on the train—I bought a bottle of disinfectant and, as secretly as I could, gargled and cleaned my mouth out until it was raw and blistered with whatever it was I had used. No one knew what had happened, of course, and I had a difficult job sneaking into the house and changing my filthy clothes, but managed to convince them that I had been in a fight in the rain and that was that.

Uncle Duff was quite jovial at tea that evening.

"A fight already! Well I declare! they'll make a wee man of ye yet."

My aunt was no fool. She didn't say a word, just went on buttering her potato pancake, but I think she knew that it had been more than a fight.

For the first month or two I was bullied constantly. Being skinny, having the wrong accent, although I was doing my damnedest to correct that daily, and never joining in the break time football made me as conspicuous as a cripple. And I was accordingly treated as such, for that is really what they thought I was. Deformed, different, weak, a cissie, to be got rid of. Tom was a help, but I felt that I couldn't shelter behind him all the time, and in any case, he wasn't always with me. He had his learning to do and was frequently taking a different Class to me.

Sitting one day on the wall of the Yard (there were no benches) I got clouted on the shin by a whirling block of wood being used as a football. I yelled out in pain and fell off the wall. I was suddenly engulfed in a swirling, kicking mass of roaring footballers who dragged me across the asphalt in the direction of the lavatory. Terror loaned me desperate strength. I fought and clawed and bit and kicked and suddenly found that the crowd had pulled away and I was struggling with one sole boy, older than me, taller, and stronger. His name, I think, was Bell. I don't know what happened, or how I did it, but as he swung me away from him with one arm to punch me in the face, I swung at him and hit him with all the force I could muster in the eye. He gave a great cry and fell to the ground, his face covered with his hands. I fell on top of him and went on bashing and thumping at him, but his cries grew louder and louder, and his hands flew from his face and flailed the air about his head. I saw that he now only had one eye. The other had apparently gone.

We were dragged to our feet, I stiff with terror at the pulpface before me; he barking in a loud hoarse voice, groping about in the air, blood streaming down his face.

Whitefaced, they half carried, half led, him across to the school. I stood alone in the middle of the yard. No one moved or spoke. They stood and watched me. Somebody pointed silently to a water tap over by the wall, and they watched in little groups as I bathed my face and washed off the blood which seemed to be more his than mine. When I straightened up they had gone. I was never bullied again. Avoided for a time, but never bullied.

Naturally there was an Inquiry in the Head's office. He was a big, heavy, jovial man. Wise and aware. He knew damned well what had happened but he in no way blamed me, he merely suggested, mildly, that fighting was not what I was there for, and that he didn't want to hear another complaint about me again. I was unaware that he had had any complaints before but was grateful for his leniency. As for Bell—well, whatever I did to his eye in my terror and rage kept him in a bandage for some time. And away from the school for more than three weeks. But I didn't care; from then on I ate my hot pie in peace and found school life peaceful, if lonely.

II

SELF-PRESERVATION became my main preoccupation now. Not merely against bullying; I had got that one sorted out by some strange fluke. Not only against the isolation which my foreignness caused among my school mates. I swiftly learned a thick, and unpleasing, Glasgow accent, and was grudgingly allowed to pass as more or less one of them. However, the fact that I played no games, read during the "breaks" rather than hacked away at lumps of wood stolen from the Woodwork Class, didn't know the difference between H2SO4 or 5 or 9 or whatever, and spent most of my time dreaming away plots and ideas for stories which never really got written, all these things set me clearly apart from the rest, and they resented it; and in their resentment isolated me.

I was supremely unbothered by this. For I liked none of them and preferred my own company to anyone else's, except, perhaps, for Tom whom I seldom saw apart from the hurried meat-pie at lunch on the dustbin walls.

My main self-defence was against Bishopbriggs. Not, you understand, against the town itself. It couldn't help what it was, a sordid, cold, unloving and unloved scatter of grey concrete council houses surrounding, like a belt of cement death, a grim, solid, dour little town of granite block and slate roofs. The town affected me only in so far as it was ugly, sad and apparently constantly in a drizzling rain. It was more the *life* I lived in the town which needed my defence. I found it almost impossible to realise the gentility and coldness of it without shock.

At home, among an easy-going family, we always showed our full emotions; it was, indeed, encouraged. I embraced my father nightly before going to bed, and we all touched, and liked touching, each other. Nakedness meant not having your clothes on. Going to the lavatory a normal, essential, function performed, as far as Lally was concerned, every morning after breakfast. And she wanted to know full details. Puppies, kittens, rabbits and everything else were "born": we aided the mothers and sat entranced at the births. Everything in life was totally normal and I was quite unprepared for the opposite side of the coin, the Repressions.

The first time I offered to kiss my uncle on the cheek before I went to bed he recoiled as if I had physically assaulted him and, with a crimson face, gruffly said, "We don't do that sort of thing here." And offered me his hand. My aunt received her kiss as if I had threatened her. She winced uncomfortably. The Lavatory became the "Bathroom". You never spoke of Birth, only ever of Death. If a woman was pregnant she was "a wee bittie under the weather". And one was never seen in the corridor of the house in pyjamas. Always, if we had to go from bed to the "Bathroom" a dressing-gown and slippers were obligatory. I am not blaming. This was how it was, and it was I who did not understand and so had to re-learn the rules. After all it was their house not mine. And their way of life. I would have to conform.

That settled, and accepted, the Routine had to be followed. Every weekend was planned months in advance. A constant cosy roster of relations or friends to be visited. Few ever came to our house because the change of Style had been a grave sadness to both my uncle and aunt and they preferred to keep their grief to themselves. Hence on the first Sunday of the month we went to Isa for a tinned salmon tea, where I read knitting patterns; on the second Sunday it was Aunt Teenie, who was a million years old, wore a black velvet ribbon round her throat, was blinded in one eye, and scarred dreadfully down her whole left cheek from an accident with a penknife many years ago when she had been a girl skating. She shook and trembled constantly, like a cobweb in a draught, and presided at a gigantic tea table covered with cakes and scones and home made bread. A silver teapot smothered by a crinolined celluloid doll, its pink shiny arms held out in supplication, a simpering Madonna. A small hand-knitted pom pom hat on its head. A brass kettle steamed gently over a spirit lamp, and we ate constantly, in more or less complete silence. It was, as far as I was concerned, like force feeding a goose. Later we retired to the sitting-room, lace and velvet draped, submerged in dark ferns, and while they knitted and did embroidery, the women, my uncle slept discreetly under his Sunday paper and I played eternal games of Solitaire with glass marbles on a round mahogany board.

The third Sunday in the month was usually at Meg's where we sometimes had a Smokie for High Tea, from Dundee, after which I was given a volume of photographs. The clasp would be unlocked, and I was offered a sepia world of bustles, dog carts, sailor suits and family groups of improbable strangers bug-eyed round bamboo tables.

The final Sunday was usually spent over at my maternal Grandmother's house in Langside. A long table of ten or fourteen of us, uncles and aunts, and elder cousins. Grandmamma at the head in black, a table laid as for a wedding; cakes and jams, scones and bread, tarts and sandwiches. We ate and talked of Family Matters and what had happened to us all in the month. My uncles were, without exception, handsome, dark and jolly. My aunts pleasant and kind and knitted. The cousins quiet and gently smiling. Later, in the big sitting-room upstairs, the fire was lit for Sunday and the younger of us played a new game called "Monopoly", or else "Snap", "Happy Families", or "Bezique". My grandmamma, who ruled her house with a deceptive firmness, sat in a chintz armchair and played games of patience. The uncles read papers and were allowed to smoke there.

This routine I accepted easily. It was not at all unpleasant, and sometimes comforting to know that every Sunday was so well taken care of. Of course, in the morning, wet or fine, it was a long walk to church. We left early for the three mile walk through the gritty Estate, out into the ruined fields, and then, quite soon, the real country started and the journey was always very agreeable, even in snow or sleet. The road to Cadder, where the church was, swung up and down gentle hills, across a tumbling, rocky river, through silent beech woods. The Service was dull, slow and incomprehensible. Church of Scotland. Spartan, undecorated. None of the sweeping colours, the gilts and blues, the purples and viridians, the soaring music and the heady smell of incense to which I had grown accustomed and incorrectly associated with every church. This was white and charcoal, a place for penance not praise. I watched the sun sparkle through the branches of the trees and make dancing shadows on the whitewashed walls. My aunt, inevitably, and elegantly dressed by Pettigrew and Stephens, used always to try and wear a different hat or a different costume, or coat, in the winter. She was hopeful that it would be noticed and sad when, sometimes, it was not. The Service was mostly a weekly check up on who was who and what they had been doing. It was a Social Affair, conducted with religious fervour and a great deal of kneeling and singing. But I enjoyed the walk in the country.

After lunch, which had been put in the oven while we were

at our Holy Orders and Social Spying, I had to write my weekly letter home. This was thoughtfully corrected by my uncle for faults in grammar, spelling and punctuation. Should I, by mistake, miss out an interesting bit of news, such as a trip to the Orpheus Choir, or a visit to a Football Match, this was delicately inserted, even if it meant re-writing an entire page, for my uncle was at great pains that my family should know that my life in Scotland was not just one long grind of scholastic chores. In this way, of course, I had no possible chance of saying anything the least critical. And my letters were dull, dutiful, a long list of totally boring excursions and activities at school.

My parents were relieved that I had settled down so well into the family life, that I was being so warmly welcomed, and that according to the note, always appended to my letters by my uncle, my school work was improving slowly but steadily. There was, they felt, no cause for concern. Why should there be? And so, although they none of them meant to, I was gently put to one side while they went on with their affairs, and those affairs revolved mostly about the Baby and "The Times". When I went back on longed-for holidays, it never ever occurred to me to say otherwise; I mean that life there was simple, pleasant, and everyone was good and warm, which they were. With my usual flair for obliteration of anything unbearable, I refused to spoil the treasured days of my holiday with remembering what I had left behind me up in the bleak, melancholy North. The moment the train rumbled over the railway bridge across the river at Carlisle my heart grew wings and sang all the way down to Watford. From there joy was so heady in my breast that the sights and smells of Euston swiftly erased all traces of any aching despair or loneliness. I was a very quick recoverer.

But of course, life at home had altered subtly too. It was no longer quite the same. Lally was now in charge of my brother, and also my sister adored this living baby doll. I was not included any longer, and there was never really time for us to be together again. Gradually, over time, a thin wall of dislike and indifference grew between us, and we started the inevitable growing-away process. It was not to be healed for some years.

The Cottage too had gone. The auction had not been successful for my parents, and strangers bought it. We moved the wheel-backed chairs, the lamps, the beds and the wooden kitchen table across the valley to a smaller cottage up on the other Down at

Winton Street. A collection of cottages grouped round a tithe barn and a well. It was not, and never could be, the same as the Cottage. But it was agreed that this should be only a halfway house until we found something we all liked, and which was really big enough for a now large family, where we would live for ever in the country because my father hated, with all his heart, the idea of living any longer in London. With this news at the back of my mind, the grief of losing the main pivot of my life was eased a little. I accepted. There was very little else that I could do. Holidays at Winton Street were almost, but never quite, as good as they had been: there was no gully, but still the same river, no Great Meadow, but another one almost as splendid, and the village was as near, and the same faces were still about in the lanes and fields. Sometimes I used to stand at the stile on the path down to the village and look across the valley at the soft smooth side of Great Meadow rising up to the crest of the hill and see the late sun flashing on the windows of the Cottage. Then, and then only, I got a lump in my throat and stumbled on down to the grocers.

"It's the wind!" said Lally one day, coming down with me. "It seems to blow much harder up here than it ever did over there. Must be straight up from Cuckmere and the sea. Breathe it all in, it'll do you a power of good."

But she knew.

*　*　*

After a year in Bishopbriggs things gradually began to deteriorate. Inevitably. I returned back from one holiday to find that I was no longer sleeping in the pink bedroom but on the Put-U-Up which now occupied the place of the piano in the sitting-room. The piano was in the dining-room. My uncle explained nicely that I was, after a year's wear, starting to destroy the furniture in the bedroom, that the chest of drawers, his only remembrance of his mother, was creaking badly because of the weight of the things which I placed in the drawers. Books and writing materials, as well as all my clothes. Also, far worse, the foot of the yellow oak bed had been hopelessly scratched by my long toenails. So it was decided that they should move back to their own room and I should from thereon sleep on the Put-U-Up.

That the culprit, or culprits, of the scratched bed end were not my toenails, but instead the scalding aluminium "pig" or the hot brick in flannel splitting the veneer, were unacceptable excuses.

"I have repeatedly told you about cutting your toenails," said my uncle, "every bath time. We are not made of money up here, you know, there's a Depression on."

He had never ever mentioned my toenails, although he was frequently in the bathroom on Friday nights which was the allotted time of the week for my "ablutions" as he called them. At first I had been rather surprised that he seemed to wish to brush his hair at such an odd hour in the evening, and when I, once only, locked the door, I was firmly admonished not to do so again because how could they help if the geyser blew up or I had a fainting fit suddenly? They, after all, were responsible. So no locked doors. I only minded because it was the one place where I could sing away and feel totally private without being a "noise" either to them or the people who lived up in the house above and who, from time to time, did complain that my piano playing, pretty dreadful, by ear, and limited to a range of three melodies, "The Wedding Of the Painted Doll", "Always" and "Over My Shoulder", all played very loudly with both pedals firmly down, disturbed their rest and also made it difficult to hear the Football Results on the Radio. The complaints were always very tactful and genteel. However, they *were* complaints and the piano stopped. So the bathroom seemed the next best thing musically. And also the mirror over the washbowl was useful for trying out expressions.

However, my new bed-sitting-room was pleasant enough, and we all settled down together again, although the constant worry that I refused to play all games, and had no friends, was still a source of dismay and anguish. I tried (not to play games naturally, at which I was useless and by which I was desperately uninterested), but I tried to make friends and even to bring them home to tea, which was my aunt's greatest desire. This, I suppose, to prove that I *had* friends. In desperation Tom once came all the way from his tenement in Paisley, and brought with him a slow boy called Gregg. They seemed the best two suited to our sort of house.

My aunt did a vast baking the night before and was astonished, and saddened, that Tom, in a tight blue suit, and Gregg in his Fair Isle sweater, sat for most of the meal with their hands under their thighs on the ladder-backed chairs, hardly spoke above a murmur and merely nibbled at the enormous wealth of Coburg Cakes, Soda Scones, Treacle Tarts and Fairy Cakes.

Unused to young people about them, they leant backward to be sociable and warm. But it was useless. All of us were inhibited with a deathly shyness. I hardly knew Gregg; he was usually busy in the Metalwork Class with a welding iron and solder while I battered mournfully at a copper disc beating it to death with a design of palm trees and pyramids. It was to be an ash-tray. Apart from that we hardly ever met, let alone spoke, and Tom was as out of place at a High Tea in Bishopbriggs as, he put it himself, "a spare prick at a weddin'".

Discovering, during desperate cross-questioning, that he was studying to be an engineer, my uncle, who was one, launched into a long lecture on valves and steam compression. Tom sat mute and merely mumbled "aye" from time to time. It was a total disaster. All the more so after they had left when my uncle found that they had, in their nervousness, picked away at the rush bottoms of the ladder-backed chairs, thereby "ruining them for all time".

I did not ask friends back again, although it was often suggested by my good, worried aunt.

The Summer Highlight for Bishopbriggs Society was the weekly Tennis Match held at the Club on the other side of the railway embankment. That is to say on the Right Side of Town. No one who was a member could be a member without being vetted. It was very stringent, and the waiting list was long. Naturally no one from the Estate was allowed on to the ash-courts, and nor did they ever try. I was allowed, with my aunt and uncle, because it was understood we all had "known better days", and it was politely overlooked that we lived in the unspoken-of area.

Every Friday my aunt did a baking: it was the rule that every lady should take some of her own baking for the Club Tea. My life seemed to be governed by the Bakings as much as my aunt's. The Club House was built of varnished wood and smelled like a coffin. It had a tin roof and a veranda, a tea urn and a cupboard filled with white china cups and saucers. Each week a different lady supervised, and each week we all eagerly read the lists typed and pinned to the green baize board as to who was playing whom. The day was filled with light, high, cries of "Good show, partner!" "Well tried, I say!" or "Love three all", "My game, I think!". The thwick and thwock of ball against gut lasted well into the evenings, for it was always light enough to play there until at least ten-thirty p.m. It grew boring sometimes, even though it was my job to retrieve, like some wretched little dog, the balls which loped and scattered about the chicken wire enclosure.

After The Tea, at which I helped to serve, and later wash up, they sat, if the weather was fine, in deck-chairs knitting and sewing until their game came up. The time passed slowly enough and I was often allowed to go home before the final game was over, to open the house and set the table for supper. I was always eager for this excuse because it meant, if I was pretty quick, that I could get back in time to put on the brown bakelite radio and just catch the nightingale singing from a Surrey wood. If it sang. It was a delicate thing to do. On with the radio, lock the front door, hang out of the window, eyes glued to the road from the tennis courts, willing, pleading, aching, for the blasted bird to sing. All Surrey flooded into the cramped, beige-and-ladder-backed room. But, as I said, I had to be quick, for apart from prudery I had learned deceit. The radio was expressly forbidden to be touched. So it was only when I had the house to myself, and played it low so that Upstairs could not hear and give me away, that I dared to put it on. And then only with a wet towel standing by, because the machine had a habit of getting warm as time went on, and the moment my uncle came back from Tennis the first thing he did was to cross the room and caress the sleek bakelite sides. Just to see. I had once been caught—the room filled with nightingales and cellos, my eyes maudlin with tears. My uncle's anger was controlled; I was being deceitful and morbid. He was polite enough in a steely way and for a short time the radio was removed to their bedroom. But I managed.

Coming back from Tennis, in the after glow of the evening, if I stayed that long, which I often did, the conversations never really varied. They were always, more or less like this:

"Have you got the key, Walter?"

"No. It's McWhirter's turn this week to lock up. He's got it."

"He wasn't playing very well today, I thought?"

"No. Not well at all. Sun in his eyes."

"But you tossed for places surely?"

"Of course we did. He lost. Kept hitting the net."

"Aha. Getting on, I'm afraid."

"Aye, that's a fact."

"Agnes's service was poor, erratic. . . ."

"Both getting on a wee bittie."

"Oh aye. . . ."

"Ah michtie-me."

"The Brandy Snaps went down very well. They always do. Gratifying. The cream makes it look more. Next week I'll try Molly's recipe for Soda Bread. . . ." Their voices would drift harmlessly over me, vapour trails of cloud above the Downs, to be smudged, faded, and eventually to evaporate in the gentle business of preparing the cocoa for supper.

* * *

School went ahead slowly. There appeared to be no marked improvement in my reports, and the little notes appended to the end of my letters home by my uncle, which I was not allowed to see—they were written confidentially after I had signed my name and sent love and kisses—grew steadily more pessimistic. He was doing his best to be helpful and generous, but really . . . the Boy didn't seem to be settling down, after all it was now more than a whole year. There should have been some improvement. There, apparently, was none. Except that I was doing, I thought, pretty well. I was, at least, trying. I wanted to get back to the South, and I knew that without some form of improvement in my scholastic world this would be delayed and delayed. I was there to learn, at a good Scottish School, and the sooner I learned the better. So naturally I went as hard as I could; I battered away at Metalwork making copper ash-trays and serviette-rings; I made bookends and unacceptable work boxes in woodwork; I threw cups and bowls on the potter's wheel, and I did French Translation and Essay like no one else in the school. My English was filled with long poems and stories which were often read out to the whole, agonised, sniggering, class. My Geography was noted for the amount of space I covered, products I knew, populations I recorded, deciduous, coniferous, rain and dry belts I had assembled. I was even congratulated by teachers who smiled and were polite, and my exercise books, for these lessons, were marked well into the eighties. What was wrong?

Apparently, I was failing all the time. The fact that Maths was still incomprehensible to me, that Physics and Chemistry and Engineering were far, far beyond my meagre comprehension, seemed not to matter to me, at any rate, against the glowing reports from the few classes in which I excelled. Albeit without much competition.

An angry, hurt, letter from my father sent me off to my Altar. I had found a small burn, or brook, some miles from the Estate, deep in a beech thicket away from sight or people. When I exercised the neighbours' dogs, the neighbours from the Old Town I hasten to add—the people on the Estate didn't keep dogs, only greyhounds—I used to tramp off across the sodden fields and corrugated plough to my sanctuary. I had, one day, idly started to dam the little burn with stones and boulders, and within a short time created a splendid pool and waterfall. Then, to embellish, as I am prone to do, something which was already attractive, I started work on a small Altar which I made from shards of slate and flat stone which I collected in a bag from the shale tips round the edges of the Bingies. As I spent a great deal of my spare time by the Pool and the waterfall praying to an unheeding God for swift release back to the life I once had known, it occurred to me that He might listen better, or listen at all, if I built a bit of the appropriate furnishings. I had been taught, in my mild flirtation with Catholicism, that God could Hear You Wherever You Prayed. Just so long as you did. Well I did. Furiously and piously. However, He seemed to pass me over on zephyr wings as I lay nightly moaning in the yellow oak bed: even more so in the Put-U-Up. So I assumed that perhaps an Altar to His Glory would be more appropriate, and more obvious, to His clearly busy Eye. Also the labour which it would cost, the lugging of the slate and shards of stone, the mud and slush of the construction would surely not go unseen? With this in mind, I built a reasonable Temple to Him. Decorated with a couple of empty aspirin bottles, to hold assorted wild flowers, a tin cross made from old bottle tops and a bit of wood, and swamped with a monotony of desperate prayer, it stood, beside my burn, a model of piety and trust.

Perhaps it was the sheer boredom, the waves of self-pity, which put Him off—for whatever else happened, my mumbled pleadings and sighs fell on totally sterile ground in Heaven.

Until one day.

A shaft of thin hopeful light slit across the dullness of my existence. One Sunday, after the long effort of the Letter Home, my uncle said, with a heavy clearing of his throat and lowered eyes, that he had been, very reluctantly, forced, in his weekly note to my parents, to say that, everything being considered very carefully, it was probably better that I should be removed from School since it was costing everyone a great deal of money and worry, and that there seemed to be no positive signs, after so long, that any good was coming from it all. He said, very politely and gently, that I had to see things that way for myself. Even my own reports were saddening; I seemed incapable of joining a team, of playing games, of making friends, or even of applying myself to the work which was set out for me to do.

In short, I was wasting everyone's time, money and patience.

The fact that I never, at any time ever, saw my school reports— they were always addressed to him, correctly, as my Guardian and he sent them on to my parents—nor ever had any discussions with anyone about them didn't seem to occur to either of us at the time. I was simply struck dumb with shock. As far as I was aware, I had worked as hard as possible and had tried my best.

The next morning, after an anguished night watching the patterns flicker on the ceiling from the Valor Perfection Stove, my uncle and I parted company as usual at Queen Street Station. At the bookstall I bought a stamp and a picture postcard on which, leaning against a pile of magazines, I wrote in pencil, "I am very unhappy here. Please, please let me come home." A swift Burberry'd arm shot over my shoulder and lifted it up.

My uncle's face was expressionless, a nicotined finger brushed his little moustache.

"Well now, Sonny," he said kindly, "why not post it?" He flipped it on to the magazines and walked away.

Dismay and guilt gave way to rising desperation. I did exactly as he said and went on to school.

It was an uncomfortable week.

Fearful of the results when this fatal correspondence would reach my unsuspecting parents I spent a lot of time walking other people's blasted dogs over to my sanctuary. Many a "Rags" or "Boy" or "Bobbie" passed a bewildered hour or two while I droned away at the Altar asking for Help and some form of Direction. The latter came in a sudden surging determination which shook me like ague. If *this* is where really trying hard got you, then it was very simple. I would just not bother any longer and let the whole damned thing slide. They could all do as they liked. And so would I. I ceased praying, wrecked the Altar, opened the dam, and played truant from school as often, and as pleasurably, as I could.

★　　★　　★

It was easy. At lunch-time, instead of eating my sodden meat pie with Tom or whoever else was sitting on the dustbin wall, I just stuck my cap in my pocket, pinned a handkerchief in my Blazer pocket so that it flopped over the give-away crest on the badge, opened my collar, stuffed my tie somewhere else, and, hands in pockets, one and sixpence and a few odd coppers saved from here and there, I strolled happily down the hill from the school into the busy crowds of George Square and let Glasgow and its allure swallow me up. It was as easy as that, and no one bothered to check. At first, naturally, I was terrified. I was sure that I would be spotted and carted back to the amiable but fearsome Dr Steel. However, with no badges or colours showing, I passed for any other boy wandering about the city. I found deceit very refreshing.

Woolworths was my usual haven. Because it was warm and bright, and filled with people. Here was Life. Pushing and shoving, smiling and laughing, talking and living. Music played all day. The record counter had a constant supply of melody. To the lingering refrains of "When The Poppies Bloom Again" I would sit on a high stool eating a Chocolate Fudge Ice Cream and beam happily at the world about me. Guiltless. It was all heady stuff.

Later, I grew bolder and went, imagine the bravery!, to the cinema alone. For sixpence, in the middle stalls with a packet of pea-nuts or a Mars Bar, I sat in my element and got two movies, all the Advertising, the Newsreel, the Forthcoming Attractions plus a pink, green and amber lit Organ Recital.

Life was *never* to be dull and drab again. I would always live like this, and the Hell with Effort, Loyalty, and "The Times".

It would be useful to say at this point that it was the moment when my whole future was laid before me. The great silver screen, the glamour, the glory, the guns and the chases. Camera angles, Lighting, Back Projection, Split Screen, Fade and Dissolve flew past my eyes twice a week and vanished like dreams. But I was the Original Audience for which these films were made. The refugee from worry, humdrum life, anxiety or despair. I only wanted to be bewitched, enthralled, be-glamoured. The rest of it washed away like silt in a tub. Nothing at all rubbed off at that time. My personal disillusion, even disappointment, was so great, my anger so deep, that I had fixed it clearly that I would try no more. They could come and get me and punish me in whatever way they all liked: I had given up. But until they did come to get me, or sent for me, I was going to have as pleasant a time as I possibly could. What on earth was the point in going on any longer? I had tried, and failed again. So be it.

It was, I think, at the Paramount, one matinee, that I made my first friend out of school. Tom had become more and more immersed in his Bunsen burners and retort stands, and I hardly ever saw him even for meat-pie lunches. While Gregg, after the disaster of The Tea, never spoke to me again. So apart from the dogs I walked there was no one, and I was wonderfully free, if lacking the bonds of friendship which I strangely craved since it was no longer to be had.

Even Tom was something.

The Paramount was a new, glittering Picture Palace with a deadly reputation. I had heard it spoken of in muted voices in many of the parlours to which I was bidden, or sent, for those Bakings and Teas. It was the meeting place of all the Evil in Glasgow, the Crooks and Thieves and Bookies. Any young girl going there alone, it was said, invariably ended up with a hypodermic in her bottom and a bunk in a boat at the Broomilaw awaiting the next tide down the Clyde for Morocco. Indeed the people Upstairs knew of one girl who, missing her companions, had foolishly gone in alone to see Robert Taylor and was never heard of again apart from the fact that an usherette had seen a dark-skinned man helping a young lady to a taxi from the foyer saying that she had had a "fainting fit". It made going to the Pictures much more interesting.

In any case I felt secure because of two things: first I was a boy, secondly I always sat in the middle of the stalls where it was lighter, and never in the shadows where, of course, anything might happen. Armed, this day, with my logic, I went to see a special showing of Boris Karloff in "The Mummy". I had seen it two or three times before, ages ago, but it was still my favourite next to "The Bride of Frankenstein". I also saw Mr Dodd.

Mr Dodd was almost entirely beige. A beige raincoat, beige face, beige hair and freckles. He sat two or three seats away from me and smiled pleasantly all through the Forthcoming Attractions. And still I didn't know.

During the interval, when the lights went pink and green and the organ rumbled through a selection from something or other, he smiled shyly across the empty seats and I smiled back, and he moved along and came and sat beside me. He asked if I would like an ice-cream, and I said yes, and we ate together in pleasant, companionable silence. He was very polite, quiet spoken and smiled a lot; and when he took my empty ice-cream tub away from me, plus the wooden spoon and stacked it neatly into his own and tidily placed it all under his seat, he patted my leg kindly and whispered with a secret wink that I was, in all probability, playing truant from school, wasn't I? Shattered with surprise that he had so quickly found me out, I lied swiftly and said that I was "off school" with a sprained ankle. That seemed to content him and the programme started again so that there was no need for more conversation.

It was very nice having someone to laugh at the film with, to share fear with, and to enjoy relief with all at the same time. He was very attentive and once, in a particularly creepy part he put his arm protectively round my shoulder, which I felt was very thoughtful of him indeed.

By the time the show was over it was well after six, and I realised that I would have to leave my new friend quickly and "limp" to the station and Bishopbriggs where my aunt would be waiting to hear from me how well the rehearsals for the school play were going. My excuse, true as it happened, for the lateness of my arrival. Mr Dodd was sad, he told me his name and that I was to call him Alec, and made an appointment for us to see the film again at the end of the week before the Forthcoming Attraction took its place. I agreed with pleasure. It was to be his Treat, he said, and after we would go to Cranstons for tea but that I could still be home in time so as not to worry my aunt.

I sailed down to Queen Street Station with winged feet, no limp now, heart high with happiness. Someone at the Altar had listened after all. I had a New Friend.

★　★　★

Tea at Cranstons was an impressive affair at the worst of times, and this was the best. Quiet, calm, warm, sparkling with silver, white tablecloths, flowers in fluted vases, motherly waitresses in crisp aprons and little caps, and a silver stand of cakes. Mr Dodd knew his way about very well and was pleasant to everyone and anxious that I should eat as much as I could for, he said, he was a Medical Student and he knew just how much "fuel" the working lad's mind had to have to keep it going.

It was very pleasant indeed. Although I had been there often before with my aunt on shopping expeditions, this was far more companionable. We talked at length of the film and discussed all the Technical Effects and the actors and Acting, we discussed the Theatre and Plays, although I had not seen very many by that time, but the feeling of lazy companionship, of comfort and of laughter was delightful. It was as if we had known each other for years instead of hours. He told me how his mother had saved and scrimped to send him to School and then on to the Medical College where he was now studying. I asked him what kind of Doctor he was going to be and he said a Surgeon because he felt that is probably where he could do the most good. When I said that I was rather horrified at the idea of all the blood and cutting people up, he very reasonably said that I might very well feel that because I clearly had not heard the Call as he had done. I was very impressed. The conversation slid back, inevitably, to the film and he astonished me by saying that he knew exactly how mummies were bandaged and how they were embalmed; it was really very easy to do, he said cheerfully, and anyone could make a mummy if they knew how to bandage. I was overcome with curiosity and asked him more and more questions; he tried to demonstrate with his table napkin but it was too small and too thick, so he suggested that since he lived nearby and had all his books and bandages there we should go at once to his place and he could show me in a trice.

I accepted immediately; already telling my aunt the lie about the play. And I still didn't know.

His flat was a rather poky room with a kitchenette in a high block over a tobacconist and sweet shop in Hope Street. It smelled of ether and stale cigarettes and was pretty untidy, for which he apologised, pulling hurriedly at the unmade bed and taking some dirty plates and a bottle into the sink. There were books everywhere, a typewriter, old shirts, and a gas fire which plopped when he lit it. On the wall there were pictures of Rothesay Castle and two men wrestling. He opened a thick book filled with diagrams of bandaging; people were swathed in them, heads, hips, legs, wrists, arms and everything else. It was very comprehensive.

Chattering happily, he pulled a large cardboard box from under the bed and spilled rolls and rolls of blue-wrapped bandages of every size all over the floor. These, he said, were just the trick to turn me into a splendid mummy and if I would just remove my jacket and shirt and vest and sit down in that chair there he would turn me into Boris Karloff in the flick of a fly's eyelid.

I dutifully, rather shyly, did as he suggested while he started to unroll yards and yards of filmy gauzes. It was not very long before I was straight-jacketed in strips of thin cotton bandage from the top of my head to my waist, arms securely folded, in the correct position of mummies, across my chest, a small slit left for each eye so that I could hazily see through a vague fringe of white blur, a small hole left for my nostrils so that I could breathe. Otherwise I was trussed like a fowl. Taking down the oval mirror from the mantelpiece he showed me the effect which I found impressive, uncomfortable, and very restricting. I could merely manage a vague motion with my head, which didn't show, and roll my slitty eyes. I could neither see properly, nor even hear for that matter, and I was totally mute.

As he turned from replacing the mirror, and as I stood to indicate that he might now unwrap me as soon as possible, I could see that he was speaking, but only a blurred mumble came to my bandaged ears and it was with some rising degree of alarm that I found myself clutched firmly in his arms and dumped on my back in the middle of the brass bed. I tried to struggle and yell out, at least to sit up, but I was totally rigid and the only sound I made was smothered in yards and yards of thick white gauze. Putting his beige face very close to my ear Mr Dodd said that it seemed a pity not to finish the job and make me a full mummy from head to foot, that would complete the Effect.

My shoes and socks were wrenched off and thrown under the bed, then my trousers, and to my silent screams of protest, he ripped off my underpants and I was stark naked before his eager, now red-faced, gaze.

Swiftly and with the expert precision of a born embalmer, he rolled me about the bed in a flurry of bandage. I was wrapped like a parcel, rolled this way and that, on my back, on my side, every which way until I was reeling with giddiness and terror.

174

I was wound tightly into a cocoon as a spider rolls a grasshopper. Helpless, inert, more a dummy even than a mummy, I lay rigid as Mr Dodd, his mouth stuck with safety pins, tucked in the loose ends; when this was done, and with great strength he manœuvred me off the bed, stiff as a telegraph pole, and set me upright on cotton feet to see my reflection in the mirror of his wardrobe door. Peering desperately through the eye slits I could see that he had made a complete and thorough job. Boris Karloff wasn't half as convincing.

Unable to stand by myself I was forced to lean against the serge shoulder of my host whose face was bathed in pleasure. Surely my heart could not beat so quickly with terror and I should still live. It had leapt from my chest and now pumped and throbbed in my throat. It stopped entirely when my horrified eyes saw, pathetically thrusting through the swaddling rags, my genitals, naked and as pink and vulnerable as a sugar mouse.

Mr Dodd placed his mouth to my ear again and said that he thought he had made a very good job of things and hoped I was pleased too, and without waiting for any kind of reaction, which I would not have been able to make in any case, he swung me, like an immense skittle, into an arc of 180 degrees, so that the whole filthy little room whirled round my head, and I was back down on Mr Dodd's bed; and in Mr Dodd's hand, inches from my eyes, was a pair of scissors. I tried to faint. I heard him say that in Real Life They Cut That Off—and lay supine waiting for Death. Gently his hands caressed my helpless body, kindly he whispered that he had no intention of doing such a cruel thing for how else, otherwise, would a boy like me be able to masturbate? He said that he knew that all boys enjoyed masturbating and that he was much too good to deprive me of the rights. My mind had become a mass of solid jelly. Nothing flickered there apart from deadly terror, shame, and grief at my wickedness. I couldn't rationalise. I closed my eyes and said three or four "Hail Mary's".

If I prayed surely, this time, God would hear? The anxious, firm, slippery fingers caressing and annointing me splintered my whole being into a billion jagged fragments. I was only aware that if they didn't stop something terrible and horrifying would happen.

Which it did. And I knew.

* * *

The unwrapping, which followed, was a slow, forlorn, deadly affair. The wretched stuff peeled off me in long swooping swathes, littering the grubby bed and the floor around it. I had been blubbing, snivelling in a silly useless sort of way like a girl, and Mr Dodd was worried and apologetic and kept reminding me over and over again that it was all all right because he was a Medical Student and understood these things.

Dressing hurriedly, stumbling with teary cheeks and snotty nose, falling into pants and trousers, lacing up shoes, yanking up socks and fumbling with my tie, I was unable to speak or even look at the bobbing figure scrabbling about among its merchandise. He handed me a comb and I raked it through my disordered hair; he said that he would see me safely home.

We didn't speak in the train all the way to Bishopbriggs. He pointed out, as we left the train, that it was not really very late and that he would come and explain things to my aunt. In horror I said that she was ill and could not be disturbed. I led him miles across the Estate, away from where I lived, to a completely strange house where a lamp glowed through a lowered blind. He waited at the gate as I rang the bell, and just as the door opened, fortunately he turned away and was lost in the gloom. The woman who opened the door was pleasant and I apologised for making an error but she smiled and said the houses were all so alike it was no wonder. Springburn Terrace, she said, was " 'way round the back".

For some time I lived in fear that Mr Dodd would come back or find where I lived. Once, on my way to the station, I thought I saw him hovering about near the Railway Arch. But I don't think it was . . . and I never saw him ever again. Neither did I ever set foot in a cinema alone for many years to come.

A few days later a letter arrived from my father to say that my mother was coming up to Glasgow within the month. She would stay with my grandmother. And had an appointment with Dr Steel at the school for the 28th. Nothing more was said. My uncle looked uncomfortable, my aunt defensive.

What could Dr Steel say to my mother that they could not, for Heaven's sake? she wondered. It seemed a waste of good money to trail all this way for nothing. She declared that she didn't know what to make of it at all. And neither did I.

12

NEITHER did the irritated Dr Steel as it turned out. Or my bewildered mother for that matter. Clearly my uncle and the headmaster did not see eye to eye on the subject of my education, and while the latter admitted, with bland candour, that I was not the brightest pupil he had ever had in his Technical School but showed distinct abilities in other subjects, the former seemed to have given me up for lost.

Steel suggested that it would be the gravest folly to remove me from the place where I had already been for two years and in which I had fought to remain against quite high odds, and that for the next year I should merely concentrate on those classes which would be the most useful to me in my later life, and at which I showed some signs, at least, of promise. I was to forget Chemistry, Physics, Maths etcetera, and if I cared, only follow the courses in English, Languages, Art, and all the varied handworks from Pottery to Bookbinding. Football, Hockey and Cricket were out and I was to be left on my honour to attend whatever classes I wished.

He wondered, mildly, why I had even been sent to a Technical School in the first place and said that at the end of the year I should be enrolled into a College of Art somewhere, for my future lay in that direction and in no other as far as he could see.

My mother's worried heart lifted; mine whipped up like a kite in a gale. Both parents agreed with the wise counsel of Dr Steel and also with the College of Art part to come later. I was transported to Heaven. And removed, very tactfully, from Bishopbriggs.

Clearly my unhappy aunt and uncle had reached the end of their patience and endurance. They wanted, understandably, to return to the calm and peace of their life as it had all been before my advent into their bewildered middle-aged existence.

Nothing was said in, as they say, so many words, but a Family Gathering was called at my grandmother's house. The long and short of it was that yet another of my mother's sisters, Aunt Hester, adopted me and took me off to live with her in a different part of the city with her husband and two children, and I spent the last year of my school days in a very happy "family atmosphere" where I was able to play the piano whenever I wished with no fear of the people Upstairs, and read every book I could lay hands on from Trollope to Austen without ever once feeling the slightest tremor of guilt that I should be dubbing my soccer boots, oiling a cricket bat, or ploughing through the miseries of Fractions or Logarithms. It nearly went to my head.

I bought a half-belted overcoat and began to talk like Ronald Colman. I graduated from "By the Chapel in the Moonlight" to "Sheep May Safely Graze" all by ear and with the bass pedal screwed to the floor-boards. I started to smoke "Black Cat" cigarettes in the train coming home from school, learned to skate, and fell deeply in love with my elder cousin Jean.

The only reason that I learned to skate was because of her. I adored her with an unthinking passion, and bought Family Planning magazines which had chapters headed "Can Cousins Marry?" "Cousins Marrying Causes Imbecility?" When I had read all I could understand I was brave enough to mention it to her while we were skating round and round the rink at Crossmloof one evening. I have never forgotten her look of total astonishment as she pulled her steadying hand from mine and fled across the ice to a large Canadian hockey player who, covered in pads and cages and maple leaves, was her real true love.

However she agreed to accompany me to the rink from time to time, but always left me when Canada arrived for his evening match. I was sad, of course, but thought that if I was patient she would come back to me in the end. Which of course she never did. I skated miserably about the place, close to the edge, for I was not all that good on my own and her adored hand was more than just a comfort. It was a stabiliser. Together we collided round the rink with all the elegance, and overt familiarity, of mating toads. I hoped that my sad devotion would show. Which it did. In a face like a squashed muffin. I hoped that people would be moved by my nightly vigil . . . the mournful, brave boy sliding about on the perimeter while his beloved one, golden hair flying, kilts swirling, spun about centrally in the arms of a great, uncouth, goalkeeper. But no one took a bit of notice. And once, in desperation, when I did try to slide across to them and take her tiny hand, I landed flat on my back and skidded with a sickening crash on my half-belt overcoat into the barrier.

I gave it up after that. There is nothing like a public loss of dignity to restore a sense of proportion. I put away the skates and took up my pens and pencils. Warmer, safer, cheaper and, in the end one hoped, far less dangerous than a marriage between cousins.

★　★　★

Life had changed radically. The Late Developer was starting, and not before time, to offer tentative shoots of manhood to a singularly uninterested world. It really didn't worry me very much that no one seemed to care because I cared myself; deeply. I was enormously interested in the change, and studied myself daily with satisfaction and an awe only equal to its smugness.

I knew, of course, early on that I would never be Handsome like my uncles or one or two of the cousins. Standard Beauty was not to be my fortune. But, I reasoned, I had height, good eyes well placed, and a pleasing smile which I encouraged daily in the bathroom mirror, ranging it from Winsome to Brave. A series of exercises which, if forced to watch today, would surely make me vomit.

Even though I was hopeless at skating, at Sports of any kind or at any single thing which needed any form of co-ordination—even in my piano playing the left hand was constantly at variance with the behaviour of the right—I felt that in my half-belted overcoat, my good blue suit, a florid silk scarf pilfered from someone, and my green felt pork pie hat with a feather, I was approaching my golden future with some degree of courage and confidence.

Not to mention conceit. Nothing, up till then, had come along to freeze the tender greening shoots of my April growth, except perhaps my cousin's clear preference for a Canadian hockey playing goalkeeper. On skates. That, to me, simply showed her acute lack of sensibilities.

Perhaps for the first time in my life that third year in Scotland had at last found me "driving my own coach". The Postillion was on the lead horse. It was a sharply pleasurable feeling.

Of course there was always the Lightning.

During this exhilarating time changes had taken place at home. My father, more and more exhausted by the demands of "The Times", by constant minor ailments, by his deep dislike of what he called the "Orientals" who had suddenly invaded his Hampstead streets far from the streets of Berlin, Vienna, Munich and Hamburg, became more and more desperate to remove himself and his family far into the country away from them all and settle into "the country house". Pressured thus by almost constant colds and chills, delicatessens springing up in the High Street, and the growing of the storm mounting in slow-building thunder-clouds over Europe, he started his search in deadly earnest.

This eventually led us all to a big, ugly, redbrick and gabled house in three acres of overgrown gardens in the middle of a common seven miles from Lewes in Sussex.

It had been for sale for a very long time since no one wanted to attempt any work on such a hideous, sullen, uncared-for lump of tile and gargoyles, therefore he bought it cheap, ignoring protests and doubts from my unfortunate mother, and moved us all in, cat, cupboards and cooking pots, at the beginning of 1936.

I was enraptured. Enraptured by the stained glass front door, a stork standing in bulrushes, enraptured by the high rooms, the solid doors, the wide staircase, the overgrown orchard, the silted up pond with a rotting punt, the bamboo grove and the magnolias pressing glossy leaves against almost every window. But best of all, everywhere miles and miles of rolling common blazing with gorse and heather, lizards, slow worms, rabbits, a secret patch of vivid Gentians and a stark white windmill on a ridge. Never better than the Cottage but the next best thing.

In a very short time everything was stripped out: painted white from floor to attics; the stained glass door, to my regret, replaced with oak; the lawns mowed, trees felled here and there, bushes pruned and the pond, my job, cleaned, and the spring which ran through the orchard unblocked. The house, after so many years of neglect and abuse, seemed to breathe and took on a new lease of life. So did my father.

Of course all things have to be paid for. Lally decided that a total Country Life was really not for her. A couple of months in the summer, the Easter and Christmas holidays, that was acceptable. But a whole solitary existence in the middle of a common and seven miles from a reasonable town was asking too much of her patience and love. And in any case, as she pointed out, we were all growing up . . . and needed her less and less . . . whereas her parents, Mr and Mrs Jane, were getting on a little and she would be better occupied looking after them in Twickenham.

The improbable baby, now called Gareth, was already banging about on two legs and had both my adoring mother and sister to look after him. All we needed now, she said tactfully, was a nice Village Girl who would come in and take over, now that she, Lally, had set us all on the way.

She left quickly, and without sentimentality, which was not her nature; and with long and earnest promises of holidays in Twickenham she went as quietly as she had arrived in our midst all those years ago in 1925 when she came to us as a Girl Guide with a whistle and her white lanyard gleaming.

In her place a Rubens shepherdess. Elsie Brooks from Barcombe. Auburn hair, sparkling eyes, cherry red lips and a skin like gently flushed alabaster. She was eighteen and turned my head completely. She lived in a little room at the top of the house with a window which looked out on the orchard. I spent many pleasant hours crouched in the branches of a Granny Smith watching Elsie change from her Blue and White into "something pretty" for her day off. In the half light, half shade of her room, I could see the firm rounded arms above her auburn head, the full, pale, breasts, the lips puckered in a soundless whistle. Ignorant of my yearning love, my muddled fantasies, she shoved in her Kirby-grips, buttoned up her blouse, shrugged into a coat and went off to catch the two-thirty bus from the crossroads for the excitements of Haywards Heath.

Once I summoned up the courage to ask her to let me take her photograph as she was hurrying down the drive to the front gates. Sweetly she sat on the arm of a garden seat, set her hat a little more jauntily, crossed one leg over the other and thoughtfully raised her skirt so that her pretty knee, gleaming in silk, blinded my lens. I asked her to smile, which she did, and with a jolly laugh gave me a wink before she hurried off for her bus. I was so overcome with adoration that a short time afterwards, wandering about in a haze of mumbled poetry, I walked into a tree.

What saddened me more than anything, more than the secret love in the Granny Smith, the longed-for touch from her hand at breakfast passing the sugar, the cherry lips caressing the rim of her tea-cup which I longed to feel pressed against my cheek, apart from all these delicious denials, was the fact that while I had clearly noticed her she had never, at any single moment, ever noticed me.

"Girls like older boys," said my sister scornfully. "You are much too young and you can't even dance or anything like that. No girl likes a boy who only builds birdcages and mucks out rabbits. You see if I'm wrong."

I decided that I would now learn to dance.

* * *

"I have met the most delightful woman on the bus today," said my mother happily. "Mrs Cox. She was an actress, just like me, they live in the next village and she has three children who are just the same ages as you all. Isn't that extraordinary?"

Elizabeth and I were po-faced with disinterest. But she hurried on assuring us that we would all like each other, and that we needed to have young people about and that Mr Cox was very rich and owned the Village Hall where they put on plays twice a year. That slightly shook my indifference, but not enough to want to have to meet the wretched children. However that had been fixed. They were all, not just the ex-actress mother, but the entire family, coming to have tea with us the following week. I said that I was busy building my new Studio, and my sister said that if they came she would go and hide on the common until they left. My mother, undaunted, said we were to please ourselves. If we wished to absent ourselves from our guests she would explain why but she considered it a great pity since we all shared the same interests, were all the same ages, and also, she added, wandering off to the vegetable garden which she now cultivated, if I wanted to dance there was no better way to learn than going to the weekly "hop" which they gave every Saturday night in their Village Hall. However if we wished to be impolite and foolish that was up to us both. Taking her trug basket and a small hand fork she left us thoughtful.

The Coxes were very pleasant. Two girls and a small boy who hardly counted because, like Gareth, he was too young. But the other two were all right. Nerine and Heather (their father also owned a Nursery Garden which grew Alpines, hence their names) liked toads and snakes, rabbits and ponds and both of them liked acting and writing. So far so good. Nerine said that the Dances were "terrific fun" and that all I needed was a suit and a tie and that she would help me to learn in no time at all. It was arranged.

Every Saturday night I dressed carefully, clambered on to my bike and rode the three miles to Newick. The Coxes' house,

"Chez Nous", was rather grand, much bigger than ours and covered in wisteria and small diamond-paned windows. Before the Dance began we sat nervously in their sitting-room sipping chilled white wine and seltzer with Bath Olivers. I was deeply impressed. Then to the Hall next door where, on a chalked wood floor, I swooped and twirled and fell over to music played on a tall cabinet gramophone amplified through two blaring loud-speakers. This machine was called a radiogram, and no one was allowed to touch it except Mr Cox himself who arranged the records and the dances and jiggled them about magically for the "Paul Jones" and "The Excuse Me Dance."

The Hall had a stage at one end with blue sateen curtains and a tall iron stove with a chimney which burned lumps of coke and made everyone choke if they danced too close to it. Around the walls droopy flags and streamers from a forgotten Christmas and little rickety card tables with plates of bridge rolls and cress sandwiches. Half time was Tea and Lemonade. The last waltz, when Mr Cox turned down all the lights, and sometimes acci-dentally turned them off, was at ten o'clock so that everyone could get their coats and the last bus home.

I was better at dancing than skating. At least I could move into the centre of the floor and didn't fall over as often. But I got very stuck with Slow Foxtrots and Quick Steps and really only shone when it came to the "Valeta" or "Roger de Coverley". I always managed to slip out and have a Black Cat while the Latin American dancing was on; this I found too fast and difficult.

Everyone enjoyed themselves very much. The men tidy in blue suits and dance slippers, the girls in glossy silk frocks with low necklines and little puffed sleeves. We were all very hot and shiny, and laughed too much, especially during the "Paul Jones" when one changed partners with dizzying, often tactless speed. The sweet smell of sweat, Lux Toilet Soap, French Chalk and Camp Coffee was strong stuff. The evenings always ended far too soon.

My favourite partner, because she flattered me outrageously, was Cissie Waghorn who came from Uckfield and who, though rather taller than myself, and two years older, danced beautifully and helped to teach me with patience and care—even getting me to stumble about in "The Conga" which we all thought rather daring and new. One night, after a very spirited, if inaccurate, Thunder and Lightning Polka she told me, sitting together in a red, breathless, heap, that I had Beautiful and Expressive hands.

They were, she said very seriously, an Artist's Hands and Creative. I was overcome. For days I walked about with them hanging limply at the end of my arms afraid to damage them in any way. They were, to me, thick, clumsy, stubby fingered hands. I now thought better of them and started doing more exercises, with the Smiling ones in the mirror. My sister found me, pardonably, repellent.

But little did Cissie Waghorn know that she had started a thread of fire which was shortly to consume my entire being. Not just my dangling, cold-creamed, heavily Expressive hands. Unfortunately it all went to my head, and for a long time I couldn't even lift a cup to my lips without giving it the importance of the Holy Grail. I seldom do anything in half measures.

What I yearned for now was somewhere to show off these things I had learned, the Expressive hands, the Mocking Smile, the elegance of the Slow Waltz. What better than on that blue shrouded stage at the end of the Hall?

All my life I had wanted to be an actor. All my life that is from about the age of four when, draped in a cast off curtain and an old hat with a pheasant's tail stuck in it, I had acted my own plays to myself in my room. Then came the progression, under Lally's care and interest, during the Twickenham holidays . . . and the plays my sister and I used to "do" up in the barn near the Cottage. Tremendously ambitious plays about the sinking of the Titanic with myself as the Captain (in a sailor's cap naturally) and my unfortunate sister playing Ottoline Morrell (in a wide-brimmed hat with roses on it and a red plush table cloth). I can't think why she had to be Lady Ottoline. Perhaps because I thought that she looked like her and that Lady Ottoline must have been the kind of woman who would have been spunky enough to stay on the ship while they played "Nearer My God To Thee". That was *my* plot anyway. And I stuck to it.

Even at my miserable Altar near Bishopbriggs there had been a form of acting even if not in its purest sense, and late in 1936 the seal was finally set on my decision in the most obvious way imaginable.

Yvonne Arnaud was my Godmother. Not, you understand, my real Godmother: there were two or three of them floating about whom I was never to see after the ceremonial presentations of silver napkin rings and feeding spoons. Yvonne adopted Godchildren as some women adopt habits. Unthinkingly, wholeheartedly and devotedly. She never held me at any Font, nor promised to keep me to The Faith, but she never forgot a Birthday, a Christmas, even an Easter, and was more adored than anyone of the "family blood". She had known my parents, in the tall brick house in St George's Road days, and so I can safely claim to have been one of the earliest of the thousands of Godchildren she was to accumulate later in her life.

She arrived, or so the posters announced, on one dull day at the King's Theatre, Glasgow, with a try-out of a new farce, "Laughter In Court". I left a note at her hotel and was bidden to an early luncheon on Matinee day.

The suite was a Kew Gardens of bloom and blossom, Yvonne sailing towards me, arms outstretched, flowing chiffon and scarves billowing about her like the vaguest of delicious dreams; her apparent delight at seeing me, her glorious chuckle, "But darling! You have grown *enormous*!" relaxed me and we sat down to lunch, she brimming with questions, I brimming with contentment and happiness, over-eager to answer her queries after years, it seemed, of silence, save for my moaning pleas to the Slate Altar.

"Why are you here and not at school? You *are* at school surely?"

"No. Not today . . . I mean I should be . . ."

"And you are not?"

"No. I'm playing truant."

Wide surprised eyes; a quick crackle of Melba Toast.

"What is this Truant . . . a game. It is a game?"

I explained briefly and embarrassedly. She looked stern.

"But darling, if you do not do your lessons what will you *become*? And they will find out you know. That is deceitful and wicked of you. Do you like Spineeche? It is full of iron and very good for your teeth."

Through smoked salmon, chicken and a raspberry ice, I confessed all; about *not* trying any longer and the stifled, bursting ambition to go away and be an actor like my mother and grandfather. The jolly smiles faded from Yvonne's eyes; she looked very serious indeed sipping her coffee.

"Have you ever tried to be an actor, my darling?"

"At school . . . in a play last term. And always at home with my sister, that's all."

"It is not very easy, you know, but if you would like to see how *hard* it is I can show you."

When the curtain rose on the Second Act of "Laughter In Court" that Thursday matinee, I was in the Press Box of the Court Room Scene. "He's too young! He's a boy," cried a worried looking man. "Put him at the back, darling," said Yvonne brusquely. "If I mix him up with the other Supers he'll look like a Juvenile Delinquent!" "That's *exactly* what 'ee 'ees!" cried my Godmother, "and so are most of the Press."

The rippling whisper of that curtain going up, whatever they say and however many times they say it, is the most wonderful sound in the entire world to an actor's ears. More, even, than applause. I was sick with excitement, shaking with terror, cool as a cucumber and, for the first time ever in my whole life, I knew precisely, as if it had all happened before, where I was and, what was more important, *who* I was. I fitted. I belonged. My stupid, slothful brain burst asunder the strings of its inertia and incomprehension and started to learn. Like an engine slowly throbbing into life, my whole frame started to glow with energy and I saw the road, very clearly, stretched out before me.

I knew, there and then in that painted Press Box, that I had found my place. Like the rattling, wobbling, steel ball in a pin table, I had battered round the pins, hit a spring and shot into my little hole. Lights flashed; the score went up. No one had to tilt.

And now with my inaccurately reflecting mirror, the endless compliments from Cissie Waghorn and the total unawareness of Elsie Brooks . . . I knew that I must step upon a stage and let an audience judge what so far only I myself and one devoted dancing partner knew. And what Elsie would not fail to know when she saw it. I was ready for the World.

Readiness was tested at the end of that year, in the village hall, with the local amateur dramatic society into which I was permitted entry, although under age, as a naked slave in the second act of "Alf's Button". An inauspicious start. Half naked, dressed in baggy chiffon knickers, a gold turban, a squint moustache, I stood impassively, arms folded across my chest holding a paper scimitar in one hand and my terror in the other. I never moved, and no one really saw me. But there is a picture of me in the local paper to prove it all. I was cold. Frightened. Idiotic. But I had started. And nothing now was ever going to stop me.

Mr Cox, who produced, said I had Presence and Stillness. Hardly difficult the latter, as I was forbidden to move a muscle on my Turkish Staircase; as for Presence, I didn't know about that but thought that he would. Cissie Waghorn was hopeful that in the next season I might get a better part and the local paper printed my name, for the first time, in its entirety, the van and the den and all. And Lally sent me a telegram. My cup was filling, if not exactly brimming. I knew, if no one else present that memorable night did, that I was on my way. All I had to do was explain it to the family and take the next train to Victoria.

My father, when approached, looked vague, then worried, finally irritated. And said categorically No. It was no job for a man, he explained, rightly as I was later to find out; it was risky, and nearly all actors were out of work for years and years, also they were common, and in any case he had no intention, after the years of sweat and toil that had gone into whatever education I had managed to scratch together from the wreckage of all that had been offered me, of letting me follow such a lunatic, mediocre, ungentlemanly career. If career it ever was to be. I was to do as he had arranged. Finish school and start the new year as a student at the Chelsea Polytechnic and through a solid Art Education, as opposed to a solid Scottish one, prepare myself for my eventual arrival in Printing House Square.

He was immeasurably gentle, he always was, but he was firm. And we all knew in the family that when he said No it was really No. There was, as Lally had said so often, No Shilly Shally about my father. My mother on the other hand was wistful, remembering her own, and her father's world. But she took his side and endorsed what he said completely. I was on my own.

"Alf's Button" faded away gently, as did the dancing lessons under Cissie Waghorn and Nerine Cox's devoted eyes, when I discovered, by asking her directly, that Elsie Brooks couldn't dance anyway and had fallen in love with a garage mechanic in Lindfield. I went back to mucking out the rabbits and making bird-cages. I was not unduly cast down. After Scotland nothing was ever going to flatten me again. I'd wait till next year. There was time. Next year I would be sixteen, and an Art Student. Student meant, in those days, that one was Grown Up.

*   *   *

The farewells in Glasgow were not at all difficult. Except for Aunt Hester and her family, to whom I knew I owed so much of this new liberation of spirit, and my maternal grandfather. I was almost indecently cheerful. I seldom ever saw my grandfather during the years I lived there. Banished, as he was, to sit by the kitchen range, and sleep in a bed set into the wall with curtains all around it (a Butt and Ben they called it), the only chances of seeing him I got were when the family were resting after Sunday luncheon and the maid was out of the kitchen.

He sat in an armchair beside the big iron range, a small black and white dog at his side, his hands clasped on a stick, dozing gently. His hair was snow white, his jaw firm, his eyes clear and steady. I never ever knew why he was banished to live in the kitchen and sleep in the cook's bed and he never told me. Not that I ever asked, it must be confessed. I imagined that it was probably a form of punishment for all the wickedness of his early life with my mother when, for so many years, they had stayed away from the family house and trailed willingly all over the country with wicker hampers and bookings for Crewe, Manchester, Leeds, Birmingham, Cardiff and Liverpool, their make-up boxes in a Gladstone bag and enough money for two quarts of beer and "digs" in a street near the Theatre. But it was never spoken of and still is not. So all this is conjecture. Our few conversations together were conducted in conspiratorial whispers lest we should be caught by one of my aunts, a maid, or worst of all, the unforgiving figure of my black-woollied grandmother.

"And what do you do with yourself, my boy?"

"Well, I write a lot. Plays mostly."

"You like the Theatre? That's good. Of course it's in your blood. Your mother had a fine talent, a fine talent, but frittered it away in marriage. A pity."

"I want to be an actor when I'm old enough."

He used to chuckle, his wicked eyes opening with tired amusement: "You'll never be Old Enough to be an Actor, my boy. Actors have to be always Young. We don't get Older, you mark my words. You will do the Classics? Those lovely, lovely words. Sheridan, Congreve; lovely things to say. I was a very acceptable Surface you know in 'Scandal', did your mother tell you? You ask her . . . very acceptable. Forbes Robertson asked me to understudy him in 'The Only Way' . . . but I missed it . . . now *there's* a role for an actor! Carton . . . do you know it? Oh! What lovely things to say. . . ."

I remember, after so many years, these words almost verbatim. Really because it was the only conversation, or topic of conversation, we ever had. Each time I spoke to him it was as if I had disturbed him in a continual ever-running band of thought. Forbes Robertson, Sheridan, the loveliness of words. It never varied. Once, when I asked him about Shakespeare (being at that time deeply into a simplified version of "A Midsummer Night's Dream") he gruffly said that it had never come his way, and was not his "style". He didn't care for the blood and anxieties of the plays, he said; life was filled with that already in the streets outside, so what audience wished to be reminded of all that lay about them when they had to pay half a guinea for a good seat in order to forget?

"Give them joy and delight . . . give them lovely words and good cheer, make them laugh, and *cherish them*!" he said firmly. "Cherish them as I cherish you, eh?" he said to the black and white dog at his knee. "Ah! Spot! What a wealth of lovely words you have had wasted on you. He doesn't take it in, you know. Not a word." He laughed without rancour.

He collapsed in the street one day walking with "Spot" and died shortly afterwards in the white-tiled glare of a public ward. An actor's life.

Aunt Hester, tall, worried, continually harassed, loving, gentle as a dove, merely held me just that little bit longer in her arms at the station. Her eyes were sad.

"You'll be off in a minute. I hate farewells," she said, and with a quick, nervous little wave, she hurried into the crowd, bumping into people. I settled back into my compartment, lit a Black Cat, and felt the train rumble over the Broomielaw Bridge. Looking out of the scummy window I watched the cranes and tugs and hulks of ships lining the sullen waters of the Clyde. I hoped never ever to see it again. And I never have.

$$\star \quad \star \quad \star$$

The three years in Scotland were, without doubt, the most important years of my early life. I could not, I know now, have done without them. My parents, intent on giving me a solid, tough scholastic education to prepare me for my Adult Life, had no possible conception that the education I would receive there would far outweigh anything a simple school could have provided. Life before 1934, the Summer Life if you like, with Lally and my sister in the country and the near effortless marking-time existence at the Hampstead school, had seduced me into a totally unreal existence of constant happiness, simplicity, trust and love. What I clearly needed, and what I got, was a crack on the backside which shot me into reality so fast I was almost unable to catch my breath for the pain and disillusions which were to follow.

To be sure it was a violent break, but it did not, I trust, find me weak: amazingly the Summer Life had made me strong; the break from it and all that was to follow, astonished me but left me unsurprised, cut me but left me unbloody, bewildered me but left me unafraid. And because of it I was able to enter the new phase of life which lay ahead of me with, if not total confidence (I have never had that), at least a thick veneer of it, and with the inbuilt belief that whatever happened to me anywhere at any time, I would somehow, willy nilly, by hook or by crook, manage to survive. For myself alone if for no one else.

The enforced loneliness in which I chose to dwell was not, when all is said and done, one long trail of misery and woe and barrenness. After all I was within the confines of my "family", my own blood. I was cared for, comfortable, well fed and looked after by people who, by their own standards, were doing their very best to assist me. I was even at times pleasured for there were trips to hear choirs, to see football matches, the Teas and Bakings, walks in the Campsie Fells and on one occasion a short holiday by the sea at Dunure. No: the life they all offered me in that alien land was reasonable, kind, uncomprehending and in many ways most generous. The fact that I rebelled against all it offered was entirely my own fault and no one else's. I *tried* to conform, but the conformation was unacceptable to us all. Compromise is a deathly weapon.

Unable to share the pleasures offered I chose to remain apart, solitary, detached. It must have been irritating and unfriendly. But that's what I did. I was desperate to preserve my Summer Life against all odds, and to some extent, to a large extent indeed, I succeeded.

But in those times of loneliness, in those solitary walks across the ruined fields, the dreadful Teas and Bakings, the reading of knitting patterns and endless games of Solitaire, I did not sit idle and let my mind float off into a vacuum. Instead I turned to my father's old teaching of the Remember Game and played it assiduously. I "pelmanised" a million details which, one day, I felt would "come in handy", as Lally had said so often. I looked and I watched continually. Looking and watching, as one knows, are two very different things. I watched.

My Grandfather Aimé had always said, "You must Observe. Always question." I started to become a professional, as it were, Observer. I was unable to question for I knew that I should not receive honest answers from people who thought questioning a lack of respect for one's elders.

So I observed and from observation answered my own queries. Not always accurately, but satisfactorily enough for me at the time. At least my sluggish brain was working for itself.

From this easy, silent game, which never intruded on anyone's conversation or alarmed them, I assembled a rag bag of trinkets into which I am still able to rummage. Aunt Teenie's dreadful twitch on her poor scarred face became the twitch on von Aschenbach's face at moments of stress, in "Death In Venice" for example; my own shyness and diffidence and loneliness at those Tennis Parties or Tea Parties became his when he arrived, alone, at the Grand Hotel des Bains. The games I played then, and the things I stole, gleaned, collected, observed, have remained with me, vividly, for the rest of my life.

At the same time I was also forced to build myself a sort of wall of protection which, until then, I had never had need of. It was unnecessary to protect myself from love, from trust, honour, warmth and companionship, all of which I had had in abundance. Now, those things were to be guarded and protected. From the moment my head hit the bottom of that lavatory pan I laid the first brick of my protection by rapidly learning a foul, but saving, Glasgow accent. The first brick went in. From that day on I didn't cease my labours, walling myself snugly into my shell slowly, deliberately and undetected.

I learned to blub without moving a muscle of my face so that even then I was not given away, and began to speak elliptically, so that whatever I said was not precisely what I meant, but nearly so. A habit to which I still, regrettably, cling, and which gets me into a good deal of trouble from time to time. However, it is a hard habit to break and one I am not very willing to try. I am still un-trusting to some degree.

Of course in the busy building of this wall I left many openings about me, so that I was able to watch, to look, to touch if I wished, and feel. But they did preclude others from getting too near and, like the winkle on the pin, pulling me outside.

And, perhaps unfortunately for me, I went on building right into adult life. An undeniably self-centred thing to do. But I am. Isolation, even from choice as in my case, incubates self-centredness like a culture. But it has been this wall, or tower really, for a wall does not necessarily contain all that it surrounds, which has allowed me to retain most of the values which I had been taught. This attitude, of course, has cost me dear at times. Living in a tower, however secure it may feel, is hardly a social attribute. It can give the impression that one is withdrawn, insular and distant. *Not* the accepted qualities for an Actor, where the very reverse is apparently required. It was said of me recently that I suffered from an Obsessional Privacy. I can only suppose it must be true. And it is doubtless because of this that I have never reached the highest peak of my profession. It held me back, mercifully, from "playing the game" to the hilt with the Bosses, the people in power. In a profession rife with insecurity this obsessional privacy was regarded with dislike and suspicion. In the years that I made money for them the Bosses grudgingly accepted this "fault", but as soon as I stepped out of line to change my direction and fight along with forward-looking Directors like Dearden, Losey, Schlesinger and Clayton, my general popularity waned and the box office receipts crashed accordingly. The films we made so passionately together were considered "intellectual". The people who had paid good money to see my Little-Boy-Looking-For-God look were *very* unimpressed, and started to stay away in droves. The films were, by and large, critical successes but box office failures. The Cinema demands that you make money for it at no matter what cost. I recall one of those over-tailored moguls, itching to "do" his "bob" at the Palace, saying pleasantly: "They don't want that kind of stuff. THEY want tits and bums. Or the Burtons." Since I was not in that category I quickly found myself unemployable. A cold wind was blowing. It was everywhere. Even the Studios were starting to crumble and close down under the almost intolerable pressures from within. By 1966 I was splendidly on the skids.

But there was a candle glowing in the window of my discomfort. Hollywood, Italy and France could, it seemed, keep me occupied with the kind of work I still wished to try to do for some considerable time. Nearing fifty, it seemed prudent therefore to follow the beckoning light from Abroad. And abroad in the first instance was personified by Luchino Visconti. My father reluctantly agreed. Either I stayed where I was and went broke, returned to the Theatre after many years absence, or tried my novice hand at Television. These alternatives seemed distinctly chilly.

"Then clear off, my dear," he said. "Start again. Go where they want you."

It had not escaped our minds that "to start again" would mean leaving England. We looked at each other bleakly. However it was not the England of my Summer Life which I should be forced to leave, it was a fast changing England. A country bent determinedly on its quiet revolution, led by people who, with avuncular joviality, constantly assured the Middle Classes that they were all doomed. And, not unnaturally, people wanted new faces; mine had been hanging about for over twenty years, and a change was needed. From all points of view, then, it seemed sensible to accept the invitations from abroad. But . . . but . . .

"Whatever you do, my dear, don't shilly shally," said my father, pouring himself a Worthington. "Do it neatly; mitre your corners."

I sold my house, paid all my bills, and left. Perhaps the final bricks in my tower.

Paradise regained is an impossibility. It is not, perhaps, always even desirable; and in any case is denied to most mortals. However, I tried. With no regrets whatsoever. The day I pushed open the door of this silent, empty house, standing on its hill since 1641, sunlight slanting across the tiled floors, a vine fretworking the wide windows, another Great Meadow lying all about, I knew that, in a physical sense at least, I had at last got back to the Summer Life.

Almost intact.

13

A NUMBER 11 bus set me down at The Six Bells, Kings Road, and from there, just across the road, past a row of crumbling Regency houses, is Manresa Road and the Chelsea Poly. Up the broad stone steps and through the big swing doors and I had started, in my own mind, my first steps towards the Theatre. Although no one else but myself knew that.

At first it was considered, and with reason, that I was too young to attend the Poly. I was not quite seventeen. However Williamson, the Principal, had seen a folio of my "work", that is to say examples of stage designs, costumes, and illustrations for plays which I had written but which, naturally, had not been performed. Vaguely impressed, as he himself said, by my sense of colour design and "inventiveness", he waived the few months needed to make me as it were "legal" and I started on my way.

Some weeks before, my patient father took me to Gamages, to a Fire Sale which he had seen advertised, and within an hour, among piles of slightly damp and smoky garments on the top floor, outfitted me in a grey tweed suit, a bottle green striped one, a sundry collection of woollen polo necked sweaters and a pair of brogue shoes, one size too large, in suede.

I was enraptured. These, and the obligatory "smock" which we all had to wear, were to constitute my entire wardrobe for some time to come. I almost slept in the bottle green suit I liked it so much, and the brogue shoes, stuffed with a little wad of paper, gave me a stature and dignity I must otherwise have lacked. At least so I thought.

This was a very different atmosphere from the school on the Hill. No hulking lumps here itching to kick something, no shared desks, no dustbin lunches. Instead, high, airy rooms, quiet, purposeful people, sitting on stools indulging in the highest form of luxury to me, just painting, drawing and even, at times, doodling away. We signed a book on entrance to each Class and on our departure for luncheon, usually a beer and a sandwich at the Six Bells or a Lyons Tea Shop near Sloane Square—not a beer there, of course, warm tea in a thick cup, but still . . . it was not a meat pie and Cola.

194

The Classes were a mixed assembly of people, sexes and ages. I was astonished, and encouraged, to find that my neighbour in "Illustration" was a woman as old as my grandmother with a smock, a floppy felt hat, a raffia bag full of paints and brushes, rubbers and pens, her sandwiches and a small flask of Brandy from which, during the morning, she would take a strengthening swig.

There were pretty girls with long blonde hair who were really not serious artists, but merely "Finishing Orf", as they called it—and who painted endless chains of pussy cats, blue-birds or bunnies, and seldom came back after the lunch break. Others, like Erica Schwartz, were far more serious. Smocked, sandalled, rather grubby, she and her companions worked industriously in "Design" covering yards of material with abstract patterns of blue and mauve which they then turned into skirts and shirts, and stamped about the corridors pinning notices on the Notice Board bearing large Hammers and Sickles. They, these industrious girls, and some men, also ran the Dramatic Society which I was allowed, in spite of my age, to join, so that I could help with the painting of the scenery and the making of the costumes and also to swell the chorus which used to sing "Red Fly the Banners O!" to the tune of "Green Grow the Rushes O!" It was all magical, exhilarating, bursting with promise. I had never, I believed, even at the Cottage, been so happy in my life before.

My first "task"—we were usually set a "task" at the beginning of every week to set us on a line of thought or design—was to design the cover for a book. In this particular case H. E. Bates' *The Poacher*. This of course, normally, meant that one had to read the book, or intelligently "skip through" it in order to get at the "essence", as it was always called. What the "essence" was depended entirely on what one *thought* it meant. And one's work was judged accordingly. I had read the book and set to, as I so often do, without much care and preparation. My sketch book was a riot of fields, woods, dead rabbits and panoramas of Great Britain from Lulworth Cove to Ben Nevis. H. E. Bates' simple tale was illustrated, by me at any rate, as the natural history handbook of the British Isles, including every single beast which lived within them and some which did not. I was enormously impressed by my own efforts and, as usual, embellished my design with guns and traps, fishing rods, gaffing hooks and snares. I left nothing out. And nothing to the imagination. At the Wednesday

Class, covered with pride and a singular lack of humility (everyone else was still at the "blocking in stage") I offered my finished cover to our patient, calm, gentle teacher, Graham Sutherland. In his neat farmer's smock, his pale blue knitted tie, with his small dark head and steady piercing eyes, I found him the kindest and most encouraging of all the teachers at the School. He was rather frightening too, because he smiled often, spoke very little; one was never certain of what he exactly thought. And he was not about to give anything away.

Patiently this day he sat beside me, dragging up a stool to my desk, slowly he examined my startling, lurid, finished cover. Gently he explained that I might have possibly missed the point of the exercise. It was not, he said, to tell the entire story of Mr Bates on the cover, but rather to leave that to the reader to find out for himself which, after all, was the author's job. Mine, he said gently, as the designer, was to suggest to the reader what he might find beneath the wrappers; to offer him some simple, uncomplicated, symbol which he could recognise enough to tempt him to read the book. Not something which would convince him that he had read it already, or worse, that he knew what it was all about and didn't want to read it anyway.

Swiftly, economically, he drew a face, a cloth cap, some rabbits' legs, a long waving line which was clearly a field of corn, and the entire subject was before me. I apologised in a mumble. He was anxious. "But are you *sure* you know what I mean? Simplicity, you see . . . just the suggestion. The essence. Not," he said gently, "a map of England with all its Blood Sports."

I started again much cast down but already agreeing, how could I not, that he was right. But *how* to simplify . . . how to find the "essence"? That was my problem, and eventually stealing from him shamelessly I did my design by the end of the week and got top marks.

But the discovery was magical, I mean the general discovery. Being treated as an equal, as an already proved, which I was not, artist, gave me back a great deal of ebbing courage. I drew and drew and covered page after page of sketch books with a wild assortment of ideas which I then was forced to condense, simplify, coordinate, in short . . . design. It was not, I was quick to find out mercifully, quite the same as merely "Drawing".

Drawing was much harder. Drawing meant, for me, the Life Class. A serious, grimy room. A wide semi-circle of stools round a battered rostrum on which reclined, or stood, in patient humility, and bored indifference, a naked woman or, at times, man. Always ugly, always thin or vastly fat, as unacceptable naked as they must have been fully clothed.

In winter they froze to liver-sausage blue in the arctic room, warmed only vaguely by a one bar electric fire, around which they huddled at the "rests" in tatty silk kimonos—in the summer they baked and broiled under the relentless glare of the sun from the skylight windows—all for a pittance an hour. Eyes glazed with boredom, they saw past and beyond us, locked into a frozen area of numbness from which nothing save the ringing of the alarm clock, to tell them their time was up, could release them.

Although, up until then, I had never seen an entirely naked woman, I was completely unmoved. I only remember being saddened by the sight of so much ugly flesh humped so dejectedly in a bent-wood chair. I found drawing their ugliness far harder to cope with than anything else. It seemed that if I started off with a head the left foot usually ended up miles off the bottom of the page and somewhere in the region of my own feet. However much I held up my pencil to measure, as I saw the other students doing with great professionalism, I never got the proportions right, and in spite of constant rubbings-out and starting-agains, the human body defeated me entirely. I sweated on and for ageless days sat in a smaller room with some others who found it as hard as I did, studying and drawing, in vicious detail, every bone and socket in a range of dusty skeletons which hung, dangling feet and hands, from wooden gibbets, swinging forlornly in the draughts.

"Try not to bother with her too much," said Henry Moore, who took us for Life and, later on, Sculpture. "She's not much good really, but it's very hard to get skeletons these days. Very hard indeed. She's pretty young, this one, mid-twenties I'd say . . . died some time about 1890. You see the rib cage? All squashed up, those dreadful corsets of theirs. How did she breathe for God's sake? You see? Squashed tight. Quite useless for you really. No Form there, simply de-formed. Shocking really. But it's the best we have at the moment." Smocked, and with a woolly tie, he too moved among his pupils quietly and gently, correcting and suggesting here and there, patient with the slow, glowing with the more advanced of us. Wanting to share his obvious delight and love of the Human Body. "This absolute miracle of co-ordination, of muscle and bone. A brilliant conception never yet beaten," he said.

But it took me a long time to come towards sharing his delight. And although I sat spellbound if he came to my board to tug a muscle or a joint into place, or scribbled a rapid explanation for me on the side of my disordered, erased, smudged drawing, his swathed, mostly faceless figures reminded me a little too sharply of Mr Dodd's mummies ever to re-kindle a dying interest in the Human Form. I served him better in Perspective, and he was encouraging and kind, and when I said, rather timidly, that I wanted to go in for Stage Design rather than any other form of art he set to with enthusiasm and bashed me into Vanishing Points and Source of Light until, little by little, I abandoned almost altogether Life Class and attended, as often as I could, and more often than I should, Perspective. Which is why, to this day, I can still do a remarkably good bird's eye view of the Piazza San Marco, Times Square or even Kennington Oval looking as if they had been struck by bubonic plague. My perspectives are empty. However I am very good at people leaning out of windows. That's about as far as Mr Moore, with all his patient efforts, ever got me.

If I was hopeless at Life Class I was making tremendous strides towards becoming a Playwright. The Cox family was exceedingly encouraging and welcomed me into their family. Every evening, after I had returned from Art School, I would cycle over to "Chez Nous" and spend a great deal of time with Nerine, who was soft, blonde, gentle and deeply interested in all my theories; discussing the ideas for a new play, the plots and even the sets. We wrote poetry together and spent hours in the depths of Rotherfield Woods talking of my Future. We never, it seemed, ever got around to hers. And at no time did we discuss the world around us which was steadily becoming more and more troubled but which caused us no apparent concern. The pronoun "I" fell rapidly and confidently from our lips. Except that her "I" was "You". Which I felt was just as it should be. Eventually, from all this airy chatter and from all these floating plans about my Future a play got written. It was called "The Man On The Bench" and starred Nerine as the Prostitute and myself as the Man. As far as I can recall it was a very long monologue for me interrupted, only here and there, by Nerine dressed in black satin and a feather boa.

The trick was the surprise ending when the Prostitute left in a huff and the Man fumbled about in the skirts of his overcoat producing a white stick. Blind, you see.

Very moving. I don't quite know why I had not given the entire plot away from the start for I fixed my eyes in a steady glazed stare at a point somewhere beyond Ashdown Forest and never let it waver. It went on at the Village Hall and was well received by a rather sparse audience who had other things on their minds since, a day or so before, Germany had annexed Austria. This irritated me more than anything else. We had a poor house, and I felt that the Message of the play was unfairly judged. However I cheered up considerably when I realised that within a few days I should be seventeen and Mr Cox had offered me my first leading role in a "real" play which was to be the September Event of the Village.

It was decided by the all male Committee of the Newick Amateur Dramatic Society, known as the NADS, to do an all male play With A Warning. "Journey's End" was selected as being the most suitable—a reasonable cast, one set, and timely in a year of mounting tensions. I was to play Raleigh. I started to learn the French's acting edition there and then.

In the meantime the rest of life was going on in its implacable way, which in no way affected me much until the death of beloved Mrs Jane and shortly afterwards that of Grandfather Aimé. A slight stroke and growing incontinence finally forced his departure from the grubby house by the West Pier into his clean, spartan, nursing home in Kemp Town.

Enraged at being removed forcefully, as he said, he gave one of his cronies in the Junk Trade a five pound note to strip out the house. My parents arrived to collect him one morning as two packed vans drove away from the mouldy square. He retained a few "Treasures" with which to furnish his room at Kemp Town; the rest were dispersed all over Sussex, some even landing up at Christie's months later. There was nothing to be done, everything was perfectly legal, and my distressed parents managed only to retrieve a Nanking jar, a black ebony table, and a pile of National Geographical Magazines. Grandpapa's spite had won. And it finally killed him off, loathing his Matron, smoking like a chimney, and wilfully peeing all over his faded Aubusson. He went almost as suddenly as he had entered, or re-entered, our lives. Singularly unmissed and shortly forgotten.

Rehearsals for "Journey's End" started amidst the growing tension in Europe. Not, perhaps, the wisest of plays to attempt on the threshold of a new war—although that did seem rather unlikely to me once I had been reassured, by gentle Nerine, that I would not be called up until I was at least nineteen, which gave me two years, and no war, no modern war that is to say, could possibly last *that* long. Also, she had heard it said at the Red Cross and in the St John's Ambulance Brigade, to which she was devoting more and more of her time, that all the German Tanks were made of cardboard and the Population were half starving, having neither milk nor meat nor butter.

My father, needless to say, did not share these opinions and was longer and longer at "The Times" than he was at home. All about us a disturbing feeling of apprehension was stirring. People were getting restless and even starting to dig trenches in the London parks. Erica Schwartz and her friends got more and more frantic and held long urgent meetings in the Common Room and begged us all to be Conscientious Objectors, which I thought might be quite a good idea the way things were moving. One of my special new girl friends, a golden blonde with a white sports car and a father who made shoes in Czechoslovakia, one day was no longer at Class and we heard that she had suddenly been ordered back to Prague. I was very depressed because she was beautiful, rich, clever and liked me to the extent of cooking me baked beans on toast on her gas ring in a crumby little flat which she rented for fun in Jubilee Place. I was astonished that she should leave without even sending me a note for we had become, I thought, very Close Friends . . . however, she went. The Govonis had been recalled to Rome some time before, but Giovanna was sent back to stay with us for a holiday to "keep up her English". The telephone now rang almost constantly from Rome with worried appeals to get her back as soon as possible. My father and I drove her down to a boat at Newhaven and shoved her up the bursting gangway filled with anxious people carrying bags and suitcases. We waited on the quay until eventually a small, weeping red-headed figure fought her way to the stern waving, sobbing and crying out "I love you. I'll never forget you. Goodbye, Goodbye." The sirens went, gulls screeched and the packed ship moved gently away from us.

She stood there waving and waving until the ship made a slow turn to port at the end of the long jetty and bore her away, out of my sight, for twenty-three years.

My father and I were very quiet driving home through the lanes to the house. He only spoke once, when we stopped at the Chalk Pit outside Lewes for a beer.

"I can't really believe," he said, "that it is all going to happen again."

The rehearsals for the NADS were cancelled. No one seemed to have the heart to read through a play which was regrettably becoming more and more timely. Added to which it was difficult to get the cast together because people suddenly had extra things to do in their spare time, and Cissie Waghorn, who had a car, dragooned and bullied myself and a boy from Fairwarp called Buster into driving about the county fitting elderly people with gas marks and explaining to them the problems of Blast and Blackouts.

Influenced by all this activity and talk of a new War, and very much by "Journey's End", I started to paint, exhaustingly, scenes from the first World War. I read every book I could lay my hands on in my father's study ranging from *All Quiet On The Western Front*, *The Seven Pillars of Wisdom*, *The War Of The Guns* to the Michelin *Guides to the Battlefields*. William Orpen, John and Paul Nash became my idols, and my bedroom was covered with reproductions of their works. I was *quite* convinced that I was painting in this fury because I was the reincarnation of a young soldier who had been killed in 1917. Nothing would budge me from the belief; the output of my work was prodigious, leading Sutherland to say that it was probably better to "get it out of my system" and exercise my imagination. He was very patient and understanding and knew full well that no reincarnation was taking place, simply a release from too much emotionalism.

In this welter of second hand grief, anxiety, and something which was rapidly approaching self-pity, the Polytechnic closed down for the Summer Recess and, armed with my paints and brushes plus a bursting portfolio of agonizing scenes in the blazing ruins of Ypres, Albert with its leaning Virgin and sundry portions of the entire Western Front, I glumly headed for Sussex, Nerine and the fitting of yet more gas masks. I felt lost, worried and disconnected. Even though my last reports from the Art School had been glowing and highly encouraging, I felt within me the interest and love for Art slowly ebbing. I knew, instinctively, that I would never be a successful painter, for the simple reason that I did not want to be. I had no dedication but a totally God-given talent which I truthfully wished could be directed towards the main love of my life: the Theatre. And my father's sudden and extraordinary decision, already planned long before I knew anything about it, to send me off to study the process of colour photogravure at The Sun Engraving Co Ltd at Watford came like a bolt from the proverbial blue and only increased my growing despair. If I had given up the idea of the career laid down for me it was quite clear that his mind was still quietly working towards Printing House Square.

Accordingly, one hot July morning, I presented myself at the Works in Whippendall Road, was warmly welcomed, and bustled into "digs" in an ugly terrace house in a long red brick street half a mile away. My landlady, a widow with tight yellow curls and a diamond brooch in her orange cardigan, showed me my room at the top of the stairs, hoped that I'd be "comfy" and said that all meals would be taken in the front parlour with herself and her son, who was a coffin polisher. Tea, she said, would be very soon and she would hit the gong when it was ready. My room, floored with dead brown linoleum, had a wide double bed, a washbowl with jug and a florid brass clock on the mantel which played eight bars of "The Sunshine Of Your Smile" at the hours and, like Bishopbriggs, struck all the quarters.

I learned absolutely nothing during my stay in the Sun Engraving Works. Not for want of teaching; people were wonderfully good and did everything they could to make me comprehend and enjoy the "job" which I was to follow through. Colour printing was still fairly new at that time and it was my father's greatest ambition, one day, to see the picture page of *The Times* in glowing colour. It was, apart from Northcliffe and all the Astors and their Newspaper, his consuming passion. As a very small child I remember, in the studio in St George's Road, my mother standing about swathed in bolts of coloured silks while my father and Logie Baird photographed her from different rooms, I presume, with an early Television Camera. It was all very home-made and it is all rather vague in my memory. However, it was a passion which filtered into the house and into all of us, and I clearly recall the pride and excitement of seeing the first colour photograph ever taken by ordinary stage lighting in a Theatre. It was a glass plate of Pavlova dancing "The Dying Swan" and she received it, apparently with gratitude and delight, according to her letter; that small rectangle of softly coloured glass (the second one) remained my father's most treasured possession, for it represented the culmination of years of experiment, bullying, cajoling and stubborn insistence for which he was entirely responsible.

But the love was not being transmitted to the son. Although I followed every single process from re-touching to the stapling and final folding of one wretched magazine as it came thudding off the machines, absolutely nothing whatsoever went in to my bewildered brain. I returned to the family home a little thinner, more determined than ever to try and avoid anything whatsoever to do with newspapers, and the cheerful owner of two blue budgerigars which someone in the Print Shop, who bred them, had given me. They had been in the house three days when Minnehaha, the cat, ate them: and vanished as swiftly as my father's hopes of his vision of my future.

A few nights later we drove down to Croydon Airport to meet one of his photographers who was, he hoped, on the last flight out of Prague. Standing in the dark waiting for the plane to come in he suddenly said: "I suppose really that this is a very demanding profession. I think one really has to want to do it very much to make it work . . . I love it so much, as you know, that I wanted you to share it with me. But it is no good forcing you: I can see that it's got to be something which is in you, and it is clearly not in you. Never mind." And that was all he ever said. A little later the plane arrived, a long lumbering corrugated iron cigar with wings. His photographer came down the gangway, tie-less, dishevelled, clutching a small case and his camera. He was very distressed.

Driving through Streatham he suddenly said: "Christ! Oh Christ! They pulled this woman off and shoved me on. It was the last plane you see. She kept screaming and crying. I held the door against her, they were all battering at the side of the damned thing, crying, begging. I'll never forget her, I'll never forget her."

A profession, I thought miserably, that you really have to want to do to "make it work".

It all stopped with Mr Chamberlain's piece of white paper, blowing in the wind, and "Peace In Our Time". Joy and relief were so gigantic that no one seemed to stop for a second to consider *whose* time he meant, his, or ours. But it was enough.

Back went the rehearsals of "Journey's End" now even more potent with message. It was a tremendous success. The Hall was packed for three nights solid, and people came from as far afield as Lewes and Haywards Heath. The emotion among our audiences was tangible. My set (I had been allowed to design it) was highly accurate after my "studies" and my own performance was warmly received. Raleigh is a cinch anyway, but I didn't know that then.

My wretched father, who detested anything which remotely reminded him of his own brutal war, was eventually dragged to see me on the final Saturday night. Sitting with my proud mother he was, he later said, very moved. Not unnaturally. But he still was not about to weaken completely on his decision about my career. An actor's life was still not discussed.

"Was I really all right?" I asked my mother.

"Yes really, you were very good indeed. I was proud."

"But when I hit that damned plate on the table and it flew into the audience . . ."

"That was *when* I knew you could be an actor, darling, you let it go as if you had meant it to go. No one moved in the audience, you know, no one at all. You had controlled the move and made them feel that it was true, and not a mistake."

"It really was all right?"

"That's what acting is all about," said my mother. "Convince yourself and convince them. Never one without the other." She was not entirely accurate, but near enough. And without quite knowing it. "Always Applauded" was stirring it up with a vengeance.

★ ★ ★

In October 1938 Elissa Thorburn, an elderly lady of moderate means, built and opened a theatre in a buttercup field just behind the Station and next to the Coach Terminus, at Uckfield. I had noticed, riding about the area with Nerine, the red brick form take place, but had quite thought it was to be a new factory or a building for the Public Works. It was, however, to be "the most modern, comfortable, best designed theatre in Sussex". Miss Thorburn had bullied and cajoled money from various sources, mostly her own, and the theatre opened with a shrill of local publicity and a performance of "Noah", by André Obey. And she used real actors from London, not us amateurs. Except that we were asked to come along and help out by playing Crowd or small parts for which she did not pay. The First Night was splendid with the Reigning Families and anyone else who could afford the not excessively cheap price of the seats.

Unhappily Miss Thorburn had already started to alienate the Local Council by refusing to put on plays which she considered suitable only for the, what she called, Hoi Poloi . . . that is to say, no "Rookery Nook", no "Charley's Aunt". It was to be "The Dramatic Glyndebourne," she said. And made a slight error here to start with. Never alienate your Local Councillors who consider that they are not Hoi Poloi but like a good "Rookery Nook"; and don't choose a small market town which never even went to the local cinema except on wet Saturdays and then only if "Tarzan" was running or the Home Team was playing Worthing at Bolton. The local councillors were bewildered by "Noah", insulted by the unhappy phrase "Hoi Poloi" and hated the cold, brick, functional theatre behind the Railway Station. Theatres, they reckoned, for the money that they had all contributed, should be gold and red and filled with a "good bit of family entertainment."

Not for them translations from the French about a Biblical figure, set in a cold warehouse. And having to wear a black tie as well in the weekday evenings was asking a bit too much all round. However they did notice that there was no central aisle, and therefore there could be an infringement of the Safety Regulations. But that point came a little later. For the moment only the anger mounted. One day, passing the theatre in as casual a way as I could manage, I found the doors open and wandered into the cool, dark, auditorium.

One working light gleamed on the stage. A tall, tweedy, woman was painting, not very well, a canvas flat. Seeing me standing among her brand new seats, only one play old, she straightened up, waving a paint-brush in my direction and told me to be off.

"Shoo!" she cried. "Shoo!" Her hair had fallen round her face like straw; she was hot and cross. I stood. "What do you want with me? Be off, boy!" Her anger was clear.

"I want a job," I said.

"What kind of a job . . .?"

"I paint scenery. I'm an artist."

"I don't need a scenic designer . . . Are you strong?"

I said I was and she told me to come across the seats and on to the stage and together we manhandled a large Austrian stove into a corner. I stayed the rest of the day there, painted a number of flats, screwed the handles on to a chest of drawers and accepted her grudging offer of a shilling an hour when I worked.

Over the next few months, in all my spare time and every weekend, I went to the Uckfield Theatre and worked with Miss Thorburn to get the place ready for the Spring Performance. It transpired that she had seen me in "Journey's End", having used as many of the NADS as she could, to save money and "to give them valuable experience" in the production of "Noah". Covered as they had been in furs and masks I had not recognised any of them, but that was not of importance. They were, I reckoned, amateurs whereas I already earned my way and was doing it as a dedication. The new production was to be "Glorious Morning", a heavy play about a Democracy being invaded by a Fascist State. It didn't bother me one way or the other until, with one bright eye on expenses, she offered me a part and said that she would pay me five shillings a performance. The fact that I was twenty years too young for the role didn't worry either of us; however I did agree that a black leather coat, a hat and a heavy moustache, would assist me in my "performance". We finished off the sets, rigged all the lighting together, and by the time the Real Actors arrived from London, at the end of April, we were ready to go. Except for the rehearsals which she, as director and producer, and sole owner of her Dream, would conduct personally.

I arrived, that first morning, long before anyone else. I was excessively nervous and it was also my job to open up the theatre, arrange the stage for the reading and see that there was lavatory paper in the lavatories and a packet of Typhoo tea in the little kitchen. There were also a dozen cups and two packets of Crawford's Custard Creams. I parked my bike by the scene dock, opened the Theatre, seeing the wide beams of sunlight streak across the blue velvet seats, set the "props" and took my copy of the play out into the buttercup field and sat under a giant oak. I felt that, as I was just about to commence my Acting Career, it might be wiser not to sit anxiously huddled on the bare stage too eagerly waiting, but to go and sit in the fields and start it all off from the peace and the calm of the country which I so loved. When they were ready, I reckoned, they'd come for me. Never be over anxious.

Someone came ruffling through the long nodding grasses behind me, whistling softly. I looked up from my script. A tall, well built, smiling man of about thirty stood before me looking oddly out of place in the buttercups dressed, as he was, in a double-breasted suit, brown suede shoes, long white cuffs with gold links and a rather faded carnation in his buttonhole. One of the actors for sure.

"Hullo," he said. "Do you work here?"

"Yes. At the theatre. I'm an actor."

"So am I. I hate First Readings, don't you?"

I didn't know but agreed. He offered me a piece of barley sugar which he assured me was excellent for energy and also for the voice. We started to walk towards the Theatre, a brick box glinting in the morning sun; there were people wandering in and out of the doors. My companion started to breathe deeply, throwing his arms wide as if he was about to take off and fly over the town. I was still wearing my cycle clips and we laughed as I pulled them off and shoved them into a pocket.

"My name's Wightman," he said. "William, but they call me Bill. I just think I'll have a quick pee before we go in, do you know where it is?"

I told him and watched his tall, burly figure going round the side of the Theatre to the Gents.

My first counsellor and adviser had arrived.

The weeks which followed, up until the opening of the play, were filled with joys and excitements. The other actors, with the generosity of their kind, welcomed me into their midst and we all settled down as one tightly knit company. An oddity of living which only actors seem to be able to achieve. This effect of permanence in a very temporary situation.

Bill Wightman became our leader; he was always jolly, kind, patient, amused and also the possessor of a modest, but adequate, private income which he always most generously shared with us. He also had a car, which, locked into the quietness of a pretty dull, if pretty, country town, was absolutely essential and proved a much needed escape for us all to rarer places like Eastbourne, Brighton or even London. Quite apart from his own considerable personal charm, warmth and wisdom, Bill's car was the Pipe in Hamelin, if he could be called, as he was, the Piper. But he was as much sought after for his advice and counsel as any of the more obvious pleasures which he could give. Every young Actor, or Actress, is plagued by the most appalling doubts and fears and only another actor can really share or understand them.

So it was with Bill. His patience was monumental, his

encouragement enormous, his good humour apparently inexhaustible, and his ear always available to listen to the problems with which we burdened him almost continually.

The play opened to critical acclaim from the local papers, and to a financial disaster. Not enough people wanted to come to a grim play about Middle Europe and the Fascists when they had narrowly avoided the problem for themselves only a few months ago. The Town was split into two groups, those who thought the Theatre was an asset to the place and those who thought a Hospital would be more useful. There were rumbles of dissent among the gentle hills of East Sussex. Talk of Rates and Taxes and Robbing the People, of Intellectuals pushing Propaganda plays in a Civic Theatre when the theatre, as everyone knew, was supposed to be there for Entertainment. There was also the vexed problem of no Centre Aisle and what would happen in a fire, they'd all like to know?

The dissent grew so strong that Miss Thorburn herself, cycling back to her cottage in Nutley one evening, was set upon by children and stoned while they all yelled "Witch! Witch!" causing her to fall from her bike and severely cut her knee and an eye.

It didn't stop her one jot. Sitting in her study, her leg up on a stool, reading through a magnifying glass with her Good Eye, she went through countless plays searching for her next production.

My father, driven to distraction by my insistence now that I should become an Actor, with so much success clearly turning my head, arranged an audition for me at the Old Vic. I still don't know how he did it but suspect that owing to his position on "The Times" and the help which he had given them in the past by putting in photographs of the Productions as often as he could, they felt a little blackmailed and I was summoned to the Theatre on Tuesday, August the 8th at 2.30. Armed with three "well contrasted pieces" as demanded by the proprietors, I walked up and down the Waterloo Road mumbling away at "Is This A Dagger?" from "Macbeth", the whole of Blunden's "Forefathers" which begins:

> "Here they went with smock and crook,
> Toiled in the sun, lolled in the shade,
> Here they mudded out the brook . . ."

which I found moving, referring as it did to the Last War, and the country life I loved; and also a frightful chunk of my mono-

7(a) Myself as Raleigh, Mr (Lionel) Cox as Osborne in
"Journey's End", Newick, 1938.

7(b) William Wightman (far right) with members of the Company.
Eric Rutherford, Peggy Pritchard, Uckfield, June 1939.

8(a) My father in his office at Printing House Square, "The Times", 1938.

8(b) Satyres Wood, the Somme, 1916. One of the many "agonized sketches" from my 1938–39 sketch books at the Chelsea Poly. This was probably pinched from an old photograph.

logue from the play I had written for the NADS about the poor blind man on his bench. Nothing light, clearly. I don't remember, for all my terror, much about the audition except that I am sure it amused them more than impressed them, and the glittering cold eyes of Tyrone Guthrie frightened me more than anything ever before. They were, to paraphrase a description of Aldous Huxley's, "pale blue and triangular, like the eyes peering from the mask of a Siamese cat". But, much to everyone's astonishment, I passed, and was accepted to hold spears and carry swords and possibly play "one of Romeo's Friends", in the forthcoming production of that play which would start rehearsals on September the 4th.

In my green Gamages suit, I ran almost all the way to Victoria, in spite of the extremely hot day, and telephoned my father at the office to tell him. He was calm and rather quiet. He said that he would write immediately to Williamson at the Chelsea Poly and hoped now that I was satisfied. He didn't say that he was.

Williamson's letter in return was regretful. He felt, he said, that I had talent far above average and that it seemed a pity to let it all go—but this meant nothing to me for I didn't even know of the letter until many years afterwards. For the time being my horizons were vast. I would start with my spears and swords and being "one of Romeo's Friends" and bit by bit, for I was in no hurry and realised that it would be a slow process, I would eventually become one of those glorious, and honoured, people who could call themselves Classical Actors. I never wanted, then, to become a Star. I never remotely sought, as so many of my contemporaries did, my Name In Lights—I didn't want the responsibilities that would bring; all I wanted to do was to achieve respect, acknowledgement, and honour in the profession for which I longed.

If this sounds naive and dimwitted then so I was. All I can say, from all this distance, is that that is what I felt and what I still feel to this day. It never changed.

My mother was, secretly, very pleased. But she hardly did more than give me a hug and remind me that my pleasure must be equalled only by the disappointment of my father who had hoped, and worked, for so long to encourage me to take over from him when his time came to retire.

Bill, in whom I now confided constantly, which must have irritated him a good deal but which he never let show, was delighted and counselled me to be patient, humble, and, above all, diligent, to work very hard and deserve the honour of having been admitted to, what he called, one of the most distinguished companies of actors in the entire world. I promised him that I would.

A few weeks before I had gone down to see him in a series of plays which were being performed in a tithe barn at Shere in Surrey. The barn was draughty, dark, up a little grassy track behind the village. The actors welcomed me into the company as if I were a member and permitted me to watch every play, and nearly every performance, free and when I liked. The plays were all rather, what the Uckfield Council Members would have called Intellectual, and so were most of the audiences, and although I was not always able to follow the plots I was vividly aware of what my grandfather in Scotland had told me sitting beside his range in the kitchen in Glasgow. The lovely words . . . I revelled in the sounds and shapes of them, in the things they evoked for me, in the astonishing beauty of them.

I fed, all that season, on words as if they were my main form of nourishment: which spiritually indeed they were. Everyone, as I have said, was very friendly, but especially one actor, a youth of my own age, whose enthusiasms and excitement exactly matched my own. In a pair of wrinkled tights with a shock of wild hair, bright eager eyes and wild gestures, he sat with me on the grass outside the Barn watching the audiences arrive up the scraggy little path and spoke passionately, and fluently, of his love and his dedication for his job. We were born, we discovered, on exactly the same day of the same month of the same year—and almost to the hour. I felt, therefore, a very close affinity to him, and although he had gone much further ahead than I, for he not only acted but wrote and had written the main play of the Season, I felt that as we both so clearly held exactly the same beliefs, hopes, ideals and burning passions for our craft, that in fact we almost were twins, and given time and the chance I would one day catch him up and together we should storm the world.

"But," he said, brushing the grass off his tights and starting towards the big stage door, "you have to be totally dedicated. Totally. Nothing else will do here." I wasn't absolutely sure what he meant by dedication, but his intensity was such that I clearly understood that to follow my profession correctly and successfully had to be almost a form of religion. This important encounter with Peter Ustinov was to prove the final blow to my patient father. My passion and determination were so great, that he finally capitulated, and I was offered the audition at the Old Vic.

$$\star \quad \star \quad \star$$

Four days before I was due to make my way along the Waterloo Road to my first rehearsal Germany invaded Poland. My father's face at breakfast was very grave, my mother's ashen.

"I don't think that this time we'll avoid it," he said.

Never had the sun shone so splendidly, never had the Common lain so still in a haze of heat and shimmering light. Never had the Old Vic seemed so far away.

On the Saturday evening, dressed in my green suit and a yellow polo neck shirt, I went off with Buster and Cissie Waghorn and a thin girl whose name I don't remember. We drove in Buster's car to a Road House near East Grinstead and had lager and roast lamb.

Afterwards through a sudden, crashing thunderstorm, we drove, almost in silence, all the way to Brighton. The town was deserted. Few cars, and those that were were dimmed out, few lights—it was a half blackout—no one walking. The holiday-makers had melted away. We were alone on the deserted promenade. Buster parked the car under a lamp by the King Alfred's School, and we hung over the promenade railings looking down at the black sea and then the rumbling, fading storm, moving slowly across to France. The car radio was playing softly and we started, very quietly, to dance together, cheek to cheek, holding on to each other Cissie and I, and Buster and the thin girl. Lightning flashed in great silent forks across the hot, swelling sea, the surf rustled and clawed on the shingle below, and to the gentle crackling strains of "Deep Purple" we slowly, unhappily, shuffled into the war.

14

THE launching of a nation into a war seemed, to me at least, remarkably like the launching of a great ship. In Scotland I had seen the slow, ponderous slide of the 534, later to be called the *Queen Mary*, as it inched down the slipway into the river. At one moment it was quite still. At the next, almost imperceptibly, it moved away from its berth, snapping poles like spaghetti, chains like cotton threads, and as it gained speed, growing ever faster, the rusty metal mass hit the water sending up a swelling tidal wave which rippled higher and higher and faster and faster across the river and engulfed the crowds on the opposite bank.

But it was all, or so it seemed, in silence. In slow motion, without the benefit of cheers, flags or bands playing. We were overawed. So it was with the start of the war, almost the same actions from start to finish.

In the first instance everything melted away. Chelsea Poly remained firmly shut; theatres, including the Old Vic, and cinemas closed; silver balloons rose gently into the air ringing London; and everyone who could, or had to, went into one Service or another. And all the lights went out.

In the first eager flush I, with others of my own age, hurried to our local Labour Exchanges to volunteer, only to be told, by harassed clerks, that we would not be wanted until we had reached the age of nineteen. I had a year to go. Buster, more fortunate than I by virtue of being nineteen already, got into the RAF and was blown to bits over Kent the following summer; Cissie went off to Portsmouth and became a WREN; and Nerine, trained and able, and becoming bossier and bossier as the days went by, was organising herself very securely into the Red Cross and Ambulance Brigade. Everyone, it seemed, was busy except me.

Life was spent in a limbo of unwantedness. Until I was organised to help clear out countless empty sheds, garages, stables and barns which had been commandeered to receive the first of the sad, bewildered, evacuees who came hourly from London, lugging crying children, bursting suitcases, and stuck about with humiliating cardboard labels. These wretched women were soon taken in charge by officious, but kindly, County Ladies who bundled them off in trucks or cars to their straw-filled shelters with cups of tea and five cigarettes apiece.

Miss Thorburn's Theatre was one of the first places to be taken over, and with its seats stripped out, filled with straw, provided miserable bed spaces for a couple of hundred. Everyone who could took in their own evacuees. We had two pale, nervous, unhappy brothers who arrived one afternoon and stayed for a year.

It might seem strange, in a country so suddenly tipped into a War, that there was absolutely nothing for me to do. I was the wrong age for that moment. Limbo forced me into solitude again, painting *acres* of battle scenes from a now out of date war, and writing reams of sentimental, over-emotional, staggeringly bad poems. All of which ended in tear-drenched despair or a row of ambiguous dots. Mostly because I didn't know how to write Full Stop.

My friends were all occupied happily enough; my sister, now a groom at a stables at Scaynes Hill; my mother with the Women's Institute and other Good Works; the house filled with our glum strangers from Finsbury Park. I decided to go to London and try and find something to do there. My father, tired, harassed, over-worked, accepted the suggestion with almost indecent alacrity. I had a year to go, he said, before my Call Up . . . however the war was certain to be over before Christmas so that needn't worry me, but he felt that I should use the year in trying to get work and see if I could make my way in the Theatre when, and if, they re-opened. He gave me ten shillings a week for a year and suggested that I leave as soon as possible.

Which I did. The next afternoon. With a suitcase, an extra ten shillings from my vaguely apprehensive mother, and Aunt Freda Chesterfield's telephone number in Kensington so that I could beg a bed from her until I was settled into whatever I was going to do.

To my relief they all seemed quite glad to see me go, so I arrived in an almost empty Victoria, the next afternoon, guiltless but very aware of one important factor. The night before I left, my father quietly said that a year was all he could afford, and that if I had not made my way in my chosen profession by that time, to the day, I was to return and do precisely and exactly what he said I would do. Starting as a messenger boy at *The Times*.

I had agreed, over confidently. As he was over confident that the war, so newly started, would be over and done with by the end of the next two months.

Aunt Freda lived in a Mansion Flat behind Pontings. She was warm, unsurprised, which was her nature, and said that there was a bed if I wanted it but that I'd have to find my own meals. There was always, as long as it lasted, bread, milk and cheese in the Fridge, and beyond that I was on my own. She would not, she said, make any charge, and I'd have to find my own laundry since she already had a full house. She gave me a key, half a crown, and hoped I'd manage, and said that she would mention me at Mass.

It was a strange sandbagged, almost empty, London through which I drifted. And every bit as dull and boring as it was in Sussex. No one had seen an aeroplane, or been gassed, or had a parachutist in the back yard. And as the first panic started to melt away under the strange calm, people began to return to the City and life almost came back to normal. Except for Air Raid Wardens, the gas masks, and the discomfort and indeed danger of the Black Out, nothing might have happened at all on that hot, last Saturday of Peacetime.

Total boredom and a longing for something green sent me off on a bus to Kew Gardens to see the Pagoda and perhaps look about in the Palm House. But I never got there in the end. Stopping for a moment at Kew Bridge, the bus provided a grandstand view of what appeared to be a builder's yard. Doors and windows, some scattered fireplaces, piles of junk and a girl painting a cut-out tree which was leaning against the wall of the yard. Beside this muddle of wood and canvas was a small squat building. Across the facade, in shabby letters, the words "Q THEATRE".

I ran down the steps, jumped off as the bus started again, and went towards a half open door into the yard. The painting girl looked up rather crossly. She was covered in blobs of green distemper and wore an old pair of navy blue trousers and a man's shirt. She was startled and hot.

"What do you want here? This is private, you know."

"It is a theatre, isn't it?"

She looked crosser than ever. "You'd better clear off . . . or else."

"I was wondering about a job . . . that's all."

"Well, don't bother me with your wondering, I'm busy and

the office is in there." She indicated a door which said Fire Exit and went back to her tree.

It was practically identical, this meeting, to my arrival in the dark Theatre at Uckfield; a lone woman painting a flat . . . threatening me with a paint-brush and suspicion. But I didn't think of that then. I followed her instructions blindly.

A dark, untidy corridor, with a fire extinguisher and a glass-fronted door with "Office" painted on it. It was half open and there were voices. Just as I was about to knock, it opened and a small, hurrying little woman came out eating a cheese roll. She looked up at me mildly.

"Yes?" She finished chewing, her eyes bright and interested, the half finished roll in her hand. I said that I was wondering if there was a job going. I'd seen the yard from the top of a bus and . . . She cut me short with a wave of the cheese roll: "Not auditioning today, dear . . . next week is all cast and we don't see anyone without an appointment . . . come again." She started to turn away back into the Office, when I said: "I meant painting, scenery and things. I'm an artist not an actor."

This stopped her. She took another bite of her roll and asked me where I came from. I said from nowhere particular but had trained at the Poly and worked in Sussex and at the Uckfield Playhouse. I made it sound like the Liverpool Rep.

"What happened to the Uckfield Rep then?" she asked with a shrewd smile. "They fire you?"

"No. They got commandeered for evacuees."

"And you did the sets, is that it?"

I nodded. I didn't say I'd done one only. She finished her roll, licked her fingers and turned back into the office. "You'd better come in and see my husband," she said.

*　　*　　*

Jack and Beatrice de Leon were legendary figures in the Theatre but at that moment, in my supreme ignorance of anything which happened far from the NADS or Uckfield, I was not to know. Jack was a silver haired, handsome man, as beautiful as a Persian, immaculately dressed always, tired, often; quiet and as shrewd as he was kind. His wife, Beattie as we all grew to call her after about half an hour's talk, read his scripts, cast his plays, arranged his staff and sometimes played bits and pieces herself.

Their whole life revolved about this converted skating rink in the Chiswick High Road, and to play at Q was considered to be one of the most important things for a young actor outside the immediate West End. My sudden arrival in their office that afternoon was providential. The regular set designer had walked off the day before, and with a new Show to open in a very short time and only one cross, tired, overworked girl to do it all there was indeed a job for me. I started work at the Q Theatre that afternoon on a verbal agreement of seven and six a week to help out in the scene dock, cart the props about, and do any odd jobs around the theatre which needed doing, from washing down the Gents Lavatory and calling the actors for the Curtain and the Entrances. I was, to all intents and purposes, by the grace of God and Jack and Beattie de Leon, launched.

The cross girl, who was not really at all cross when I got back to the yard, but relieved that she had someone, even someone so inexperienced, to help her, said that her name was Tanya Moiseiwitsch and that we were starting out on a musical called "The Two Bouquets" by Herbert and Eleanor Farjeon. It was, she said, a sod with three big sets, one of them being, as she put it succinctly, "the entire bloody Twickenham Regatta". It was on this backcloth that I was put to work, squaring up Eel Pie Island and half the river Thames. My Twickenham. My first truly professional job. If that wasn't fate, I wondered, what was?

There really wasn't a great deal that I could do to help Tanya. She was very much more experienced than I, and as she was in the middle of the job I mostly scurried around boiling the glue, mixing the size, squaring up, and getting her cups of tea. But I had the impression that I was useful even banging in nails and stretching soggy, size-wet canvas. After a very short time my endless stream of questions started to dry up and I moved more and more about on my own.

Apart from the Scene Dock there were other jobs to be done. I bought a new toothbrush and used my old one with a tin of Brasso (supplied) to bring the taps and pipes to shining life in the Gents. No cigarette ends were ever allowed in the sweet flowing china canal of my Gents. As soon as graffiti appeared, which was not often and usually between the matinee and evening performance, I blotted them out with a wipe of distemper, polished the mirrors and swabbed down the cracked marble floor after every interval. There seemed to be quite a lot of bad aimers.

Adjacent to the Gents and opposite the auditorium was the Club Room. Q, like a number of other smaller theatres, had no licence or Bar but they were allowed to have Club Members . . . which meant a Club Room . . . which meant that if you were a Member, for very little extra per year, you were entitled to the use of the Club Room, as much drink as you could afford to consume, a snack or a meal before the Show and the month's programme of events mailed to your door. I rather think you also received a slight reduction on your seats. In any event the Club Room, presided over by fat, jolly, Vi, thrived. It was not large, about eight tables and a corner bar, a gas fire, two or three armchairs and a long couch. I carted plates about, wiped down the tables, set the salt and pepper straight, saw they were filled, emptied the ash trays and collected the "empties", thus saving Vi a certain amount of work and assuring myself of at least one good meal a day.

If it had not been for Vi and the Club Room it is more than probable that I would have starved to death. Seven and sixpence a week, although a good deal more in 1939, was not very much. However, I managed pretty well. Aunt Freda's free bed was a godsend of course, but I didn't always use it . . . especially if we were in the middle of rehearsals when there simply wasn't time to get back to Kensington. If there was a bed in the play of the week I was particularly lucky and slept, with the mice and the creaks, on that in the Prop shop. Or even on the couch from the Second Act. Never, however, in the Club Room which Vi locked firmly every evening before she left.

I don't think that I can have looked all that clean, thinking back. I shaved in cold water in the Prop Room . . . used my own Gents, of course, and managed a bath once or twice a week when I got back to Aunt Freda's. First thing in the morning, before anyone but the milkmen were about, I was up and setting my little iron stove alight with bits of wood and paper and then heaved up the coke. Made the bed or couch on which I had slept a dreamless night, and started off down the Chiswick High Road for my breakfast. A packet of Maltesers from the local newsagent, just opened and stacking the papers for the delivery boy to collect, a packet of Woodbine, cheaper than Black Cat, and then a half bottle of milk, or a pint if I could find it, snitched from any old front door step on my way back to the theatre.

Not long ago I was asked by one of those anguished middle-aged people who seem to dominate Television interviews if there was one really "awful, shaming, thing which I had ever done in my life and which still made me blush". In the course of over fifty years there have been one or two. But the one single one which makes me really blush is the pinching of pints of milk and the thought of the perplexed morning faces when those doors were opened. However I reckoned that I needed it more than they did. I hadn't even got a door to open . . . let alone a doorstep or a bottle of milk idly sitting trustfully there. And I never, ever, took the only one. I took from the Rich. Those who had ordered a pint and a half or anyway two bottles. I felt that was fair.

I enjoyed waiting at table, a napkin over my arm, my hands clean, the typewritten menu offered, the little pad and pencil. All rubbish really: Vi only ever had two meals on her Menu. Grilled Gammon and Egg or Grilled Kidneys, Chops, and Two Veg. The veg depended on what she had managed to get that morning on her way to work. But it all set a "tone", I felt, and sometimes I got a tip. Which Vi allowed me to keep. If I told her. If I didn't she never knew. It depended on the state of my week's money. Sometimes the actors would send me out to the pub next door for a bottle of Guinness or a round of sandwiches and were often very generous with a couple of pennies or even, mostly from the women, a threepenny bit . . . and all in all by the time Saturday Pay Night came along I had usually managed to break even.

As time went on I graduated more towards the actual Stage itself. Helping out the ASM, playing "God Save The King" at the end of the Show on a scratchy old ten inch HMV . . . and, on some terrifying occasions, actually "Holding the Book" of the play in the Prompt Corner and prompting the actors who "blew" a line. That was the nastiest part of all. The feeling of anxiety was too acute for comfort and sometimes I wondered if my own fear was affecting the actors on the stage for it always seemed to me that I had to prompt a performance more than the real ASM. Many of the plays only had a week's rehearsal, so it was a pretty nerve-racking night, a First Night at Q.

Taking the book at rehearsals was more relaxed and better for my learning. Day after day I sat through the play, in between waiting at table and swabbing down my Gents, and less and less I spent time in the Scene Dock. I was infinitely more use as, and more interested in being, general dogsbody. I was, of course, getting closer and closer to the Stage in this manner. Which was my intention. My pay packet, however, stayed firmly the same every Saturday Night. Three florins, a shilling and a sixpence. Sometimes the sixpence came in coppers.

Until one afternoon Beattie came bustling into the Club Room where I was wiping down the tables and waiting for Vi to get my lunch of left-overs out of her oven.

"Shouldn't you be on the stage, dear? It's Dress Rehearsal," she said worriedly. I explained that one of the actors wasn't feeling well and that the rehearsal was put back half an hour.

"Oh I know all about that," she said. "It's the photographer's assistant, isn't it?"

She hardly ever addressed small part actors by their names, but usually by the name of the role they were playing. "Well, he's got an appendix, that's what. You know the lines, dear, don't you? There are only a couple anyway, and if you don't know them you've got plenty of time to read them up before this evening. Hop off and see if his suit will fit you; if it doesn't wear your own and carry his hat. Off you go. We're up in a couple of hours."

Breathlessly I reported this news to my director, a red-haired young man in a wrap-around camel hair coat called Basil Dearden, who was assiduously modelling himself, with considerable success, on Basil Dean, a director noted for his brilliance, sarcasm, acidity, and apparent abhorrence of actors.

"Christ Almighty!" he said. "Now I know there's a war on: they've started to ration the Talent!" And to my eager face he quietly said, "Well, don't stand there, piss off and see if the blasted things fit", starting a deep friendship which only ended with his death more than thirty years later.

J. B. Priestley's "When We Are Married" brought me, with two thin lines, a few physical miles nearer to the West End. I don't remember very much about it except that the suit did fit and that I spent over an hour making up and sitting in a real dressing-room with real lights and real actors all about me. I also had to call the Half, the Quarter, and the Acts. I felt as tinny as the Bishopbriggs clock. Too busy to be frightened, I did what I could and was allowed to stay on till the end of the Production. Quite suddenly, and as tiresomely simple as that, I became an actor proper. Although I still had the Gents and the Club Room and the errands to run for the other actors . . . but as the parts got larger, for they did as time went on, I gradually had to give up the other jobs and found that I was being paid seven and six to play quite large, for me at that time, roles. Young actors were getting hard to find easily. The war had netted quite a number already.

"There's a nice little part for you next week in 'Saloon Bar'," said Beattie one day. "You are a bit young for it but I think you'll get away with it. Alf the Pot Boy. See what you can do." I did. And enjoyed it thoroughly and made up my mind, halfway through the week, that I would go and ask Jack de Leon for a rise. After all, I reckoned, I was now an actor with a quite respectable line of roles behind me . . . a rise was not unreasonable. But on Saturday night, my pay packet had no jingly coins inside. In terror, in case it was my Notice or something, I ripped it open and a shilling fell out on to the floor. Anxiously I scrabbled in the little buff envelope. There was one green, crackly pound note. A guinea! I'd done it.

I bought Vi a gin and lime, had a giddy whisky myself and crossed the dark street to the telephone box outside the Station. My father answered as he always did, "Bogaerde here." I told him what had happened. "And next week there's a better part in a better play and if I get it they'll double the salary to two guineas." There was a silence on the line, I heard the pips go and my father's voice saying, "I suppose you realise that you have spent your profits. I'll tell Mother. Ring off now. Very good." And the line went dead. But I knew that he was impressed. He was also accurate in his accounting. No more gins and whiskies, nor did I telephone them again.

* * *

The war didn't end that Christmas as so many of us had hopefully predicted, and it seemed, from where I could see, that the German tanks were hardly cardboard, and for a nation on the very brink of starvation they were doing uncomfortably well. It was an ominous, dark, waiting time. For everyone. For me it meant that Call Up loomed nearer and nearer and the chances of my making my mark in my chosen profession began to look very shaky indeed. The war, I was sure, was going to go on for ages, at least until I was over twenty-one—which was the limit I had set myself for "success". Not stardom, never that, but calm, assured, character-lead stuff. The kind of actor who is never out of work, always comfortably engaged, and always able to play almost any rôle within the wide range of Character. Never too many pressures, never too much splendour, nor too much responsibility. "Always Applauded" would suit me very well. And when Beattie gave me my first really big role, in a revival of Priestley's "Cornelius", I knew that I had found my exact position. Lawrence, the office boy, was what I wanted always to play. No play to "carry", a good moment in each act—the perfect rôle. I enjoyed it, was good in it and liked very much the compliments which started to arrive from my fellow actors. On the last night I saw Beattie in the Club Room with her book of the week's takings. "We had a good week," she said. "Funny with a serious play. But we always do well with Priestley." As Vi came out with us, pulling on her coat and getting her torch and gas mask ready I said to Beattie: "It was a *marvellous* week for me. I really feel now that I am a proper actor." Beattie shot me a distant, flicker of a smile. "Do you, dear?" she said. "That's nice."

We played one week at Q and then moved up north to the Embassy Theatre at Swiss Cottage and played a week there. They did an equal swap with us and so most plays had a good two weeks run before we had to start all over again. The Embassy was more of a theatre really than Q. It had a balcony and red plush and I had no responsibilities whatsoever back stage, so my week playing there, unless we were preparing the next production's set, was pretty quiet; I only had the Shows to worry me. And "Cornelius" was, I thought, pretty well buttoned up.

It was buttoned up. So was my acting career for the time being. Beattie informed me that there was nothing "for me" in the next three Productions but that I could carry on, if I wished, in the Gents, in the Scene Dock, and helping Vi in the Club Room. I was not over anxious. What to do? I needed advice rather quickly. Fortunately Bill Wightman had taken lodgings in a sombre yellow brick house not far away from the Embassy Theatre in Fellows Road. He was between jobs but offered me Ovaltine and chocolate digestive biscuits in his comfortable room overlooking the back gardens of Swiss Cottage. And copious advice. He agreed with me that it might be wiser to try and press ahead with the Theatre rather than go back to the Gents and boiling glue and carrying trays to more fortunate players, and suggested, very mildly, that he knew of a woman who was running a Rep Company in the country and who might be willing to give me a job. She was, he said, finding it too much of a struggle to keep going, and that he and a friend were considering making an offer to purchase the place outright thus ensuring himself a permanent job and a permanent theatre. She had not definitely made up her mind to sell, and in the meantime she was short of a Juvenile. Perhaps I should go down and see her before I committed myself to Beattie and the Gents.

The next day, after he had telephoned and made an appointment, I took the train down to Amersham in Buckinghamshire and went to meet Sally Latimer who looked at me doubtfully and asked if I could do an American accent. I lied and said yes. She asked me what else I could do, and misunderstanding her in my anxiousness, I said that I also painted sets and worked at Q and could wait at table. For twenty-two shillings a week I got the job, and as soon as "Cornelius" closed, at the end of the week, I told Beattie and waited for the storm. There was no storm from Beattie.

"All right, dear, good luck. Remember, if you ever want to come back we'll see what we can find for you. I'm busy now dear, so let me get on with it, will you?" and she continued checking the "pull" of a poster for the next production.

It was a little over six years later that I took her up on her generous offer. On Demob leave, in my worn Service dress, a reasonable row of campaign medals on my chest, three pips on my shoulders and ten shillings in my pocket, I stood in a line of elderly women whom she was interviewing for Char Ladies. Nothing had changed, the same rubber floor, the same smell from my old Gents, the tatty silver and black paintwork, the faded stills from "Peg O' My Heart" and "Abies Irish Rose" with Beattie in a bow and gingham. Nothing seemed to have altered at all since Arromanches, Arnhem, Berlin, Bombay, Singapore and Sourabaya. As I reached her, last in the line, she looked up pleasantly from her little note book.

"Hullo dear," she said. "Been away?"

*　　*　　*

The Amersham Rep was based in a converted grocer's shop near the station. It had no balcony, no "flight" and a very small, narrow, stage. The Green Room and the actors' dressing-rooms, one for the men and one for the women, were down in the basement and the scene dock was a lock up garage. It was what you might call a very intimate theatre, and the atmosphere of it was more Family than Theatrical. The Front of House staff were local townspeople who worked free for the love of us, and Sally Latimer, a tough, slight, firm-jawed woman ran it with total dedication and her partner, a tall, blond-haired girl who wore flannel trousers, a blue blazer and smoked incessantly, called Caryl Jenner. We did one play a week, opening on the Monday night and starting rehearsals on the morning of the same day for the next week. It was not an unusual occurrence to find yourself rehearsing Laertes at eight-thirty a.m. and going on stage a few exhausted hours later, to open "cold" as Maxim de Winter in "Rebecca" with the Set being erected about your ears. But we never stopped, and the theatre was a success attracting at its height even the London Critics to some performances of New Plays including, and often led indeed, by the Emperor of them all, James Agate. It was clearly a place in which to learn, to work, and to love. I did all three.

I got Digs up the road in a semi-detached called "Beechcroft" behind the pub, and for five and six a week received a single bed under the roof, use of the bathroom, and a hot meal after the show which was usually scrag end of neck with barley and carrots kept hot in the oven over a low gas. I was in seventh heaven. I did my American Accent, pretty frightfully, in "Grouse in June" and started rehearsals as soon as that was over for "Call It A Day" the week that Italy declared war and the Germans invaded Belgium and Holland. It was frighteningly clear that the cardboard tanks were making shattering progress, and by the end of the week had ripped into France and were less than two hundred miles from tranquil, unsuspecting Folkestone.

We were intermittently glued to Dodie Smith and the BBC. It didn't seem as if we had very much time left. We opened to smaller houses than usual and found the laughs rather difficult to "get". In an atmosphere charged with emotions of every kind, filling the air with the sullen zig-zags of summer lightning I, inevitably, fell deeply in love with my Leading Lady, a red-haired Scots girl a couple of years older than myself called Anne Deans. With a stunning lack of timeliness I announced our engagement to the astonished company during a coffee break in the Green Room on the very day that the shattered British Army started its desperate withdrawal to Dunkirk. I seem to remember that Annie was about as astonished as the Company, but was carried away by my eloquence and passion and needed, as she said, cheering up.

That evening we went down to the local equivalent of the Ritz, a chintzy, warming-panned, huddle of exposed beams and gate-legged tables called The Mill Stream, and over eggs, chips and sausage and two expensive Carlsberg Lagers celebrated my some-what emotional announcement. I apologised for not having a ring but Annie was ahead of me and produced one, from her handbag, which belonged to her mother and which she had had the foresight to acquire just before I had collected her from her digs in White Lion Road. Slipping it on to her finger she accepted me as her future husband. I reeled with pleasure and ordered another Carlsberg Lager each.

Walking home through the blackout up the steep hill to the Recreation Grounds near which she shared two rooms with her mother, we made happy, if inaccurate, plans for our future deciding, sensibly I thought, not to get married until I was really and truly Called Up. But to go on with our Careers and announce it in the newspapers as soon as possible.

After a passionate farewell under a pollarded oak outside her front gate, I walked back to the Theatre and telephoned the news of this momentous piece of trivia to my parents who were unable to hear the telephone owing to the fact that they were both far out in the garden, standing holding hands together in the still hot night, feeling the earth trembling beneath their feet, and listening to the guns rumbling in France.

*　*　*

One morning while I was out "shopping" for props for the next production (we used to go and beg and borrow anything from a grand piano to a patchwork quilt from the generous people in the neighbourhood) a telephone message arrived at the theatre asking me to call Q Theatre urgently. Feeling, I don't know why, that the message might be private and not wanting it to be heard all over the Box Office, unlike the Engagement Announcement, I went up to a call box at the station and called Q. Beattie was very calm, almost disinterested.

"They want to take the Priestley play into the West End. You know, the one you did here last season. 'Cornelius'. They want to know if you are available. I said I'd find out, dear. You'd have to start next week of course."

I walked down the hill to the converted grocer's shop in a trance and asked Sally Latimer if she would release me from the Company, which, after a sour look and some understandable grumbles, she finally agreed to do. Annie was delighted but somewhat wistful. "Oh dear!" she said. "It's just like the flicks, isn't it? Where they want one half of the act and not the other . . ." But I was beyond subtleties of this kind. I had already packed the green suit, my washing bag and a "good" pair of black shoes I had pinched from the theatre wardrobe, and as far as I was concerned had already opened in the play and caused a sensation.

★   ★   ★

Bill Wightman got me a room in his lodgings in Fellows Road. His landlady offered me the one hot meal at night, a bed under the stairs on the second floor, and said she didn't normally take actors but would make an exception because Mr Wightman had recommended me strongly. She asked for ten shillings a week, and to my astonishment, I agreed.

Miss Hanney was bossy, curious, and kind. All her lodgers, there were six of us, were "professional" gentlemen, she said, that is to say they were Lawyers, Accountants or men who were "good at figures". We all sat down together, on the bong of a gong, at one big table in the front room and were served a meal of thin soup, meat and two veg, and cabinet, suet, or treacle, pudding. No one spoke much, and the only sound was the clink and clonk of the knives and forks against thick china. But I ate heartily for my daily diet was still much as it had been at Q—supplemented now and then by a sandwich in a pub or a hard-boiled egg.

The rehearsals started in the green room of the Westminster Theatre and, although I had played it at the Q and at the Embassy, it became startlingly clear that while *I* might have been tremendously enthusiastic about my performance no one seemed to be in the West End. It was not, it was felt, quite up to West End standards—and for a time it appeared that I would be given the sack. And, indeed, I would have been, had it not been for the great efforts of Ann Wilton, who had played with me at Q and felt that I did have a "spark", as she called it.

Patiently, every day at the Lunch Break, she coached me all

alone in the Green Room, encouraging me, forcing me to project, to move, even to think, listen, and time a line. She knew, as I dimly did myself, that On The Night I'd be all right. But I was holding back too much at rehearsals and no one, except herself, had the least idea of what I might possibly do. She told me bluntly that I was to be re-cast, and begged me to try harder than ever. I did. And with her help and patience finally won through.

My agonies were not unnoticed by everyone in the Company. Sometimes one of the student actors from the Mask Theatre School, who had a small part in the play, came timidly down into the Green Room and sat in the corner watching Ann's desperate efforts to force me into "attack" . . . he was a pale, tall, blond boy with anxious blue eyes: his own shyness was so great that he too, under the irritable eyes of our director, Henry Cass, was starting to wilt and was also in danger of getting sacked. So we were both in the same boat, except that I was in a far more unpleasant position, for at least I was supposed to be a Professional Actor already, and he merely a Student. Our mutual dilemma brought us close together and although he did all that he could to breach his shyness and reserve, Paul Scofield was eventually replaced while I, thanks entirely to Ann Wilton's supreme belief and care, was coached through the whole of the rehearsals until our modestly triumphant opening on August the 24th, 1940.

If Ann Wilton taught me two of the most important lessons in the Theatre, devotion and dedication, Max Adrian, who was also in the play, taught me quite another. But not less essential or timely. Humility. Overimpressed with my modest notices in the Daily Press, and well aware that the audiences not only liked me but thought I was funny, I started, within a very few performances to attempt to take over the play from the Principals. I mugged about, invented bits of, I thought, irresistible business, extended my laughs and behaved as if I was a one-man show at the Palladium. One matinee, unable to bear my behaviour any longer, Max, who played a humbled, timid little clerk, took up a great leather ledger and brought it crashing down on my totally unsuspecting head with an infuriated cry of "Never do that again, I say!" Bewildered with the suddenness of the blow, the stars literally reeling about my head, I slammed into a wall and slid, winded and stunned, to the stage amidst the largest roar of delighted laughter I had ever heard in a theatre in my life. At my own expense. A salutary and necessary lesson for which I was ever grateful.

The sirens went between the shows on the following Saturday. Just before the Second House. We all excitedly clambered up to the roof and looked across the rooftops mellow in the evening sun. Far away down the river the sky was peppered with little puffs of smoke; the rattle of guns and the drone of planes carried clearly through the traffic from the street below. The All Clear had not sounded by the time the curtain rose, and by the end of the first act it was impossible to continue for the noise outside. Stephen Murray, who was playing the lead, interrupted the performance, went to the edge of the stage, and told a sparse audience that if they wished we would continue the play or else they could leave, have their money back, and we would ring down the curtain. The play continued. To our astonishment we realised that the roof above the stage was entirely made of glass through which the steadily burning sky of London was reflecting with a carmine glow. At the end of the play the audience were asked if they wished to come below to share our Shelters, great caves below the theatre which were once supposed to be Henry VIII's Wine Cellars. Crouched together, audience and Cast and one large Alsatian dog which someone had brought with them, we sat through the long night, miserable, hungry, and very aware that the war had really started at last. It was, in a strange way, almost a relief. But start it had: and the next day, after the night's toll was known, everything closed down again, and the War took charge of our lives. "Cornelius", along with many other shows, folded for good, and I was once again back where I had started, with an ever diminishing area of opportunities.

Lying in my small bed under the stairs in Fellows Road, feeling the house shake and tremble with every near miss, I decided that it might be wiser to swallow my pride and see if Amersham would have me back: it was in the country, Annie was still there, and all told I had only been away from them for about six weeks. When my window blew in and the door slammed itself out of the room across the mahogany banisters I decided that there was no time like the present. And as soon as it was light I walked to Baker Street and got the Metropolitan Line to Amersham on the Hill.

★   ★   ★

Sally Latimer took me back. Juveniles were getting harder and harder to find, and although I was so to speak Under Sentence,

I was better than nothing. I remember that at the bottom of every programme it was stated that: "All The Actors In This Production Are Either Unfit For Military Service Or Awaiting Call Up", which made us all feel a bit second-hand. However it did stop the occasional complaining letter from patriotic Townspeople.

Annie was delighted to see me and behaved as if I had come back from Dunkirk rather than Swiss Cottage. So far the war had not touched Amersham very much: a string of bombs had fallen in an orchard up at Little Chalfont, and at nights the sky in the north east was scarlet with the flaring glow of burning London. But otherwise everything was relatively peaceful and we played to packed houses every night. I started with Caryl Jenner on the sets for "You Never Can Tell" and Bill Wightman, who had failed in his effort to purchase the Rep from a reluctant and determined Sally, came down to play The Waiter while I played McComus in a white wig and a mass of Leichner Carmine wrinkles which gave me the appearance of something between badly laid crazy-paving and a vicious razor attack.

My money had been raised to two pounds five shillings a week and I moved out of "Beechcroft" to an ugly bungalow in the White Lion Road where I slept in a bleak little front parlour on a camp bed surrounded by framed passe-partout signed photographs of Claude Dampier, Gillie Potter, The Crazy Gang, and George Lacy as The Dame in "Mother Goose". My pleasant new Landlady had clearly been on The Boards herself.

All this, of course, was in order to be a little nearer to Annie in her digs under the pollarded oak by the Recreation Fields. Our "Romance" was becoming something of a strain, since we found it almost impossible to be on our own anywhere. I volunteered to be on almost constant duty as a Fire Watcher for the theatre, which meant that I spent the whole night in the Green Room waiting for Incendiaries to obliterate us and Annie to arrive with a Thermos of coffee, a quart of beer and a cold meat stew which we warmed up on the electric fire and ate off "prop" plates with "prop" spoons and forks. Hardly a conducive setting for Romance, and it was not altogether satisfactory. Neither were our performances on the following days. Wan and hollow-eyed, we blundered about the stage—until Sally decided to alter the Roster and insisted, rightly, that we rested for the Theatre's sake.

After "You Never Can Tell" it was agreed that a change of pace was needed and that we should "do" a Revue. Everyone went to with a will and we wrote sketches and songs and pinched other people's material disgracefully, opening with a rousing number which was called "Joan of Arc" and was, we all felt, very topical. Dressed in black berets and raincoats, for some reason best known to ourselves, and set against the wobbly backcloth of a white Eiffel Tower and a vaguely inaccurate Notre Dame which I had painted all by myself, we sang the opening bars of our Song, which went, as far as I can remember like this . . .

> *"We can hear you calling,*
> *Joan of Arc,*
> *Over the Sea,*
> *Out of the dark,*
> *To the Land of the Freeee . . ."*

Perfidious Albion all right. It made everyone feel very sad, and was hardly a rousing opening for an Intimate Revue . . . nevertheless we were a success and even toured it on Sundays, when the theatre was closed, round various army camps and hospitals all over Buckinghamshire. It was patriotic, exhausting, self-indulgent, and Always Applauded. I wrote a supposedly hilarious sketch for Annie and myself called "Doon the Watter" which was to accommodate our hardly ever used Glasgow accents, and she did a rather violent Clog Dance to the "Petticoat Song" from "Miss Hook Of Holland". There were sketches and blackouts, and a plump girl from Rickmansworth did a thoughtful dance with a long cigarette holder to a scratchy recording of "Rhapsody in Blue". At the end the entire company assembled with many outstretched hands and wide-flung arms to a passionate rendering of "We'll Meet Again". Oh dear. Oh dear. But we all thought we were splendid. Perhaps we were.

After the Revue a change of pace again and a turgid piece called "Grief Goes Over". All I can remember is that my wife died with her baby, or having it, I can't recall, and that I was comforted, in a long sad Third Act by my mother, played by Miss Latimer herself in a fur coat and a Herbert Johnson hat, in which I was able to indulge myself in some pretty hefty masculine sobbing, wearing my father's tails borrowed for the occasion. I must admit that though I cannot remember the play I do remember thinking that I looked pretty fine in Tails, though they did not fit and Anne had to pin them together with safety-pins. The fact that I looked like a Cypriot waiter totally escaped me and

I enjoyed myself nightly giving a performance of self-indulgence which would have made a Fire Eater blush. However, our sad little play was not popular, and the last Saturday night, much to my sorrow, was sparsely attended. There were a good many empty seats scattered about which, as it turned out, was just as well for me.

★　　★　　★

If Lieutenant Anthony Forwood, R.A., on leave from his Battery at Hornchurch, and slightly bored after dinner, had been able to get into the Regent Cinema for the last showing of "Edison The Man" that Saturday night, it is fair to say that this book would have ended at the paragraph above. As it was, he bad-temperedly wandered down the hill to the Theatre and bought a seat, easily, for the last two acts of "Grief Goes Over" and sent his card round to the dressing-room. On such frail threads hang one's destiny. Ivy who worked in Front of House came through the Green Room with a tray of empty coffee cups and the card, which she flipped through the curtained entrance to the Gents dressing-room. "Chap out front sent this round for you," she called. "Says he's a representative from Al Parker the agent. He's waiting."

The card was an ordinary visiting card. But Al Parker was no ordinary agent. At that time he was the "chic-est" agent in London and his clients were nearly all Stars. My heart leapt. The company were impressed. Annie shot up to the stage to peer through the Curtain and have a look at the visitor while I cold-creamed my tear-ravaged face and struggled out of my father's tails.

"He's tall, blond, in full regalia," she reported, "and not Jewish."

"What do you mean, regalia? "I asked.

Annie was struggling into a black lace frock because Saturday night was "our" night together at the warming-panned Mill Stream, and she always liked to look her best on the dance floor.

"He's an officer of some sort, and Ivy says he's a local and they live up at Chalfont and are very rich or something; he's giving her a lift home in a few minutes so don't be long or we'll never get to the Mill and I'm starving."

Someone lent me a clean white shirt and someone else a tie and in my only suit, the black stolen shoes, and clutching the card, which had impressed me by being embossed and not printed, I went up to the auditorium to meet Mr Parker's Representative who was sitting very uncomfortably, for he was over six foot, in the last seat of row A.

I was quite unprepared for the elegant splendour reclining in the too-small seat before me. Booted, breeched, tunic'd, buttons and badges glittering brightly in the meagre light of the dim auditorium, his hair shining like a halo, he extended an indifferent hand, told me his name and said that he had been in Front and thought I was "interesting". I sat nervously in the empty seat beside him. "Far too young, of course, but a very strong— Quality?"

"Well . . . I'm too young, I expect, but you know . . ." He waved his vague hand somewhere in the air.

"There's a war on, I know. And the tails were frightful, of course."

"They are my father's."

"That's what they looked like. Have you got an agent?"

"No. It doesn't seem worth it: I'll be called up pretty soon."

"When? I mean, how soon?"

"Next birthday. March."

"Well . . . that gives us a little time. I represent Parker in London. I'm looking out for my own clients for after the war, if you think it's a good idea I might represent you. You need experience, of course, but you have got a . . ." again the hand waved loosely in the stale air of the theatre, "a Quality, I suppose. Do you want to talk about it?"

I said yes very quickly and he unfolded from the seat and stood before me, a glittering figure. He murmured with a suppressed yawn that we couldn't talk here and that as his home was very near, and he was giving Ivy a lift back because she lived at the end of his lane, perhaps I'd care to come back with him, meet his grandfather and have some cocoa?

Annie was grumpy, but reluctantly agreed that I should go as long as I didn't stay long and got to the Mill Stream before the sausages ran out. She said she'd go on with the others and keep me a place at the table. Sally, unimpressed, reminded me coldly that the Set had to be dismantled before midnight because we had to start the rigging for rehearsal the next day on "Children To Bless You".

231

We dropped Ivy off at her house half way up Cokes Lane and through a misty October night bumped along a rutted drive through hundreds, or so it seemed to me, of cherry trees until we reached the low, rambling, creeper-covered house where he lived.

In the glimmer of the dimmed headlights, through wisping mist, a torch bobbled among the trees and a woman in a headscarf and wellingtons waved a tin bowl at us.

"Forgot the ducks again!" she said cheerfully. "Enjoy the show?"

We clambered out of the car and slammed doors.

"Cousin Phyllis," he said. "This is a chap called Bogaerde. Is there some cocoa or anything?"

Cousin Phyllis went ahead of us wagging her torch and we followed through wet grasses. In the low heavily timbered hall, she clumped off somewhere to get "the refreshments" and my companion said that his name was Tony which would make things easier, and ushered me into the study, a snug room, down a deceptive couple of steps, a fire glowing in the grate, Stafford-shire figures, and his grandfather, Pip, sitting in an armchair, late eighties, bearded, clasping a thick walking stick, one leg up on a padded stool. He was polite and warm, and I was almost im-mediately at my ease. We sat talking about the Theatre and the War until Cousin Phyllis, chatting and eager, brought in the tray with cocoa and fruit cake and Forwood said that Herbert Farjeon was getting the Cast together for another version of his Revue, "Diversion", at Wyndhams in a few weeks' time. There was, he said, a pretty good chance that he could get me into it, as a glorified chorus boy, if I was free and wished to do so.

I agreed immediately. He was pleasantly unsurprised. "There is only one thing else," he said, "if I do get you in I would naturally wish to represent you, be your agent so to speak, after the war. Would you agree to that?"

Sitting round the study fire that evening, Pip starting to nod off, one veined hand occasionally slipping from the wooden stick, Cousin Phyllis thoughtfully sipping her cocoa, Forwood sprawled in a deep armchair hardly bothering to stifle a yawn (he had to be on duty at dawn in Hornchurch), I felt so immediately secure, the atmosphere was one of such familiar trust that it never remotely occurred to me to say anything other than "Yes" with-out qualification. We shook hands, I remember, which was the only form of contract we have ever had, and shortly afterwards, full of cocoa and cake, and the warmth of the welcome, I was driven back through the orchard down to the Mill Stream where, with a very casual salute, as if this sort of thing happened every evening of his life, he dropped me in the car park and swung the car out on to the main road. For a few moments I stood in the foggy night before the blacked-out restaurant door. "Where or When" came faintly through the latticed windows. I watched the Mercedes turn left on to the main road and roar back up the hill to the ivy-covered house at the top of Cokes Lane.

Suddenly I had an Agent. The possibility of a West End job again, and something intangible which might, or might not be . . . "a quality". I felt, with a burst of joy, that I owned the world. I didn't know that eight years later I should also own the house.

15

"A-ONE, A-Two, A-Three, BACK! Four, Five, Six, TURN!"
The voice was a metronome, relentless, cold, mechanical,
occasionally human only when it rose to a desperate cry on the
words Back! or Turn! usually applied to myself. I was as graceless
as a duck; the other five appeared almost balletic in comparison,
probably because they had already been through it in the First
Edition of the Show. I was suffering greatly from my usual
complaint: lack of co-ordination. However, I bumped and
staggered about and watched the others with a sense of despairing
envy. Having got this far I was going to get the steps right if it
killed me and everyone else concerned. A dim back room in a
pub off St Martin's Lane, some mirrors, a bashed piano, the front
removed, bent wood chairs insect-like round the walls, dirty
coffee cups, a bald-headed man in shirt-sleeves banging out the
opening number of the show. It was a Judy Garland movie,
completely familiar to me: as if a dream was repeating itself. The
stars, Dorothy Dickson, Bernard Miles, Edith Evans, Joyce Grenfell and the Director, Walter Chrisham, didn't come to the chorus
rehearsals . . . they fitted themselves in a few days before the
opening, and the whole Company only got together for the
Numbers. I was in about five and both the Opening and the
Finale. Not overworked; and in between fittings for a full dress
Kilt, my first Tails, a bathing suit, a dinner jacket and sundry bits
and pieces, I spent most of my time in the room in the pub trying
to get my feet to do what the metronome voice implored them
to do. It wasn't easy. I began to doubt the wisdom of Tony
Forwood. I might have "Quality" on the stage at Amersham,
but it seemed not to be much in evidence half a mile from
Wyndhams Theatre, Charing Cross Road.

Annie had been sceptical when I told her of my good fortune
that evening at the Mill Stream. To begin with I *was* an hour late,
the sausages *were* off and she felt the whole thing boded ill. Agents
from the West End, she pointed out, were pretty sharp people,
who seldom kept their words, and a Revue didn't seem the best
place for a straight actor to begin his attempt on the West End.
And if I did get the job, she asked pointedly, what would happen

to her? I would be in London and she'd be stuck in Amersham on the Hill and we'd never see each other? It posed a great many problems, I could see, so I obliterated everything for the time being. I still had a whole standing Set to dismantle that night, and decided to enjoy what remained of Saturday: after all I might never hear another word from Mr Parker's Representative on his Ack Ack site in Hornchurch.

Which was where I was wrong. A few days later he telephoned to say he'd fixed it, and then a telegram arrived from Bertie Farjeon saying he was happy to welcome me to the Show, that rehearsals commenced in two weeks' time, would I please confirm soonest. Sally Latimer was understandably irritated, but agreed that I could leave at the end of the following play. Annie looked glum and said that she would try and get a job with ENSA . . . I packed my suitcase and arrived back at Fellows Road, Swiss Cottage, and repossessed my bed under the stairs.

The first rehearsal, on the stage at Wyndhams, was pretty frightening. All in our Best, Edith Evans magisterial in mink, Dorothy Dickson in fox and an Orchid, and our Director, Wally, elegant in pale blue silk. The six "Chorus" sat on one side of the stage, the Élite on the other. We were all perfectly friendly and integrated, but everyone knew their places, and a feeling of discipline, position, and West End reigned quietly. This was no harassed Uckfield, no Rough and Tumbled Get The Show Together Amersham. This was as polished, smooth and organised as a well designed, luxurious, motor-car. Or so it seemed to me.

I was greatly heartened to find that one of the six of us was my friend in wrinkled tights from Shere, Peter Ustinov, and even happier to find that we were sharing a dressing-room together. We were the only men. The other four were girls . . . and one of them was particularly wise and understanding of my timidity and gracelessness, to such an extent that she even attempted to make herself as idiotic as I felt and was, in order to encourage me, although I well knew that she was far more experienced than she pretended. It was all done for me and I loved her very much for it. Her name was Vida Hope, and hope was exactly what she offered at every clumsy, inexperienced, rehearsal. Thus, with drums and a piano in the orchestra pit, we started out on the big adventure. I knew that I had a lot to learn and a long way to go. Never mind. Get on and do it.

Sitting there in the Stalls waiting my turn to work, watching the polished poise of Miss Dickson "walking through" a dance routine with Wally, plotting the moves, the turns, the steps, the movement of an arm, precisely, calmly, and with complete confidence and assurance made my heart thud with excitement. I sat there every day and never missed a second of any part of the Show . . . from Irene Eisinger throwing wide imaginary shutters in a Mountain Chalet singing "Tales From The Vienna Woods", to Joyce Grenfell making her Entrance, taking her positions, and making the Exit . . . to the most magical of all, Edith Evans, sitting under a working light on a wooden box, her mink over her shoulders, snow boots on her feet, declaring in that liquid voice of astonishing range, Queen Elizabeth's speech before the Armada. I glutted. I watched and listened constantly; all that seemed improbable was that I should ever master the A-One, A-Two, A-Three and TURN of the very ordinary Dance Routines . . . but I worked. Somewhere along the line I had been given an infinite capacity for trying, or perhaps it was Ambition.

My mother was very pleased at this turn of events, and my father forced to admit that in a little over a year I had, at least, managed to survive in my chosen profession, and with some small subsidies from himself, usually half a crown here and there when things got really tight, plus a florin and a hurried meal in her kitchen from Aunt Freda, I had managed to pay my way, supplementing my meagre income (we were not paid for rehearsals) by working in a couple of cheap restaurants near Leicester Square and pocketing the tips while clearing the tables and washing down the counters.

The only person who wasn't altogether happy with the way things had transpired was Annie. Trailing about the country from one Army Camp to another meant that she hardly ever got to London, and when she did we only seemed to manage a grabbed lunch in a pub or, on one or two occasions, tea with Bill Wightman in his room in Swiss Cottage where we drank his hoarded Earl Grey's, ate digestive biscuits, and asked, constantly, his advice about the vexed problem of our Engagement. His advice one day, given with great care, was that we should both wait until I was twenty-one . . . or until the war was over, and until we had both gone a little further, one way or another, in our jobs. It would be restricting and frustrating now at this moment to get married, he thought, especially as my Call Up was imminent and who could possibly tell how we should both feel, with so much before us, when Peace returned?

The astonishing thought that Peace would return, with Victory, at such a dark time of the war, was unquestioned. That evening, during a fairly savage air raid, and a pleasantly emotional supper at the Café Royal, Annie put her engagement ring in her handbag and replaced it with a Red Indian's Head in solid silver. As a token. We felt sad, brave, and both, I think, relieved. The next day she went down to Borden Camp and I went on to Wyndhams to continue with my A-One, A-Two, A-Three, TURN!

★　★　★

Whenever I could afford to, I went home to Sussex at the weekend to get a couple of nights relaxed sleep. The Air Raids were now becoming a fact of life, more and more frequent and disturbing. My window had again blown in, and was hermetically sealed with thick black paper, and Miss Hanney, one evening at supper, informed us all with relish that when the Private Hotel on the corner had been hit they found one of the maids stuck all over with knives, spoons and forks like a hedgehog. A weekend on the Common in my own house seemed desirable; there, in my room with the McKnight Kauffers and Nevinsons and Nashes pinned on the walls, the bits of Staffordshire I had started to collect from barrows off the Kings Road, my sombre library of war books and pamphlets on rearing everything from a Natter-jack Toad to a Goat gave me a great sense of comfort and security. And the war, although constantly present with its red waning glow in the north sky beyond the Forest at night, seemed a long way off.

In spite of all the changes the Family were still very much there. The Evacuees had finally left, the eldest into the Merchant Navy and the younger, miserable and lonely without his brother, packed up to risk his life again in Finsbury Park. My mother was now in ARP as a Warden with a tin hat and full instructions on what to do in the event of a Gas Alert. She had also mastered the art of making Molotov Cocktails, and the shed near the garage was filled with her collection of bottles and fuses, plus a strong smell of spilt petrol. Since the Invasion Threat of the summer had passed somewhat, she now concentrated on splints, bandages and hot sweet tea for shock. She was really quite enjoying her War. Gareth was at a Dame school in Newick, wrinkled socks and a satchel; Elizabeth groomed horses at Miss Umfreville's Stables; only my father was absent, sleeping as he did mostly at *The Times* if the Raids were too heavy or yet another reverse somewhere forced him to relinquish the security and peace of his own bed. Elsie wandered about the house mournfully, her alabaster skin dull, her eyes sad, her Mechanic in the RAF. Otherwise it was all much as it ever had been. And yet . . .

The cold, clear, December sun slanted through the dusty windows of my ramshackle hut up in the orchard. It was, predictably, called Trees and I had built it with my own hands from bits of junk picked up here and there, furnished it with a couple of chairs, a table, a marionette theatre of imposing size, shelves for books and a glass vivarium which had once contained lizards and a grass snake called Bill who ate them all.

Today it stood empty and forlorn. A smell of damp and rotten apples from a great tumbled pile of windfalls in a corner, mildew on the faded carpet, books curling limply, cobwebs draping the dusty curtains of the theatre, the vivarium cracked and empty. I picked up a forgotten copy of *Theatre World* for October '38, the pages glued together with wet, Marie Tempest and John Gielgud almost completely devoured by snails. Things weren't at all as they had been. My sister came wandering up through the lichened trees and peered through the dusty windows.

"I've been looking for you," she said.

"What for?"

"Just looking. To see where you were, that's all." She sat down and scraped some mud off her wellingtons with a stick. "Doesn't it smell awful. All mouldy and horrid."

"So do you. You smell dreadful."

She laughed, and threw a lump of mud into the ragged garden outside. "That's horses. I groom three, you know, and do the saddles and things."

"It's dung," I said. "DUNG . . ."

"spells Dung!" she finished. "Do you remember, Lally and the stallion?"

"Of course I do. I expect he was really quite safe, the stallion, it was only Reg who tried to frighten us out of our wits."

"He was called Dobbin, wasn't he . . . so he can't have been all that awful." She looked round the place. "Isn't it sad though? All this . . . I never come here now, you know, it's too sad and creepy."

We sat for a while in silence looking out of the door down through the trees to the little stream and the bamboo break riffling in the cool wind. Presently she got up and went to the window, pressing her face against the glass.

"Do you think you'll get killed? In the Army, I mean?" The snails had eaten right up to Marie Tempest's neck.

"I don't know. I could just as easily get killed in the Blitz. A lot of people do."

She was playing noughts and crosses with herself in the dust. "But the Army's different. With guns and things. I expect it'd be quick, wouldn't it? If you did get killed?"

"I hope so. Would you care?"

"Mother would."

"But would you too, I mean?"

She crossed out a game with a stroke of her finger. "Yes. I'd cry, I expect."

"I hope you would. But you'd still have Gareth, wouldn't you?"

She wiped the game out with her fist in big circular movements. "He's too little."

"But he wears a satchel now, he'll be grown up soon."

"It wouldn't be the same because he doesn't remember the Cottage . . ." she pulled on a pair of woollen gloves slowly pushing her fingers to the ends ". . . or the gully or Great Meadow. Do you remember Great Meadow, wasn't it lovely then . . ."

"And Lally's ginger beer! Wasn't it so lovely then . . ."

"Except you were rotten to me all the time."

"I was not! I liked you very much indeed."

"When you stuck the knife in me . . ."

"Oh that . . ."

"Well, I've still got the scar. Lally said it will show in an evening dress."

We wandered out of the damp studio into the clear hard light and, dodging under the branches, walked back to the house for lunch. I took her woolly hand and she looked at me with surprise. "I hope you don't get killed, that's all," she said, "because when it's all finished you might become a Film Star or something, like Lloyd Nolan or Robert Taylor and then I could come and live with you in Hollywood and we'd have real palm trees in the garden."

The idea suddenly cheered me up; she was being so silly that it almost made sense. I pushed her suddenly and she gave a scream and slithered about on the muddy path.

"I hate you! What did you do that for when I was being so nice to you? I might have got this coat all mucky, and it's my school one too . . . but you don't care, oh no . . . you're just vile."

We heard Elsie through the trees banging on a tin tray with a spoon to call us in for our meal, and Rogan our terrier came bounding up the path, tongue lolling, tail wagging. I put my arm round her neck and pulled her to me. "I'm sorry . . . I didn't mean it . . . really. I was just suddenly feeling happy again." She shrugged me off a bit, but not much and we walked on to the house. "It's a funny way of showing it, that's all I can say," she said. "It's stuffed cabbage today and there's no H.P. sauce. Oh this war! It *is* a bit of a nuisance."

★　　★　　★

At the final run through before the dress rehearsal we heard the stick of bombs ripping down somewhere behind the theatre across St Martin's Lane. The final one, we felt sure, would hit us; on hands and knees under the Stalls we heard it, with gratitude, crash into the Hippodrome opposite. The lights flicked and went on again, we scrambled up from our graceless positions, Miss Evans straightened her hat and Peter raised his hands to catch a small disc of paper which came gently eddying down through the dusty air. He read it out aloud. "Do Not Accept This Programme Unless The Seal Is Unbroken." We all laughed stupidly and the rehearsal finished. Tony Forwood, who was attending this performance before he moved, the next day, to Yeovil, suggested that we all clear off and find shelter somewhere, and that if anyone wanted a lift he had a car outside and enough petrol. Miss Evans said she'd like a lift to Albany where she had a flat and we left the theatre to enter an inferno in Charing Cross Road. The whole world seemed to be on fire, the sky crimson, dust and smoke like a thick fog, the glass canopy round the theatre shattered into inch long splinters, rubble, broken branches and fire hoses everywhere. The Hippodrome was burning fiercely, people cursing, coughing and running, wires looped across the street and everywhere belching heat and smoke. Five of us piled into the miraculously untouched car standing by the curb, but by the time

9(a) Self and Natalie Jordan, "Grief Goes Over", Amersham 1940.
9(b) Lieutenant Anthony Forwood R.A., Summer 1940.
9(c) The Playhouse, Amersham on the Hill, 1940.

10(a) Stephen Murray, Jenny Laird, Max Adrian, Ann Wilton, myself and Dorothy Hamilton in "Cornelius". Westminster Theatre, August 1940. (Photo: Angus McBean)

10(b) "In for a Dip". Myself, Vida Hope, Joan Sterndale Bennett and Peter Ustinov, Diversion No. 2, 1940. (Photo: Tunbridge & Sedgwick) we had bounced and bumped to Leicester Square, past the ruins of the Café Anglais and the flaming roof of the Leicester Square Theatre, we knew that we were stuck. Wally suddenly remembered that there was a small Afternoon Drinking Club not far away in Orange Street, and rather than be buried alive in Tony's soft-top Mercedes, it was suggested that we make for its shelter. He was, he said, a member.

Streaked with dust and flakes of oily soot we clambered up a couple of flights to a discreet polished door, and were admitted, resentfully, into the calm of a dimly lit room. A thick carpet, a small bar in one corner, a white baby grand in the other. Soft, warm, safe. A pale young man in a blue angora sweater was playing "Our Love Affair"—he looked up with polite surprise but went on, his identity bracelets gleaming softly. At the bar, brushing down the dust and bits of glass, Miss Evans ordered an Orange Juice from the slender bar man with a sun-tanned face. The rest of us had something stronger and the young man at the piano rippled into "Run Rabbit Run" defiantly. Bombs fell intermittently, shaking the room, making a glass tank of wax lilies jerk and wobble in the blast. Eventually Miss Evans decided that she must, simply must, get back to Albany, which was, as she pointed out "just down the road" and that she would walk since no traffic could move in Piccadilly. We went with her offering company in one form or another all of which she firmly refused, and the last we saw of her was her tall, determined figure, walking swiftly down the crimson street, until the swirling smoke and dust hid her from sight. She was back the next morning on the dot and "Diversion" opened to a packed house and great acclaim. Apart from the Windmill up the road, we were the only theatre open for business in London.

Dressing-room number four at Wyndhams was hardly palatial, but Peter and I settled down, one on each side, and started a small salon. Rather he did. I was far too timid. He had vast energy which astonished and embarrassed me, and although he had two numbers of his own in the show, as well as doing all the bits and pieces as I did, he still found the time to write another play which he handed, sheet by sheet, to an enraptured Joyce Grenfell who sat at his feet on the cramped floor in blue velvet. People were always dropping in to see him, to talk in varied languages, argue and drink tea. It was all very Russian. Vida brought lunch from the pub next door and we had picnics which seemed to last most of the day. We were in the theatre most of the time anyway: two shows daily, three on matinées, all gauged exactly so that the audiences were well away by the time the Warning went, which it did regularly every evening between five-thirty and six. If it was hard and tiring I never knew. I was far too busy and far too happy. Although I had nothing much to do, a few lines here and there and the tag line of a not very good sketch, my days seemed filled to bursting, I was in euphoria. It came as something of a shock, therefore, one day to receive my Medical Exam Papers and a command to report at some obscure address in Brighton. A sorry undignified affair in a converted shop off North Street. Naked and ashamed, we shuffled along in a smelly line before white-coated, weary Doctors who prodded, lifted, and pressed various parts of our flinching bodies and passed us fit for duty. In one of the cheap restaurants where I cleared the tables, I had heard rumours from some of the Actors who made up most of the clientele, that the best thing to do before a medical was to drink endless cups of black coffee an hour before, thus increasing one's heartbeat, or else to swallow castor oil mixed with a certain amount of soot, which would make one cough and leave a warning sediment in the lungs for the X-rays. Neither suggestion seemed to me to be worth the risk, so I didn't bother. But that morning in Brighton in the cold, stone-floored shop, I almost wished that I had heeded my advisers. Too late. I was fit and well and returned to the show chastened but healthy.

Peter's energy being almost limitless, he also did an act in the evenings after our shows were over at a small cellar night club called "The Nightlight" opposite the stage door of the Hippodrome. He suggested that as I found the evenings boring and dull, since the final curtain was at 5.30, I should try for an audition and get together an act for the Club. This would add to my earnings and be good experience. With a sudden spurt of imagination or something, I wrote a pretty dire monologue based on the character I had played in "Cornelius", called "Lawrence". In a battered felt hat, a draggly rain coat and a tartan scarf I presented myself for my audition one morning in the empty club. It is well known that a Night Club in the morning is as near Hell as one can possibly imagine: illusions are stripped away, the sheer tattiness and ugliness of everything is laid bare. Standing on the minute stage, in my uninspired costume I went through my hastily written, hastily learned, act. I was supposed to be an Electrical

Addict and did the whole monologue holding two bits of flex. The trick, if that is the word, was that at the end I put them together and blacked out the house. To immense applause, I hoped.

It must have been a pretty tough time for the Nightlight because I passed, and opened there two evenings later on a bill with Peter Ustinov, Ord Hamilton, and a Hungarian lady who sang a song about a "Teenie Weenie Martinee". . . . I got paid five pounds a week. Life, apart from the Medical and the Bombs, was looking very rosy indeed.

The Nightlight was nearly always filled. It was a dark, low room below two shops, down a single winding staircase, and after the Café de Paris got hit it was closed because of the dangers it held. One bomb on the Nightlight and everyone would have perished. But while it lasted, so did I. And "Lawrence" got polished and embellished with every exposure. Not always for his own good. Tony Forwood was delighted at my enterprise, shattered by my performance, but put it all down, charitably, to Good Experience and refused all percentages until After The War. Which from where I was standing seemed to be getting longer and longer and must surely engulf me. Which it did. One morning Peter and I, both the same age and both in the same Initial Category, went down to Charing Cross and signed up. It was a daunting moment for us both, only very slightly lightened by the fact that when we got back to the Theatre we were treated as if we had just relieved Mafeking and Vida had brought a bottle of champagne. The pleasure was increased, a few days later, by the news that we were both to be Deferred for three months because we were in the show and were helping to boost Morale. Which made me, at any rate, feel excessively important. However, May was not all that far away . . . and in one degree I was almost glad at last to know that I had to go. Everyone it seemed was in Uniform. I was beginning to feel uncomfortable and out of place in civilian clothes. A very earnest actor suggested one evening at The Nightlight that I should become a Conscientious Objector, and gave me a pile of leaflets explaining the facts. The idea of digging ditches in Scotland, of all places, of becoming a Stretcher Bearer or working for the Forestry Commission and allowing the Germans to rape my sister horrified me, and I settled for the idea of a short, undemanding, anonymous, career in the Army. The shorter the better. Preferably in the Cook House.

"You mustn't give things up, you know, ducky, when you get in," said Vida one evening in the kitchen of the little flat in Belsize Crescent where she lived with a girl friend and sometimes cooked me a meal after the shows. "You must go on writing and drawing, however difficult it may be. Write anywhere . . . you can always take a bit of paper and a pencil with you: don't just flop about cleaning your equipment or whatever they do in their free time . . . you must keep your mind going." She bounced two fried slices of Spam and some potatoes on to a plate and set them before me. "And start with poetry . . . men always do in the Army, it makes them very emotional and odd. Some of the best poetry was written in wartime you know."

I remembered, glumly, Brooke, Blunden, Sassoon and all the others whose works I had learned by heart during my "re-incarnation" period and wondered how on earth I could ever approach such standards, and what horrors and fears I must endure in order to commit them to paper. And, as I pointed out, I felt that I would have to have someone to write to, or for . . . I could not envisage just writing for myself.

"Well! Write to me," she said. "Write everything to me. I'd love it, you know that: I'd try and help you, criticise, you know . . . I used to be in Copywriting so I know a *bit* about words. Not much but something. Send me your first poem. Make it a promise now and write everything and anything which comes into your head. But put it down, ducky, get it out. Don't let it rot there . . . I know you, you're terribly lazy unless you have the incentive . . . well, it's easy. I'll be the incentive, you see."

Walking down to Fellows Road after supper I knew that what she had said was true, and that I would try to follow her advice: I would take note books and pencils and some paints perhaps when the time came. And I'd try and join a Concert Party . . . she said they always had Concert Parties and that they would welcome a professional with open arms . . . if there wasn't one perhaps I could start one . . . first a sort of Revue . . . songs and sketches, that sort of thing, then later maybe a simple play. Which I would direct, naturally, and Star in. Thinking in this manner I felt very cheered up. The future didn't seem so daunting with these possibilities ahead and she had very generously given me herself as my Incentive, and although a raid was in progress during my long walk back, and the air lethal with red hot fragments from the Ack Ack guns on Primrose Hill, I felt happy and sure again, and protected, for she had also very thoughtfully provided me with her umbrella.

* * *

On April the 14th I left Wyndhams with Peter: our Deferment was almost up, and they had to train replacements for the show. The whole cast signed our programmes as a souvenir, and I left the theatre with a heavy heart to the strains of the Opening Number as a thin youth leaped about in my place showing signs of being far better than I had. It rose somewhat when Miss Hanney said that a Miss Deans had telephoned and would I call her back urgently the moment I got in. Annie was at Drury Lane which was the Headquarters of ENSA. She said that there was a part going in a new tour of "The Ghost Train" and if I was out of "Diversion" why didn't I come along and try? If I was in ENSA, she reasoned, I would almost automatically be Deferred again and this could go on for as long as the tour lasted, which was for six months at least, by which time the war was bound to be over and I needn't go. It was very persuasive. Especially as I was free, miserable and at a loose end. A couple of days later I attended a slim Audition on the stage at Drury Lane and got the part of the Juvenile with Arnold Ridley directing his own production. But I was not a good choice, and it was not the happiest of times. Cold dreary barns of theatres, long bus journeys in rain and fog, miserable hostels and endless stations. I felt even guiltier playing to uniformed troops than I had felt walking the streets of London, and by the time we got to Amesbury I welcomed the telephone call from my father, to say that I was requested to report for Military Service at Catterick Camp, Yorkshire, on May the 4th next. I wanted no further deferments. When the final curtain came down, for me, on my last performance in "The Ghost Train" I felt a surge of joy. Someone had made a decision for me; I'd do just what I was told from now on in . . . until it was over.

* * *

Gareth said he wanted a German helmet or a coconut, depending on where I got sent. My father said that for at least twenty weeks the nearest I would get to Action of any kind would be the barrack square or assault courses on the moors. The best I'd be able to send him would be a bunch of heather or, at worst, a picture postcard of Darlington.

He was slightly amused that I had been sent to a Signals Unit. I was amazed. "What did you put on your form when you signed up? I mean you don't know a flag from a cat's whisker! You can't even get the Home Service on the wireless. I really can't see you tapping away at Morse Code."

"I just put 'Actor' down where it said 'Profession' and then the schools where it said 'Education' . . ."

"Which you hardly had."

"Well . . . I don't know *why* they sent me to a Signals Unit any more than you do. I'm told the Army is a bit funny in that sort of way."

It was decided that, very probably, the Glasgow Technical School had tipped the scale in my favour away from the ignominious Infantry into something a little more Specialised.

"Will you try for a commission, if they ask you?" said my father, pouring the wine for my last family dinner. "I believe it is not very fashionable among people of your age today . . . the Class thing?"

"I'll try. I mean I'd like to. It's a bit more comfortable, isn't it . . ."

He folded his napkin and slid it into a silver ring. "That depends. Not always. It carries a good deal of responsibility. You don't come first, you realise, the men under you do. Your troop or platoon or whatever it is . . . and I never thought that you particularly cared for responsibility . . . actors don't very much, do they?" He was not being in the least unkind. Accurate. I had to agree: but assured him that a new life lay before me, and that the two years which had passed so swiftly and so filled with experiences, had opened my eyes. I would make a very determined effort to succeed somehow, whatever I had to do. I would treat the whole operation exactly as I had tried to treat the Theatre . . . with auditions, energy, elbowing and climbing; it wasn't so very different. The survival of the fittest, as with beasts, and I'd try to survive.

Strangely enough on that final evening, I really didn't think it was going to be all that difficult. One chapter had closed at Amesbury, another was about to open. I was, I felt, quite ready.

He didn't seem as sure but on the other hand was happy that I had decided not to be a Concie, as he called them, and agreed with me that with determination, hard work and a good deal of luck, anything was possible. Even an unlikely commission. I said that those were the Theatre rules. He smiled, shook his head and rang the little bell for Elsie.

We went down to the pond with the last of the wine and our glasses. It was a still, warm evening, even though it was yet so very early in the year. May bugs skimmed the surface of the water, bumping and zig zagging over the tightly closed waterlily buds which, I suddenly realised with a sharp thrust of regret, I would not see in flower, for the next time I came home it would be winter. My mother sat on the swinging hammock, a jacket about her shoulders, sewing a button, or something, on one of Gareth's shirts. The rusty springs creaked as she moved gently back and forwards. Across the pond, rustling about in the new spring sedge, my sister hunted for a beast with Rogan, his tail wagging, feet splashing in and out of the water. Ripples bobbled the lily buds and we could hear her voice clear across the soft evening air: "Ratty! Where's Ratty! Seek the rat, seek him . . ."

It was infinitely peaceful, safe, impossible to believe that at this very hour tomorrow I would be hundreds of miles away starting the process of becoming a soldier and melting my identity into a Mass. This I firmly resolved, there and then by the pond, never to do. I would keep all that these people, this place, the Cottage, Lally, and all the rest had given me, and I'd never let any of them go. They would be my salvation and my comfort if, and when, things got too hard.

My father spun his cigarette butt out across the pond. A tiny, glowing ember, arking in the dusk, a final second before extinction in the rushes.

"I expect," he said, clearing his throat (he had been thinking too), "they'll send you to the Far East when the time comes. But that's pretty safe really. I don't *think* we'll have much trouble there because the Americans are bound to come in with us sooner or later . . . usually later, like last time, but they'll come in, of that I'm sure. And with them there *and* Singapore, you'll have a pretty easy time. Gareth may get his coconut."

The Far East was light million years away to me sitting there in the falling dusk. I even felt that I would prefer Yorkshire. "Anyway," said my father, starting to collect the cushions and empty glasses, "your war won't be like mine. Mine was all defensive. Ten yards back and forth a year in the mud. This is an Attacking War. I don't think you'll have much time for boredom . . . once it starts again it'll all be over before you can say Jack Robinson . . . unless I'm *very* much mistaken." He started up the bank towards the house, calling to the dog.

My mother rolled up her sewing, closed the workbasket and pulled the jacket tightly round her shoulders.

"It suddenly gets awfully cold. It's far too early to sit out yet. But so pretty. Bring up the other cushions and that ash-tray, it will look so sordid . . ."

We walked slowly up to the house. The sky was velvet blue. A star was up. The air still. A moorhen, startled by our steps, hurried away on green legs to the water. When we got to the lawn my mother stopped and took a deep breath. "How lovely it is!" she said. "It's going to be a fine day tomorrow, you see. Just as well: I've got six rows of Winter Greens to get in: should have done them last week . . . never mind." She reached out suddenly, pulled me to her and kissed me hard. "Just you think of your poor old Ma tomorrow: I'm really past the age." I knew that it was her way of saying goodbye. There was to be no fuss in the morning.

* * *

There wasn't. Elsie called me punctually at seven-thirty with tea and a biscuit and I lay comfortably for a moment watching the shadows of the rowan tree flicker across the ceiling. Then remembered. And fear flooded into me like a fast running tap.

There was nothing at all to pack save my washing gear, one towel, a pair of pyjamas all in an empty suitcase for the return of my Civilian Clothes, according to the bit of grey paper which had come with something called the Movement Order. In the Morning Room everyone was very bright and cheerful. My mother brilliant in a cotton summer dress. No one spoke of War, of Army or Soldiers. Breakfast was a sort of Hell.

At the car we stood about awkwardly. My father stuck the empty case into the boot: the light across the Common sharp and clear. Cobwebs dew-silvered. I said something about it going to be a perfect day for Winter Greens and climbed in. No kisses, no final embraces: my mother called out cheerfully, perhaps too loudly, "Bye darling!" and my sister, holding Rogan in her arms, waggled one of his forelegs into a wave. I didn't look back.

Nor did I try to speak until we had passed "The Anchor" on Scaynes Hill. Then I fumbled about and lit a cigarette.

"I'm sorry . . ." I said. My father looked troubled.

"What about?"

"Well . . . *The Times* . . . you know . . ."

"Oh that!" he sounded relieved. "You don't have to worry about that now, my dear. Can't force people, you know. It doesn't matter."

"But you minded?"

"Oh . . . just a bit . . ."

"Well I'll try and make up for it, in the Army . . ."

"I know you will. I don't mind what you do in life as long as you do your best. That's all that matters."

"I promise." We drove on through a spinney of greening larches.

"You're not worried about being killed, are you?" He sounded as if I wasn't.

"No! Goodness no . . ."

"And you know about the VD thing, naturally . . . that's as bad as any Jerry bullet . . ."

"Yes I know about that. I'll take care."

"And keep your writing going, letters, a diary that sort of thing. I did."

"And painting. I've slipped a tin of watercolours into my coat."

"Excellent. There is an awful lot of sitting about in the Army, you'll find . . . fifty per cent boredom, someone said. It'll be good to have something like that to do, you'll see."

In the train he rifled through his brief-case to find his *Times* and brought out a small green sketch-book. He chucked it across to me. "Useful size. I had one. Just fits into your haversack or a pocket. You might find it handy."

We parted at Victoria with no words and a rough hug. I got a taxi to Wyndhams where I left the empty suitcase with Doris at the stage door and then met Vida outside Warners. She was wearing a hat with a white rose and a veil. It didn't suit her, and she knew it. We took arms and walked down to Lyons on the corner and the "Olde Vienna Café" which we liked because it was full of red plush, gilt, and newspapers stuck on bamboo sticks. It was also cheap and you could have as much coffee as you liked if you bought a bit of gateau.

"They'll cut all your hair off, ducky, you know that of course. And to the bone because you're an Actor and you do rather look like one." She pushed back the spotted veil laughing: "But it'll suit you." She touched my hand to show that she thought I was nice enough anyway.

"Given you my address, haven't I?"

"Catterick Camp, Yorks."

"I'll know more after tomorrow. Have to change at Darlington."

"Ghastly place. Mills and doom."

"And then Richmond. There's a castle . . ."

She tried a bit of the gateau with a fork but it squashed and she pushed it aside.

"A theatre too. Regency but they don't use it."

"It's not a Date or anything?"

"No. No. They store things in it. Furniture, that sort of stuff."

"What a waste."

"It's all a bloody waste . . ."

We sat and looked at each other. The sub-Coward dialogue faded. I tried to rally.

"How long do you think the Show will last?"

She picked up the too hot coffee-pot, swore, and fumbled for her napkin to wrap round the handle. "Another couple of months. Depends on the Raids really. Peter's in Kent, did you know? Infantry. I must say the new boy looks a bit silly in your kilts, they come down to his shins." She stopped quickly. "When you come back, you know, I think you ought to have a try at the Cinema. Your kind of work is just right for their what-do-you-call-it . . . Technique. It's very intimate. You might do awfully well. Do you fancy yourself as a Film Star?" She laughed as if she knew the answer.

"You've got to look like Clark Gable or someone . . ." I said. She collected her gloves and handbag from the seat beside her. "Nonsense! Look at Wallace Beery! Or Lon Chaney! They'd snap you up. When you're marching about up there doing your drill I think you ought to have a . . . well: think about it." She made her mouth into a round O and carefully smoothed it with her finger. "I think you'd be spiffing on the Flicks, I really do . . . with those big sad eyes of yours, ducky, you couldn't miss. *I'd*

250

know it's because you've forgotten something, but *they'll* think it's because you've lost something . . ."

At King's Cross we pushed through a sea of khaki and blue, crying children, anxious women, trundling tea-urns, trolleys, hissing steam, and hundreds, it seemed, of men carrying empty suitcases. My lot, I thought. The Conscript Special. At Platform 10 there were three men singing "Tipperary" and waving a bottle about and a woman passed us with a white face, weeping without expression, holding a bunch of bluebells.

Vida said: "That's your train, isn't it?"

"Yes . . ."

"Well I'm not very good at this part. I'll just go." I kissed her on the cheek through the veil and saw that she was crying too. Quickly she waved a hand before my mouth. "Don't speak . . . and write . . . remember to write to me . . . the poems . . . send them to me . . ." She turned swiftly and went away. Bumping into people, fumbling in her handbag. Aunt Hester at Queen Street . . . the same wrench of sadness. All gone. I couldn't run after her.

The man at the gate looked at my bit of paper. "Change at Darlington, sonny," he said.

*   *   *

A full compartment. One elderly woman in the corner by the window, knitting something fluffy. I looked at the sketch-book which I had in my pocket. He had written on the inside cover. My initials, then "from" and his initials, U. v. d. B. At the bottom he had put, "With Love" and the date. A lump, large as a fist, rose unbidden to my throat. I stared out of the dirty window. Somewhere after Luton I lit a cigarette but the knitting woman said she'd vomit if I smoked and this was a Non Smoker.

I stood in the corridor leaning against the door. On both sides other men were doing the same. Hands in pockets, bodies lurching with the train, staring out at the racing fields, woods, scattered houses, billows of white smoke ripping away from the engine. No one speaking, or singing, just leaning, bodies rolling with the motion, having a "jolly good think" as Lally used to say . . . Think. Think. Not of today, of tonight, of tomorrow, just Think. Of the good things. The partridges in the glass case at Twickenham, the Zeppelin from Potters Bar . . . Winter Greens;

is she doing them now, bending between the rows . . . No. Not *that*. Well; Great Meadow then, the way it rises high up from the road to the gate by the privy . . . the feel of wet grasses against bare legs . . . you could write a poem about that. Vida's poem. How do you write a Sonnet. "Shall I Compare Thee To A Summer's Day . . ." How do you paint love? You can paint death and life but love? People in love, holding hands, lying with each other . . . but that's not Love. How do you paint the intangible, how do you paint all the love which I have had and which this sodding train is taking me away from . . . No! Think! Constructively. What will it be like after? When you come back. The Haymarket? His Majesty's? Maybe the Old Vic after all . . . a Star Character Actor like Edith Evans . . . there will be time, plenty of time then . . . this'll be a dream in a year or a bit . . . perhaps I *should* try the Flicks . . . be a film actor. More money. Huge money. Sometimes a hundred pounds a day even . . . will there be beds or bunks . . . or just straw on the floor or something . . . Usually bunks in the Barrack Rooms, one on top of the other, like rabbits . . . Elizabeth said that we could have real palm trees in the garden in Hollywood . . . and swimming pools too I suppose . . . Florida Palms they are called . . . Swimming pools and a Mess Hall . . . like the ones at Larkhill, Amesbury . . . like the Tuck Shop at School. But no Lavatory. Sweet God! . . . No lavatories . . . they wouldn't dunk me at nineteen would they . . . everyone has a different accent in the Army . . . a Melting Pot . . . like Hollywood. They like English accents there. You won't be dunked in the Lav. in Hollywood. Think of Ronald Colman, Leslie Howard, Dame May Whitty. . . . Soldiers are equal. I wonder how soon they will let me telephone? It has started to rain. Good for the Winter Greens. . . . Not that. Funny how the drops slide down the window so dreadfully slowly when the train is moving so fast. Centrifugal Force or something. See how they slip, slowly, slowly, drop by drop . . . and then stop quite still like this one . . . and as suddenly tear away and run down the window into oblivion in the sill. Like a life. My drawn reflection, behind me No Smoking: back to front it looks strange. ⅁ᴎⅠꞰOMƧ Oᴎ. That's how Nosmo King found his name . . . if I'm killed let it be quick . . . not a leg or an arm or a bit of my face . . . that would muck everything up for Afterwards. Just as long as it's quick. Obliterate. Obliterate quickly . . . it's raining heavily now . . . lambs in the fields like small sodden handkerchiefs . . . high chimneys of a brick works . . . six table legs in the dark sky . . . must be Bedford. . . . Afterwards won't be a Barrack Room. That's Now. Think of Afterwards. A Dressing Room not a Barrack Room . . . a Star on the door would be quite nice . . . just imagine that. There you are, and you are just about to turn the handle and, very slowly, you go in. . . .

16

IT was pitch dark and smelled of conditioned air and beer stains. Glitters of light slitted through the shutters. I felt my way across the room, hit a table, and pushed open the windows. Hot smoggy air came up from the Studio Yard. In front the yawning doors of A and C Stage. Six men pushing half a snow-capped mountain trundled up the yard. A woman came running down, a bundle of sequined dresses over her arm, a paper cup of coffee in her hand. To my far left, the carpenters' shop. Planks and sawdust and gilded doors leaning against the concrete walls. To my right, high up, the misty smog-smudged ridge of the hills. The great wooden sign striding the skyline, one letter missing, long since fallen. Hol-ywood.

I had arrived at last. I was there where it all started. The most oriental city on earth West of Calcutta. My heart fell with despair. Six months to go.

Joe came barging in opening doors and drawers, switching on lights, trying taps and pulling the lavatory chain. He plumped up cushions and looked round the room carefully. Hands on hips, blue jeans bursting, a gold cross round his neck winking in the thin sunlight. He jangled his identity bracelet and shrugged.

"This is a good room, you know. Masculine. All the Male Stars have rooms like this, very Butch. This one is *reely* nice, you know? They're doing you good so far. Two ice boxes you got, television, radio and a shower *and* a bath . . . that's a First Class Room. You get judged by that here, you know. If you get to have just the john and a shower and no ice box you don't *reely* rate. Not at all. This is Star Stuff. You like it?" He seemed indifferent.

It was pine panelled. Fake plaster pine panelled. Tweed carpet like old porridge. Chairs and settees covered in violent tartan. Hunting prints on the walls, a sword, a galleon in full sail, two ice boxes disguised as corn-chests, lamp shades with maps of the world on them. I found "England" squashed up beside "Norway", a small table with a flat bowl of plastic sweet peas and dahlias. The bathroom off. Plain, white, Butch. All very Male.

"Fine."

"Well it's gotta be. This is what you are allocated. This is what you got. This is what you stay with. Get it? It's *reel* nice. But I'll just check something." He was back in the bathroom turning on all the taps, pulling the plugs. He beckoned me to come in to him. In the roar of water he said, in normal tones: "Just check we ain't got any bugging things here. If we have you gotta keep your trap closed unless you run water, get it? That blurs the tape." He strode into the dressing room and yanked at the pictures. Henry Alkins were pushed about. No microphones. The air-conditioner above the door was pulled apart. Satisfied, he lifted the bowl of sweet peas and dahlias. They came up in his hands with a long black wire which ran down through the table-top. His face was triumphant. But the wire was unconnected. No plug at the end . . . thin twists of copper. He replaced the bowl and motioned me into the bathroom again.

"You see that? Wired. And there is another air-conditioner just over the window. Even for a *reely* good room it don't rate *two* air-conditioners." Back he went, up on a chair and struggled with the second air-conditioner. The vented front came away in his hands revealing an empty metal box behind. There was dust and a dead moth. Worms of fabric dust . . . he scattered thoughtfully over the carpet. "I reckon it's all been disconnected . . . when Levison was alive, every sodding room was connected to a Central Pool. So they could know if you was 'happy' or if you was 'worried about the script' or anything like that. Just so they could 'help' you if supposin' you was too shy to ask out for something . . . but I reckon that's over now. Things was different with McCarthy . . . but you seem unhooked. Just watch out, though. If you do have something reely important to say, just do it in the john. No use you taking any chances. Saul Gallows didn't want you in the Movie, you know that, a Limey with a British Accent . . . so you just gotta be careful and keep your nose nice and clean? You ain't Gay, are you?" I shook my head. He patted his crotch. "Just thought I'd ask, that's all, most everyone is in this town . . . but we'll get on fine. There's a nice guy who tested all the girls for the part of the Countess . . . but he ain't against you. You'll like him, his name's Rod Raper . . . that's what the Studio call him . . . we just call him Al. You'll meet him I reckon. Reel nice kid. He won't hold nothing against you."

I slumped into one of the tartan chairs and Joe jangled a

bracelet, fixed the blind over the window and presently left me to my Masculine-Plaster-Panelled-Gloom.

Beside one of the map-lamps lay a large piece of paper. Cautiously I took it up and read it: Production 9678. Pre-Production Day 1. 8.00 a.m. Arrive Studio. D.R. 2. Block A. 8.30 a.m. Music Conference. Room 2456. Block C. V. Aller. Dummy piano. Playbacks. Key Board. 10.00 a.m. Make Up. Room 2784. It went on until it simply said "Car. Main Gate. 6.30 p.m." Trapped.

Room 2456 was dim, painted brown with a brown carpet and three pianos. The blinds were down; electric light gleamed dully on the scratched wood of the Broadwood. On one wall a faded colour photograph of Myrna Loy, on the other a View Of Naples. A tall coat and hat rack. A gramophone. Two chairs and Victor Aller. We had met briefly before at what was called a "General Meeting To Get Acquainted". He was to teach me the Piano and never leave my side night and day until the final Shot was in the Can. He was totally at my disposal. Small, benign. A Russian Jew with glittering rimless glasses and beautiful hands, he sat quietly at the Broadwood playing something sad. I didn't interrupt him but sat quietly in the chair beside him. He switched music and went into something extremely fast, short and vaguely familiar. He placed his hands on his knees and smiled at me.

"That's Chopsticks."

"Oh."

"You know it?"

"I think so . . . somewhere."

"Everyone knows it. It's a child's exercise. Play it."

"I have never played a piano in my life. I couldn't."

A pause like a century.

"You gotta be Liszt."

"I know that."

"Liszt played piano."

"Yes."

"You don't dispute that?"

"No."

"He played piano like no one else played piano."

"I believe . . ."

"And you don't?"

"No. Never."

256

"Well we gotta start then. That's what I'm here for. To teach you to play piano and fast. And like Liszt."

"Thank you."

"Don't thank me till I have." He played some scales rapidly. I watched his hands, dull with fear. "These are just scales . . . we'll have to do a lot of this, just to exercise your fingers . . . show me your span."

"What's that?"

"Shit! Put your hands out in front of you and spread your fingers . . . that's a span."

I did as he asked. My hands looked supplicating. They were.

"Nice span you got. You play tennis?"

"No."

"Football?"

"No."

"Ping pong . . . table tennis?"

"No neither."

Another long stupefied pause. The air-conditioner hissed and throbbed.

"You play that game you have in England. With a bat and a ball . . . like rounders?"

"Cricket?"

"Yeah. Cricket. You play that?"

"No."

"Shit." He played another set of scales.

"And you gotta be Liszt?"

"They tell me so."

"In five weeks we start shooting in Vienna. You going to be ready?"

"What do you think?"

"Not in a million years let alone five weeks. You got eighty-five minutes of fucking Music in this Production. Eighty-five minutes of music not including conducting Les Préludes and the Rákóczy March."

"They said they'd use a Double for my hands. They would only shoot me in long shot or so that my hands were hidden by the key-board. That's what they said."

"Where did they say they would use a Double?"

"They said so in London when we all first met . . . and in New York when I met the Front Office in Mr Gallows' office. We'll use a Double, they said."

"They didn't tell *me*. They told me I was hired for six months to teach you piano, to teach you to play like Liszt and to Conduct. I got the Contract. You wanna see my contract? Six months I have. I am at your total disposal. I don't have a wife, two kids, or a cardiac condition . . . I just have you and two pianos and eighty-five fuckin' minutes of music to get into you before the end of the six months."

"I'm sorry."

"So'm I. Shit. A Double. No one told *me* about a Double. They said categorically you would be required to play it *all*. That's what they told me. Fuck the Front Office and Gallows. They just don't happen to be here in California. They don't know. Charles Vidor says you play and you play, I assure you."

"Well. I'd better start. I mean, perhaps you could show me, very slowly, a bit of something I have to play . . . not Chopsticks. It's too fast."

"So is the fuckin' 1st Concerto . . ." He started, very gently and softly to play. It was good. He played with deep feeling and tenderness. I listened and watched. Horrified. How could I ever remember where the fingers went. Which keys to use, the black or the white?

He stopped. And glittered at me.

"That's the Moonlight. That's the slowest piece you got in the whole eighty-five minutes. Try with me. Put your hands on the keys . . . look, like this . . ."

For the next half an hour he quietly and kindly told me about sharps and flats, about bass and span, about thighs, and back, about wrists and fingers, about tempo and allegro and Christ only knows what. I was stunned into voiceless silence. I grew eighty fingers, I sweated, I hit my knees but I never once hit the keys or got the right hand doing anything at the same time as the left. It was a grim half-hour. The glitter in Aller's glasses was like sheet lightning. But cold.

"You have as much co-ordination as a runaway train for Christ's sakes. . . . Do you dispute that?"

"No."

We went on trying until my time, according to the piece of Paper, was over. I got up from my chair unsteadily. He sat in his looking stunned. His fat lower lip sticking out like a sulky baby. I thanked him and started to the door.

"Remember I'll be here all day. Right until six-thirty p.m.

And then I'm available to you all evening at your hotel or here or wherever you like. I don't finish until you do. I don't leave the Studio until you do. I'm here all the time for you to practise. You got five weeks and not a chance in hell. See you later. Remember I'm here all the time, just waiting." He started to play something slow and sad again, his head up, his eyes fixed on Myrna Loy.

*   *   *

Joe helped me into my trousers. Skin tight black taffeta. A white frilly shirt . . . a jacket cut like an hour-glass. We did up zips, hooks and eyes, he fixed an expert silk cravat, and tucked Kleenex round it to prevent the make-up staining the white cloth. Agony to sit down, legs stiff like a milking stool, glossy patent boots slid on, and trousers strapped under. Gloves, sixty pairs all hand made in Paris, France, were chalked and eased on to my swollen, fat fingers. He said I looked swell. I felt silly and too tight, and scared to death. It wasn't my Test we were doing . . . I already had the fatal role . . . we were testing ladies for The Countess. But I felt as terrified as if they were testing me for Cholera.

In the Make-Up Room a silent man in a white coat like a surgeon had covered me in a pink nylon robe, read a list of instructions in his hand, studied some enormous black and white blow-ups of Liszt aged twenty-seven and started to work. We didn't speak. Except once, when I said, politely and quietly, "I never wear make-up in England." He didn't stop covering my face with a scented sponge. "You do in Hollywood," he said. The final result in the mirror looked like a mad Rocking Horse. My hair had been washed and rolled in curlers and baked and combed and tinted and primped and finally covered with a thick spray of lacquer so that it moved almost independently of my head and body. A great bouffant, faintly pink, tea-cosy of a hairstyle. Liszt at twenty-seven. A mad rocking horse in a pink candyfloss wig. I was humbled to the dust. Joe didn't help by saying I looked cute . . . and when the whole paraphernalia was put together, taffeta trousers, frilly shirt, pink hair and hour-glass coat, I looked and felt like something out of an Army Drag Show. But worse.

The Test Stage was small, made of corrugated iron and

concrete, and built in 1914 when the Studio first developed on the site of an Orange orchard. It was blinding, hot, and smelled of dust and wet paint. There was a quarter of a room. Flock wallpaper, gilded panels, real mahogany doors, thick carpet, bowls of plastic lilac, a piano, naturally, and a fat silk settee. They were busy hanging a chandelier when I walked onto the set and found my chair. Green canvas, my name printed across the back. Awkwardly I sat down, heart heavy, but beating like a mad yo-yo. Someone came up and shook hands and said he was Buddy and welcome to Hollywood, and a nice looking woman with rimless glasses and a stopwatch round her plump neck said her name was Connie and I looked just dreamy. I thanked her and apologised for not being able to get out of the chair because of the tightness of my pants.

"Mercy me! So British of you! Never you mind a bit. Mr Vidor won't be too long: he just went to see yesterday's Test on one of the Chopins. Do you want a cup of coffee? I'm so glad you're on the Production, I just loved you in that film about the Doctors! So English and quaint. Oh here's Mr Vidor now. I'll get you some coffee."

Charles Vidor was shortish, sixty-ish and, as far as he was concerned, stylish. Grey spiky hair like a hedgehog. Manicured nails blushing a gentle pink. Rings glittering. A flat platinum watch. A viewfinder in gold hanging round his neck inscribed with the names of all the films he had directed with it: dressed entirely in grey. Cashmere, silk shirt, immaculate flannels, crocodile shoes, a cigarette in a long paper holder. He smiled across the quarter room, spoke to someone arranging a jar of plastic roses, slapped someone else on the back and sat down beside me in his own canvas chair.

"You look cute," he said and patted my knee absent-mindedly.

"I feel ridiculous personally."

"You look great, kid! Great. I like the hair. You look just like him ... like the pictures we got up in the office ... you seen them? You look just like him. Claude-Pierre said so too and he should know. Claude-Pierre is French from France and he's done all your costooms and he KNOWS. You know the velvet we got for your waistcoat when you play the Campanella bit cost fifty dollars a piece? Fifty dollars for a bit of Paris velvet? Can you beat that? My wife wouldn't spend that much on a bit of Paris velvet and God alone knows she *spends*. You look great." He reached into his cigarette case and fitted another long thin cigarette into the holder.

"About the Campanella . . ."

"What about it?" He was casual and didn't meet my eye.

"Mr Aller says that I have to play the piano. You won't be using a Double."

"That's correct."

"But you said that you would. I can't play the piano. Or tennis or cricket, even a mouth organ."

"Be reasonable! This is Today! Movies can't be faked now. Television brings it all close to them . . . We want you to be the first to *really* play. Everyone else had a double in the old days, but this is Today! We'll start on a close up of your head, anguish, passion, all the music registering there . . . your love for the Princess . . . your mother . . . your agony of mind over the Church . . . and then we pan down, without a cut, mind you, and see your own hands, your very own hands, actually playing the music he wrote! It'll be a sensation. So moving . . ."

"But when do I have the time to learn all this stuff. There is eighty-five minutes Aller says . . ."

"Aller is the greatest teacher in Hollywood. He taught Cornel Wilde to be Chopin. He worked on two of my last pictures, I trust him implicitly. If he says eighty-five it means he *can teach* you eighty-five minutes. And we'll have a Box Office Smash such as you have never seen before. You want to be a Movie Star? Well, you have to work for it." He lit his cigarette and waved cheerfully across at someone else arranging yet another pot of flowers.

"Don't put the fuckin' things behind the chair, Al, they'll stick out of her head when we do the Close shot . . . move 'em to the little table by the drapes there . . . fine . . . you're a good kid."

I sat in a state of rigid despair. There was nothing more to say; yet. I'd have to wait. Try a few more times with Aller. Connie came with coffee in paper cups, she offered sugar in paper wraps, and plastic spoons. She sat beside us on a small stool, twinkling like a Japanese lantern, all sweetness and light with the eyes of a ferret. We sipped coffee.

"What was the Test like, Mr Vidor . . . did you find your Chopin yet?" She swirled coffee with a pencil beaming brightly at us both.

Vidor stretched his legs thoughtfully, and smoothed his creases. The crocodile shoes shone and gleamed like Connie's eyes.

"There's one might do. Australian guy. Good looking, but I didn't like the wig. He looked faggy. You know?"

Connie nodded seriously.

"I don't want a faggy Chopin, be difficult with the George Sand . . . know what I mean? A woman with a feller's name and wearing pants . . . it could be very difficult. I got Wallis to check out some other Chopins and a few George Sands . . . maybe we'll do a couple more tests tomorrow. I can't be sold on that Australian yet."

Connie finished her coffee. "Maybe Make-Up or Hair could fix a different wig for him?"

"We're checking just that. He's in Hair right this minute."

There was a slight disturbance somewhere across the quarter room. Women came huddling into the lights . . . a lot of chatter and fixing . . . in the middle of the group a small pale girl dressed in yards of blue silk with her hair plaited and an expression of sheer terror. One of the Countesses. One of the finals who would be tested that day with me. We all stood and were introduced. She was French, had flown in a day before, was sick with fright, tired, bewildered, and ready to weep. Vidor took her away gently, and talked to her kindly. His arms round her shoulders, his viewfinder hitting her breasts.

We started Testing shortly afterwards. I sitting in a chair, she arranging plastic roses on a piano. My voice seemed to come from the soles of my patent leather boots . . . hers from below the Seine. After a couple of long shots they moved in to close stuff and during the break two people walked onto the set, greeted everyone with large hand waves, hugged Vidor and, with eyes like unforgiving steel nuggets, perched themselves on two tall bar stools and watched us. Our first Audience. Tony Curtis and Jack Lemmon. No one introduced anyone, and apparently no one was about to do so. The Test proceeded before them as they sat immovable, unflinching, on the stools. It was rather like being something in a Fair Ground. Only they didn't actually chuck anything at us. It might have been better if they had. After a great deal of flower arranging, and waving of hands, and a long imploring speech at my feet, the Countess came to the end of her "bit" . . . and we started all over again on mine. The Film Stars slid off their stools, called "See yah!" to the crew, hugged Vidor, made a joke, roared with laughter. And left. The set went back to work. We continued.

★   ★   ★

I ate a beefsteak-tomato and some cold chicken in my Olde Worlde Male Dressing Room. Joe pottered about opening a can of beer, folding my costume, gathering together boots and button hooks. The beer tasted of thin yellow water, the tomato of water, the chicken of cold roast water. I was soggy with it all and with the day. I still had to go down and face Aller who I knew was still sitting in that hateful room waiting for me at the damned piano. Joe looked sympathetic and slid into a chair opposite me.

"Hate the Test?"

"Yes . . . everything."

"First days are always the same kid, always the same. Even for Henry Fonda, or Gary Cooper, it's always the same. You'll be fine tomorrow when you see the stuff. And after all," he added reasonably, "you *got* the part. I mean it's not as if you haven't *got* the role, is it? You *got* it. They *signed* the contract. You're *IN*."

"I'm in all right. Up to my bloody neck. Eighty-five minutes of music I've got. That's what I've got, and those bloody silly pants and gloves and this god-awful hair . . . and all the Campanella and the Moonlight and the Rhapsody . . . Jesus! Have I got it!"

Joe slid the pants on to a hanger. "The music is different. Try. If you can't make it sure as hell they'll use a Double. Only be warned. Rod Raper, you know the one who has been Testing for you while you were in Britain, well Rod knows it all . . . the Music . . . he's been practising for weeks. And he's good, I mean good. Worse than that he's determined. I don't mean no harm to Rod . . . he's a sweet kid. We have assed about a bit, I mean he's sweet, he'll do anything. But like I said . . . he knows the Music. And he'll fit the costooms . . . he'll kill his Daddy to play this role . . . I'm just tellin' you this because Tinsel Town is a funny place . . . you can never be quite sure who's holding the knife. Get me? Try the score, shit if Rod can do it you sure as hell can. Rod came straight out of a Department Store in Dallas . . . used to sell shirts and underwear until someone asked him to model the goods one Sunday. He didn't know a piano from his asshole. About the only instrument he did know how to handle was his cock. So you can see that he's a very ambitious boy. And there's another thing you better know, though I shouldn't even mention a word." He leaned over my crumpled form and whispered very close to my ear; there was a strong smell of "Arpege" and collusion. "They got a big Contract Artist standing by to take over if you screw it all up. A real nice guy . . . got a couple of good Movies behind him, and he's under Contract, he's all set . . . I shouldn't say this but you better know. They got all his measures down at Western Costume and everything would fit except maybe the boots . . . so watch it." He straightened up and tumbled cuff links and dress studs into a small cardboard box. When he spoke again his voice was normal, for him, and flat as a steel blade. "You better pay heed to old man Vidor. Want another beer?"

*   *   *

Aller was sitting in a crumpled heap reading *Newsweek*. Reluctantly we went to our pianos. And he started, again, fingering the Moonlight. I watched in anguish. Nothing seemed possible. If Rod Raper could do it, why couldn't I?

We "worked" for two hours. My hands were sweating, my arms ached, Aller's voice was dull and defeated.

"You got no co-ordination at all. It amazes me. Positively amazes me. I seen a child of four with more co-ordination than you. Do you doubt that?"

I did not.

"If it's not too personal—could you tell me how you even got this far?" I was mute.

"I'll try and give you some simple scales . . . you'll try and learn them . . . and then go over them again and again tonight on the piano in your hotel room. Maybe tomorrow something will break through. Maybe you're tired; first day after all. Now let's start with this . . . it's the simplest scale of all . . ."

*   *   *

La Campanella had no charm whatsoever, and by the time we got to part 2 of Rondo Capriccioso I slumped gently out of my overstuffed white tweed chair and lay, eyes closed, tears welling, on the thick white pile of my Bel Air Hotel Bungalow. Room

264

Service hadn't cleared, and half eaten scrambled eggs stiffened in their grease, cigarette butts lay like corpses drowned in cold spilt coffee, and on the Record Player the disc revolved gently, only the hissing of the sapphire point endlessly obliterating the genius of Liszt.

Taking another record from the high pile beside his chair, Tony Forwood stepped over my recumbent form and slid it from its crackly yellow sleeve.

"Well . . . let's just hear a bit of the Etude in D Flat . . . it's slow."

"Slow." I was beyond help or care.

"Slower . . . it's the Theme Song, for God's sake . . ." He slid it on and moved the start button.

"I'm packing it in. Call a meeting tomorrow, with all of them, Vidor, Aller, Feldman . . . it's not too late. I'm here under false pretences. They said they'd use a Double . . . I can't do it . . . I played by ear years ago at school . . . but I can't be accurate to *one bloody note* and act all the crap they've written in five weeks. I'm packing it in . . . we'll get the Pan Am flight back tomorrow night. I've got five weeks to learn half Liszt's bloody output, plus all the rest."

In despair I reached up and finished off the Hennessy bottle and shoved it upside down into the wastepaper basket. Un Sospiro droned through the room mournfully.

"I don't want to be a Movie Star! They keep asking me if I want to *be* one . . . for God's sake! I'm nearly forty! I never wanted to be one, not from the beginning . . . and always on my own terms . . . this is on their terms . . . I want to go back to those Dull Little English Movies they keep sneering about . . . maybe I *am* a late developer but it's too late to develop into something I don't want to be . . . Call Vidor tomorrow, and Feldman, call them now, tonight . . . help me!"

Wearily Tony switched off the player. I watched him hopefully, cunningly, through a haze of Hennessy and self pity, this time tomorrow I'd be on that Pan Am flight out of this monstrous place filled with monstrous, ugly, people. Carefully he slid Un Sospiro back into its yellow cover, not looking at me, preoccupied, worried, thoughtful. I knew all the danger signs.

"What is it?"

"Well . . ."

"Well what, for God's sake?"

"Well . . . no one's ever done it before . . ."

"Done what?"

"Eighty-five minutes of Classical Music . . . without a Double."

"Oh shit! Who'll know? Who'll care?"

"You will," he said evenly and placed the record carefully back on the pile.

★ ★ ★

Victor Aller looked up from his piano without welcome. He finished off whatever he was playing and sat silent.

"Your eyes look funny. Smog?"

"Yes . . . it's bad today."

"When I first came here it was all Citrus orchards . . . sky was blue . . ."

"Could you go through my bit of the Campanella . . . slowly for me?"

"Sure . . . but it gets hellish fast."

"I'll just watch . . . watch your hands . . ."

"Here we go. La Campanella . . ."

"Play it three or four times, will you . . . at that speed?"

I stood there watching those beautiful hands moving across the keys with elegance, love and confidence. He looked up at me and smiled through his glittery glasses:

"What are you doing, waiting for the lightning to strike?"

"Something like that," I said.

INDEX

This index is in the main a guide to Part 2. Because of the problem with names, as explained in the Preface, it does not include everyone mentioned in the text.

Adrian, Max, 226, Plate 10 (a)
Agate, James, 223
Aller, Victor, 256-9, 261, 264-6
Amersham Playhouse, 222-4, 227-30, 235, Plate 9 (c)
Arnaud, Yvonne, 184-6

Baird, Logie, 202
Bates, H. E. (*The Poacher*), 195-6
Bennett, Joan Sterndale, Plate 10 (b)
Bishopbriggs, Scotland, 150 ff, 159, 163 ff, 176, 177, 185
Blunden, Edmund, 208, 244
Brooke, Rupert, 244
"Bunty Pulls The Strings", 130, 132-133, Plate 6 (b)

"Call It A Day", 223
Cass, Henry, 226
Chelsea Polytechnic (now the Chelsea School of Art), 131, 187, 194 ff, 209, 212, Plate 8 (b)
Chrisham, Walter, 234-6, 241
Clayton, Jack, 192
"Cornelius" (J. B. Priestley), 221-2, 224-7, 242, Plate 10 (a)
Cox, Mr and Mrs Lionel, Heather and Nerine, 182 ff, 186-7, 198-9, 201, 212, Plate 7 (a)
Curtis, Tony, 262-3

de Leon, Jack and Beatrice, 215-16, 219-22, 224-5
Dean, Basil, 219

Deans, Anne, 223-4, 225, 227-31, 234-5, 245
Dearden, Basil, 192, 219
"Death In Venice", 148, 191
Dickson, Dorothy, 234-6
"Diversion" (Herbert Farjeon), 232, 234-7, 241
Drury Lane Theatre, 245

Eisinger, Irene, 236
Embassy Theatre, Swiss Cottage, 221, 225
Entertainments National Services Association (ENSA), 245
Evans, Edith, 234-6, 240-41, 252

Farjeon, Herbert, 216, 232, 235 (*see also* "Diversion")
Forwood, Anthony, 230-33, 240-41, 243, 265-6, Plate 9 (b)
Forwood, Ernest Harrison (Pip), and Phyllis, 232

"Ghost Train, The", 245
Glasgow, 129, 150, 153, 170 ff, 177 ff, 185-6, 187-9, 210, 246 (*see also* Bishopbriggs)
Govoni, Giovanna, and family, 133, 135-7, 200
Grenfell, Joyce, 234, 236, 241
"Grief Goes Over", 229-30, Plate 9 (a)
"Grouse in June", 223
Guthrie, Tyrone, 209

267